The Genesis of John

The Genesis of John

Novel Commentary

By
STEVEN GRANT

RESOURCE *Publications* • Eugene, Oregon

THE GENESIS OF JOHN
Novel Commentary

Copyright © 2019 Steven Grant. All rights reserved. Except for brief quotations in critical publications or reviews, no part of this book may be reproduced in any manner without prior written permission from the publisher. Write: Permissions, Wipf and Stock Publishers, 199 W. 8th Ave., Suite 3, Eugene, OR 97401.

Resource Publications
An Imprint of Wipf and Stock Publishers
199 W. 8th Ave., Suite 3
Eugene, OR 97401

www.wipfandstock.com

PAPERBACK ISBN: 978-1-5326-8594-1
HARDCOVER ISBN: 978-1-5326-8595-8
EBOOK ISBN: 978-1-5326-8596-5

Manufactured in the U.S.A.   04/18/19

For Yahweh, the One who provides:

Existence
Sentience
Salvation
Endearment
Nurture
Clemency
Eternity
Our essence

Contents

Acknowledgements | ix
Hebrew Names | xiii
Preface | xv
Introduction | xvii

1. Rabbi and Disciple | 1
2. The Project | 4
3. Light | 6
4. Glory | 9
5. Baptism | 12
6. Illumination | 15
7. Three Couplets | 19
8. Life | 21
9. Adam in Eden | 24
10. Adam in Jerusalem | 27
11. Disciple Servant | 29
12. Apostle and Proselyte | 31
13. Messiah Begins | 33
14. Born Anew | 36
15. Burial Spices | 39
16. Irenaeus | 41
17. Wilderness Mikvah | 43
18. Ethos Not Geos | 46
19. Nephesh Not Genus | 49
20. White For Harvest | 52
21. Junia | 56
22. Physical Atonement | 61
23. Spiritual Atonement | 65
24. Ya'aqobe | 69
25. Physical Feeding | 72
26. Physical Rescue | 76
27. Spiritual Feeding | 80
28. Spiritual Rescue | 84
29. Evening Meal Invitation | 88
30. Sermons of Sukkot | 91
31. Water of Life | 95
32. A Spiritual Invitation | 99
33. Light of the World | 104
34. Rejection of the Light | 108
35. The Blind Receive Sight | 111
36. Those Seeing are Blind | 114
37. The Light of Ya'aqobe | 117
38. Living Psalm 23 | 120
39. Who is Elohim? | 124
40. Lazarus in Languish | 128
41. Lazarus Lifted | 132
42. Recollections and Repairs | 135
43. Anointing the Son | 138
44. Glorifying Adonai | 142
45. Proclaiming Adonai | 146
46. Pharisees and Scribes | 149

47	Patience and Passover	152	
48	Betrayal and Honor	156	
49	Love and Peace	160	
50	Plans and Perseverance	164	
51	The Vine and the Advocate	167	
52	Overcomer of the Cosmos	172	
53	Timeless Prayer of the Redeemer	176	
54	Arrested	180	
55	Inspected	184	
56	Tormented	189	
57	Resurrected	193	
58	Chavah's News	198	
59	Project Planning	202	
60	Yeshua and Yehoshua	205	
61	Propagation Preparations	209	
62	The Southern Messengers	213	
63	Copies Complete	218	
64	The Northern Messengers	222	
65	The Enclave Apostle	227	

Endnotes | 229
Bibliography | 235

Acknowledgements

Genuine success is positively influencing people toward a vast exposure and deep experience of truth. These iterative, newly found affinities motiviate and enhance our benevolence for others.

There is nothing more potentially powerful than the truths of Yahweh. If this book has any success, it is in part due to the individuals below for their contributions.

George Goldman, PhD - Encouragement, openness,
and manuscript review

Tom Hoffman, MDiv - Manuscript review

Leslie Thompson, Rogue Creative - Logo and marketing advice

Hebrew Names

Andrewas - Andrew Miryam - Miriam Yehoshua - Joshua
Chavah - Eve Netan'el - Nathaniel Yehuda - Judah
Kaypha - Peter Phillipus - Philip Yeshua - Jesus
El'azar - Lazarus Shimon - Simeon Yochanan - John
Marah - Martha Tauma - Twin, Thomas Zvad'yah - Zebadee
Ya'aqobe - Jacob

Preface

Dear Reader,

Please understand that I have included information in this preface and the introduction to enhance the journey on which we are about to embark. I have endeavored to keep the Preface and Introduction short and succinct to provide the most expedient path to the genesis of our adventure. As noted by the logo and title of the series this is *Novel Commentary*. This series is a rare combination of fictional creative writing and critical interpretation of scripture. A novel does not typically provide an original translation or observations on scripture and a commentary does not typically aim to entertain by employing fictional creative writing. This book endeavors to weave the major elements of *Novel* and *Commentary* in a cohesive codex enticing the reader to read the commentary from cover to cover. You, dear reader, are now my judge if I have accomplished this unique task. My deepest hope is that this book is simultaneously illuminating and entertaining.

While *Novel Commentary* is the series, this book is entitled *The Genesis of John*. The genesis of the idea for this work began with noticing the differences and apparent contradiction that John has with the rest of the gospels. Matthew, Mark and Luke share a high percentage of the same information or motifs, which gave birth to their collective reference as the Synoptic Gospels long ago. John shares only 5% of the motifs in the synoptics[1] and this percentage is obviously less when compared to any individual synoptic gospel. This lovely, unique difference that John has with the other gospels, in my opinion, is on purpose.

In addition to John's uniqueness, there is also a glaring contradiction when comparing John to the Synoptics. This unsettled chronological conundrum was the spark of my passion to write this commentary. Either a cursory glance or an in depth study reveal an undeniable chronological

---

1. Out of the 250 narratives provided by the Synoptics and John, only 12 of the narratives in John are also in the synoptics.

progression to all the gospels. They all record the advent of Messiah at the beginning of their account and the resurrection of Messiah at their conclusion. When chronology is considered, the one glaring contradiction between John and the Synoptics is the placement of Jesus' cleansing the temple. John records this event in chapter 2 at the beginning of his work. Matthew, Mark and Luke record the cleansing in chapters 21, 11 and 19 respectively, just before Jesus' arrest and crucifixion.

This raises the question, "Were there two cleansings of the temple, one at the beginning of Jesus' ministry and one near the end?" None of the four gospels record two accounts, and the similarities in all the gospels seem to make it clear that they all refer to the same event. Did John's scribe shuffle some sheets around by accident before binding the work in a codex? This mistake seems unlikely with what we know of the strict scribal practices, and possibly infringes on some aspect of the doctrine of inspiration. The reconciliation, I believe, to this chronological conundrum lies in the double entendre in the title of this work. *The Genesis of John* not only refers to one possibility of the accounts creation but also reveals the influence that the Genesis scroll had on John, the author.

As mentioned before this is *A Novel Commentary*. The novel or creative writing aspect of this book will provide a fictional account of how John and his amanuensis produced the gospel of John. The commentary aspect will provide a fresh translation from, primarily, the Nestle Greek text; keeping John's affinity for Genesis in mind. Observations along the way will contain both novel and commentary aspects and will hopefully provide some illumination expected of a commentary on the scriptures. This commentary is critical in content but I have placed academic clarifications in the end notes while reserving footnoted comments to help the reader understand the context of the creative journey. My goal was to produce a commentary that anyone could read from cover to cover like a novel, being both entertained and illuminated.

Introduction

Novel Commentary primarily views scripture from a Hebraic perspective. Jewish and contemporary hermeneutics, combined with cultural and contextual awareness, guide the interpretive statements within the fictional account. *Novel Commentary* also uses a biblical theological method in that it is historical, chronological and focuses its observations within the context of a singular work or author.

The Genesis of John introduces a primary premise that John used Genesis as a comprehensive literary pattern for the compilation of his gospel. Indicators that Genesis was a source document for the organization of the fourth gospel are vivid and numerous. One of the most obvious indicators is the opening phrase where both books use, "In the beginning" for their first words. I believe John intended this shared opening to be an intentional literary pointer for the reader to consider his use of Genesis in outlining his gospel. As mentioned in the Preface, the impetus for this commentary was the apparent contradiction of the placement of the cleansing of the temple account in John compared to the Synoptic gospels. The answer to this contradiction resides in the analogous outline that John shares with Genesis. For Genesis, the first six days of creation are the *Introduction*, the accounts of the patriarchs are the *Body*, and the Joseph narrative is the *Conclusion*. This observation is fodder for argumentation, however, for the purposes of this commentary, the point is that John wrote his gospel with a similar outline in mind. For John, six events of Messiah's life form the *Introduction*, the narratives during the feasts are the *Body*, and the *Conclusion* is the last chapter which corresponds to the Joseph narrative. A simple comparison is below.

Genesis	John
Introduction - 6 Days of Creation	Introduction - 6 Events of Messiah
Body - Accounts of the Patriarchs	Body - Accounts of Messiah
Conclusion - Joseph Provides for Israel	Conclusion - Jesus Provides for Disciples

Addressing this outline in reverse order, the *Conclusion* for John is chapter 21 and parallels the provision motif of the Joseph story, which provides the conclusion for Genesis. The *Body* of Genesis is segregated by the Hebrew word "Toledot" and means "account of" or "generations of." This word divides Genesis into, arguably, six accounts of the patriarchs. Genesis records the events of the patriarchs in chronological order. The *Body* of John is segregated by the Greek word "Heyorte" and means "feast." This word divides the gospel into at least six festal narratives. John records the events of Jesus in chronological order during certain feasts over the three years of his ministry.

Finally, both Genesis and John have *Introductions* that use six motifs to provide an overview before starting their detailed accounts. While the *Introductions* provide a chronological overview, this timeline is independent from the chronology of the rest of the book. The Genesis *Introduction* records the six days of creation. The *Body* of the book starts the detailed patriarchal narrative mid-way of the sixth day just before the creation of Adam. Chronologically, the end of the *Introduction* overlaps the start of the *Body*.

In John's *Introduction* we see six key events beginning with Messiah at creation and ending with Messiah cleansing the temple. The *Body* of the book starts the detailed narrative of Messiah at the first Passover of his public ministry, essentially between the fifth and sixth event of the *Introduction*. Just as in Genesis, the chronology of the *Introduction* overlaps the chronology of the *Body*. The reason the cleansing of the temple account is at the beginning of John's gospel is that it is the last event of the *Introduction*, which overlaps the start of the chronology of the *Body*. A detailed comparison is below.

Introduction xvii

Genesis

Introduction—Days of Creation

1	2	3	4	5	6
Light	Glory	Water	Illumination	Life	Renewal

Body—"Toledot"—Patriarchal Narratives

1	2	3	4	5	6
Adam	Noah	Shem	Abraham	Isaac	Jacob

Conclusion
Provision
Joseph

Chronological Progression ⟶

John

Introduction—Key Events of Messiah

1	2	3	4	5	6
Light	Glory	Water	Illumination	Life	Renewal

Body—"Heyorte"—Festal Narratives

1	2	3	4	5	6
Passover	Atonement	Passover	Tabernacles	Dedication	Passover

Conclusion
Provision
Jesus

One last observation for this introduction, also represented above, is that the six events of John correspond to the six days of creation. Both the days of creation and the key events of Jesus, in each *Introduction*, share the motifs of Light, Glory, Water, Illumination, Life and Renewal in that order. "Renewal" for John is the cleansing of the temple account.

These six analogous narratives will become clear as we progress on our fictional journey, which begins now. Let your mind drift toward Israel and picture the calm waves of the Mediterranean Sea softly saturating the shores near Ephesus. Not far from Ephesus there is a small, rural, rustic, first century village saturated by the dusk of the day. Imagine the barely visible narrow, rough dirt roads and clay brick adobes with flat pitched parapeted roofs. The smell of burning cypress lingers in the air while the shimmer of candlelight alters the linen covered windows. The calm cool spring darkness is giving way to the slice of sunlight cutting across the distant horizon.

I

Rabbi and Disciple

Yom Chamishi[1]

Yochanan[2] opened his eyes to another barely breaking morning anxious for prayer and dictation. His amanuensis, Polycarp[3], lay on the raised mat not far from him, positioned near the only door of the adobe. Yochanan set his feet on the cool dirt floor, stood gradually, stretched silently, and reached for his linen cloak and wood walking stick. His hand grasped the knobbed area at the top that was smooth and discolored from the oils of his right wrinkled palm. As he moved slowly and silently past his disciple he was again thankful for this dedicated scribe and realized that Polycarp was living up to his new name; he was becoming very fruitful indeed. "Yahweh[4] is gracious," he whispered ever so slightly, as if it were a soft exhale directly from his soul, as he remembered the meaning of his own name.

 The Father's grace had certainly produced fruit with this pairing of an aging Rabbi and a young disciple scribe. Approaching the doorway, he noticed the worn gapped cedar boards of the front door and the tearing leather hinges that would soon need repair. He dismissed this readily because of more exciting thoughts. Today, instead of the cold pitch of the rooftop he

---

 1. Hebrew for Fifth Day—Thursday

 2. Hebrew name for John

 3. Irenaeus, Tertullian and Jerome testified that Polycarp (many fruits) was one of Yochanan' s disciples

 4. Covenant name of Adonai (God)

wanted to feel the early barley all around him as he knelt to pray. The feeling of First Fruits[5] was still lingered in the air, which brought a new excitement for everyone in the small Jewish enclave on the outskirts of Ephesus. He slipped on his worn sandals and crossed the threshold of the adobe. As he lumbered to the side of the nearby field closest to Jerusalem, he knelt in the dark fertile soil, looked up and began to pray.

Stirring with a sense of purpose Polycarp awoke and looked immediately toward his Rabbi's mat while rising to his knees. Suspecting Yochanan had already left, he felt shadowed with aloneness even before he saw the empty mat. Turning to face Jerusalem, he recited his morning prayers. After taking some of the brittle branches that he had gathered last night, he stirred the remaining glowing ashes of the fire and set them on the embers. He lowered his large thin, cloaked frame to the rim of the charred fire pit and blew a long strong, focused breath toward the coals. Ash lifted into the dark air as the thin branches grew bright with the coals. He then lifted the nearby half-full water kettle to the hook at the top of the iron tripod that straddled the pit. He made careful preparation the night before, knowing Yochanan would want to get an early start with the new project. After laying out some black olives, honeycomb and challah, he threw a measure of barley in the small water kettle just as the door abruptly swung open and let in the morning sunlight.

Yochanan, silhouetted by the incoming dawn provided by the opening, entered the small adobe and greeted his scribe with a quick but meaningful embrace.

"Shalom Saphar, I see you have breakfast ready, thank you." Saphar was the Hebrew word for scribe and had become Polycarp's nickname with the new project. Yochanan took from the prepared plate, gently broke off some of the challah, looked upward and chanted,

"Barukh ata Adonai Eloheinu, melekh ha'olam, hamotzi lehem min ha'aretz."[6] Polycarp responded,

"Amen." The two enjoyed their breakfast in silence.
Finishing their meal, Polycarp said,

"I am anxious to get started Rabbi."

"I'm glad for that Saphar, but first let us take a walk to the market and talk about how we are to go about this important project."

Polycarp gathered the wooden plates, quickly rinsed them with the water in the basin across the room, and removed the kettle from the fire,

---

5. Biblical feast just after Passover that initiates the counting of the Omer to Shavuot (Pentecost)

6. Blessed are you Yahweh our Adonai, King of the universe who brings forth bread from the earth

which had burned down to a steady umber glow. Then, grasping the rusty iron latches of the four wooden window coverings, he let in the glowing sunshine by swinging each shutter open as wide as the creaking hinges would allow. The smell of the morning dew rushed the room. Yochanan grasped his surprisingly heavy staff and the two treaded down the now bustling dirt road toward the market.

2

The Project

Polycarp welcomed these times of walking and talking with Yochanan. There was a privileged formula during these strolls of Yochanan teaching, plus Polycarp absorbing, which equaled blessings for both.

"We must continue to proclaim the good news of Messiah Saphar. The circulation of the account of Yocnanan Markos[1] is a blessing. However, no matter how many produce accounts there will never be enough to contain all that our Master accomplished. I cannot escape the nudge, no, the compulsion of the Spirit, to lay out more than a historical string of amazing events over the years. Now, this we will do, however, there is an additional depth to our Master's accomplishments I wish to convey. He was, is, and ever will be the Son of Yahweh. As the Father gave us all that we see, so the Son gave us all that we could be. He provides a great spiritual opportunity to the sons of Yaakov[2] as well as to all who believe."

As they made their way through the fragrant market, Polycarp purchased a variety of fruit from the smiling vendors for lunch. He wanted to purchase a few more things for dinner but Yochanan cut the walk short of the typical time in order to prepare for the project. They both headed back to the adobe kicking up the morning dust with a slightly quickened pace.

"You see Saphar, the Father and the Son created worlds for us to enjoy; this world and the next." Yochanan turned toward his disciple while continuing the pace. "Where do we see the Father's creative work?"

---

1. Hebrew for Mark—the author of the gospel
2. Hebrew for Jacob

"B'resheet[3] of course" replied Polycarp.

"Yes, and I wish to convey that the spiritually creative life of Messiah parallels the physically creative work of Adonai. It is this worldly, or better said, other worldly connection between the Father and the Son we will reveal. The six days of creation reveal important things about the Father. Similarly, six events of the Sons life provide this same revelation. This is how we will introduce our version of the greatest story of history."

As they crossed the threshold of the adobe, Polycarp pulled the distressed but sturdy wood scribal desk and cross-legged chair from the wall and situated them in the corner of the living area. Yochanan handed him the parchments, quills, and ink, after sitting down in his usual rough sawn cedar, cotton padded chair. After the normal blessing by Yochanan, Polycarp made a simple title on the first page, "According to Yochanan."

---

3. Hebrew for In the Beginning—i.e.—Genesis

3

Light

"Now Saphar let us look in detail at the days of creation and the life of Messiah. Do you remember your training of the first day of creation? What is the theme of that day?"

Polycarp responded quickly. "Adonai, from wherever the darkness was, created *Ur*, light, the physical light of Adonai."

"Correct, light is the theme of the first day." Yochanan raised his hands, as was his custom when quoting scripture, and recited some verses from Genesis.

> In the beginning, Elohim created the heavens and the earth, and this land ᴬ was formless and empty, and darkness was before the abyss. And the Spirit of Elohim was hovering before the waters and Elohim said, "HaYah Ur (Let there be light)," and there was light, and Elohim saw the good light and so Elohim made a difference between the light from the darkness. Elohim called the light day, and the darkness he called night and there was evening and there was morning, the first day.[1]

"Just as the Father spoke and created physical light for the cosmos so the Son came as the Word of Adonai to reveal Adonai's spiritual light. We need physical light for this world to find our way and the Son came to shine spiritual light and reveal the way to the Father." Yochanan paused briefly, his eyes focused on the door, but his mind was looking back through the

---

1. Genesis 1:1–5—My own translation from the Aleppo unless otherwise noted

years. "I remember when Yeshua[2] started His mission; all the elements of creation were present. I want people to make this connection to B'resheet so we will use the introduction used by Adam so long ago. Are you ready to begin Saphar?"

"Yes Rabbi."

> *In the beginning was the Word, and the Word was with Adonai* [B], *and the Word was Adonai. He was in the beginning with the one and only Adonai. All things emerged* [C] *through him, and without him not even one thing that has emerged, emerged. In him was life, and the life was the light of humanity* [D]. *This light beacons in the darkness, and the darkness has not overcome it.*

"The physical light created by the Father so long ago helps us realize the spiritual, saving light of Messiah. Saphar, Yeshua's presence illuminated my purpose when I was near him. It became clear that my greatest joy was in obeying his commands. Now Saphar, let us continue with the mission of the Baptist who introduced the Master as the genuine light."

> *There was a man, having been sent from Adonai, whose name was Yochanan. He came as a witness, to testify concerning the light, that all might believe through him. He was not the light, but came to testify concerning the light that he was the genuine light, which enlightens the entire human race, and that he was coming into the world. He was in the world, and the world emerged through him, yet the world did not know him. He came to his own people, and his own people did not receive him. But to whoever received him, he gave spiritual power* [E] *to become children of Adonai, to those believing in his name. These were born, not of blood nor of the will of the flesh, nor of the will of man, but of Adonai.*[3]

"How privileged we are, my disciple, to be able to see the physical light of Adonai and receive the spiritual light of Messiah. Only this light can lead anyone to salvation. His spiritual presence and his illumination affected everyone around him and it continues today. I see his light in you and it will continue until he returns." Polycarp nodded in agreement, as he finished his scratching of the parchment. Yochanan gave a sideways glance at Polycarp and asked, "Do you recall the theme of the second day of creation?"

---

2. Hebrew/Aramaic for Jesus
3. John 1:1–13 My own translation from the Nestles unless otherwise noted

"If I remember correctly Rabbi, the second day records the creating of the cosmos or heavens from the division of the waters."

"Correct Saphar, and Adonai said..."

 *Let there be extension^E in the midst of the waters, and let it divide a space between the waters from the waters." And Elohim made an extension which divided a space between the waters that were under the extension from the waters that were above the extension and it was so. And Elohim called the extension sky and there was evening and there was morning, the second day.*[4]

---

4. Genesis 1:6–8

4

Glory

"There is much that could be said about this glorious picture Saphar, but what did King David say in the first scroll of the Psalms of this sky, what we sometimes call the cosmos or heavens?" Polycarp thought for a moment and after quickly running through the Psalms of book one in his head he answered.

"David sung that the heavens declared the glory of Adonai, and the sky above proclaimed his handiwork."

"Correct again. As this sky, or heavens, physically revealed the glory of Adonai, the Son would spiritually reveal the glory of the Father. Dip your quill Saphar and make the necessary person changes as I relate the events."

> *And the Word became flesh and tabernacled with us, and we beheld his glory, glory unique from the Father, full of favor and truth. Witnessing concerning Him, Yochanan cried out saying, "This was he of whom I spoke, 'The One who was born after me has higher rank, because he existed before me.'" For from his fullness we have all received, favor upon favor. As the Torah was offered through Moshe, favor and truth was born through Yeshua Messiah. No one has ever seen Adonai; the unique One* [G] *of Adonai, being in the cleft* [H] *of the Father, He has made him known.*[1]

Yochanan lifted his left palm upward, toward the open window and said,

---

1. John 1:14–18

"This sky, or heavens, physically displays the glory of the Father. The cosmos displays his majesty and his creation reveals his grace in providing us physical life and sustenance. Likewise, Messiah spiritually displays the glory of the Father. He revealed the Father's righteousness and pours out his favor in providing spiritual life and sustenance. Adonai revealed his love by sending his perfect Son to dwell with fallen humanity. The character of the Father was unveiled in Messiah's total devotion to the Father's commands. Messiah's favor, sacrifice and power are present because he completed what the Father sent him to accomplish. He manifested the Father through his life, death, and resurrection. This world's glory will someday be done away with, but Messiah's glory will never fade." The two paused in thought and worship at these words. After a moment Yochanan said,

"Let's continue with the testimony of the Baptist."

"Yes Rabbi."

> And this is the testimony of Yochanan, when the Judeans [1] sent priests and Levites from Jerusalem to ask him, "Who are you?" He confessed, and did not deny, but confessed, "I am not the Messiah." and they asked him, "What then? Are you Elijah?" He was saying, "I am not." "Are you the Prophet?" And he answered, "No." They therefore said to him, "Who are you that we might give an answer to those who sent us? What do you say about yourself?" He said, "I am a voice proclaiming in the wilderness, 'Make straight the way of the Master,' as the prophet Isaiah said." Now those having been sent were from the Pharisees. And they asked him and said to Him, "Then why do you baptize if you are not the Messiah, nor Elijah, nor the Prophet?" Yochanan answered them, "I baptize with water, but among you stands one you do not know, even he who was born after me, the strap of whose sandal I am not worthy to untie."[2]

"Rabbi, it is because the Baptist was Essene that they did not know him?"

"Rest assured disciple, they knew him. However, they did not comprehend the meaning of certain scriptures, or the role Adonai had chosen for the Baptist. The lack of understanding by the Priests and Levites is not surprising. Their king Herod, as son of Edom, could never claim the legitimate dynasty of Yehuda Maccabaeus. Most in his court did not have the proper heritage or perspective to understand the scriptures fully. However, all that was required to gain a proper understanding would be to search the

---

2. John 1:19–27

scriptures with an open heart and mind. Saphar, please make a note of the location where these things took place."

 *These things took place in Bethany across the Jordan, where Yochanan was baptizing.*[3]

"So, we have seen the light and glory of the Son, on this side of the Jordan, so to speak, and how it compares to the Fathers light and glory. Remember, Saphar, that the light of the Holy One, blessed be He, and the glory of the Holy One are linked just like the first two days of creation. In fact, the six days of creation provide three periods of two days each. We will follow this same pattern as we continue our introduction of our beloved Messiah."

---

3. John 1:28

5

Baptism

Yochanan felt the subtle pain on his hips and adjusted to a better position in his chair. Polycarp took this opportunity to reach for the water jar. They both anticipated the sweet well water's refreshment.

"I believe I know your next question Rabbi," he said as the sound of the fresh spring water bubbled from the clay pitcher to the wooden cups, "What is the theme of the third day?" Polycarp paused out of courtesy and when he was sure Yochanan was waiting for him to continue, he said. "The theme of the third day of creation is water, and if you agree with some of the other Rabbis it was also the baptism of the world."

"Correct Saphar, for the third day Adonai said. . ."

> "Let the waters under the heavens be contained [1] into one place, and let land appear." And it was so. Elohim called the land Earth, and the water pools he called Seas. And Elohim saw that it was good. Elohim also said, "Let the earth sprout tender plants perpetuating their seed, and trees bearing fruit from their seed within, each according to its kind on the earth." And it was so and there was evening and there was morning, the third day.[1]

"Notice that Adam uses the verb 'be contained' for the gathering of the water but once it is gathered he uses the noun 'pools' since it is now contained. This is the first use of 'Mikvah'[2] in scripture which is why many Rabbis believe this is the record of the world's baptism."

---

1. Genesis 1:9–13 Abridged
2. Hebrew word for immersion or baptism throughout the Old Testament

Baptism

"Very interesting Rabbi for I know what happened after the Baptist answered the priests and the Levites, sent from the Pharisees. He baptized the Master." Yochanan paused and then responded in a soft, thoughtful voice,

"He allowed the Baptist to fulfill what was written so He could continue his obedience to the Fathers' commands my young disciple."

"Yes Rabbi, forgive me."

"Of course, Saphar." Yochanan looked at Polycarp and smiled. The wrinkles became deeper around his cheeks and temples and a sparkle appeared in his deep emerald eyes as he said, "It was a day of days."

Next,[K] he saw Yeshua coming to him, and said, "Behold, the Lamb of Adonai, who is removing the sin of the cosmos! This is he of whom I spoke, 'The man who was born after me has higher rank, because he existed before me. I also did not understand him but for this purpose I came baptizing with water, that he might be revealed to Israel." Also, Yochanan testified saying, "I saw the Spirit descending out of the sky like a dove, and it remained on him. I also did not understand this, but he who sent me to baptize with water said to me, 'If you see someone whom the Spirit is descending and remaining on, then this is the One baptizing with the Holy Spirit.' And I have seen and have testified that this is the Son of Adonai."[3]

"As the Father spoke life into being and baptized our world at creation so the Son was baptized at the start of his ministry. The father provided us with physical water and new life on the earth. The Son, the word of Adonai, provides us with living water and new life by redeeming creation. From baptism to baptism, Adonai orchestrated all that has happened. He can comprehend all of time and eternity and he parallels certain events in these ways."

The two again paused in thought, and then Yochanan continued.

"Even as the Spirit hovered over creation, so this same Spirit came and remained on Messiah. While I have described the Spirit as a Dove, it does not fully describe what we saw. Language is so limited for the things of Adonai. The events of this day were amazing, but to many they were confusing. Some thought they understood the Baptists words 'he existed before me' but most stood still, puzzled by what they beheld. Whether they knew it or not, we were all witnessing Adonai's anointing of the Anointed One. It was after this event that the people started using the word 'Messiah' for Yeshua. Wet your quill Saphar."

---

3. John 1:29–34

> *At that time, Yochanan was standing with two of his disciples, and having looked at Yeshua walking, says "Behold, the Lamb of the one and only Adonai!" And the two disciples heard him say this, and they followed Yeshua. Then Yeshua, having turned, beheld them following and says to them, "What do you seek?" And they said to him, "Rabbi" (which translated means Teacher), "where are you staying?" He says to them, "Come and you will see." So, they went and saw where he stays, and they stayed with him that day, for it was about the tenth hour. Andrewas, Shimon Kaypha's brother was one of the two who heard from Yochanan and followed Yeshua. He first found his own brother Shimon and says to him, "We have found the Messiah" (which translated means Christ). He led him to Yeshua. After staring at him Yeshua said, "You are Shimon the son of Jonah, you shall be called Cephas" (which means Rock).*[4]

"These men witnessed Yeshua being immersed in the water and the Spirit. They were convinced it was the anointing of the Father and they hoped he was the Messiah. While there were a few unique people that sought out Yeshua during his ministry, he came to seek and save the lost, which is of course all of humanity, regardless of ancestry. Those who would accept his offer would become luminaries to this dark world, reflecting the light of Messiah. Let us move on to the next day, Saphar. What is the theme of the fourth day?" Polycarp responded quickly.

"The theme is light. The Father created physical luminaries in the sky for the earth."

"Correct, and just as Adonai created physical light for the earth Yeshua was the spiritual light of this world to illuminate how to get to the next."

---

4. John 1:35–42

6

Illumination

 *And Elohim said, "Let there be lights in the extension of the sky to divide a space between the day from the night and let them be for signs and for feasts and for days and years and let them be lights in the division of the sky to shine upon the earth...and Elohim set them in the division of the sky to give light on the earth, to have dominion over the day and over the night and to separate the light from the darkness. And Elohim saw that it was good and there was evening and there was morning, the fourth day.*[1]

"Just as the Father provided physical light for His creation so the Son would provide spiritual light for all souls. He also selected those who would carry forward His mission of illuminating the grace of the Father on earth. Do you remember, disciple, where the Master chose to venture once He started His ministry, after He was baptized?"

"Yes Rabbi, and many still wonder why He went first to Galilee."

Yochanan slowly rose from his creaking chair and shuffled to a bookshelf. He pulled a scroll from one of the shelves. Unrolling it slowly and carefully, he then studied it in silence for a time before answering. Polycarp sat quietly waiting, but noticed that Yochanan had selected the Isaiah scroll. It seemed to be his favorite of the Nevi'im.[2] He then responded to Polycarp.

"The word Galilee has its root in Galil which, in part, means encircled. Galilee was, at that time, encircled by Gentiles and filled with a mixture

---

1. Genesis 1:14–19 Abridged
2. Hebrew for "Prophets" one of the three divisions of the Old Testament

of every nation on earth, including the tribes of Ya'aqobe. Yeshua went to Galilee to be a light. He became the spiritual light for Israel and for all the nations just as Isaiah said."

 "And now Elohim says, he who formed me from the womb to be his servant, to bring Jacob back to him; and that Israel might be gathered to him—for I am honored in the eyes of Elohim and Adonai has become my strength—he says: It is too light a thing that you should be my servant to raise up the tribes of Jacob and to bring back the preserved of Israel; I will make you as a light for the nations, that my salvation may reach to the end of the earth."[3]

Yochanan went back to his chair and sat down.

"This is exactly what the Master did Saphar. Yeshua not only came to provide salvation to Israel, the easy or light thing, but He also completed the difficult or heavy task of being the light to the nations. He was providing the opportunity for salvation to all adam, all humanity. He went to Galilee to shine to all humanity and chose souls to hone into spiritual lights for this world. Because of His light, they would shine to the ends of our world. They would not only reveal the difference between light and darkness but also help separate adam[4] from the darkness. Remember, the Spirit remained on Him and those who sensed it wanted others to see this light of redemption. The first to see this light were Phillipus and Netan'el. Here is what they saw."

 *Next, He desired to go to Galilee. He discovered Phillipus and says to him, "Follow me." Phillipus was also from Bethsaida, the city of Andrewas and Kaypha. Phillipus found Netan'el and says to him, "We have found him of whom Moshe in the Torah and also the prophets wrote, Yeshua, the son of Yehoshua of Nazareth." Netan'el says to him, "Is there any good thing able to come from Nazareth?" Phillipus says to him, "Come and see." Yeshua perceived Netan'el coming to him and says of him, "Behold, truly an Israelite in whom there is no deceit!" Netan'el says to him, "From where do you know me?" Yeshua answered and said to him, "Before Phillipus called you, when you were under the fig tree, I saw you." Netan'el answered him, "Rabbi, you are the Son of Adonai! You are the King of Israel!" Yeshua answered and said to him, "Because I said to you, 'I saw you under the fig tree,' do you believe? You will be enlightened to greater things than these." And he says*

---

3. Isaiah 49:5–6 ESV
4. Hebrew for Mankind

> to him, "Truly, truly, I say to you, you will see the starry sky opened, and the angels of Adonai ascending and descending on the Son of Man."[5]

After finishing these words of the dictation, Polycarp thought for a moment and said, "Was Netan'el thinking of the Proverb that says, "In the light of a king's face there is life, and his favor is like the clouds that bring the spring rain?"

"That is an interesting observation Saphar. Phillipus may have been thinking of this proverb, but his mention of Moshe and Torah was a direct reference to another Proverb that says, 'A commandment is a flame and the Torah is the light.'[6] Torah, Light, the Word of Adonai, Yeshua revealed all of these simultaneously. While Netan'el was the first to proclaim him as King, Phillipus was the first to recognize him as the spiritual light for the world. Just as the celestial luminaries provide physical light so Messiah provides spiritual light."

"Rabbi, to be around Yeshua when he evidenced his supernatural ability must have been astounding. However, I cannot help but think there was some other significance between Netan'el and Yeshua because of the messianic references."

"Your instinct serves you well Polycarp. It was inexplicable how Yeshua had seen Netan'el, but it was purposeful. None of us fully understood the fig allusion until much later. I am sure you remember that one of the first trees mentioned in B'resheet,[7] along with the trees of life and morality, is the fig tree. Its leaves covered the loins of Adam and Chavah. Yeshua not only saw Netan'el under the fig tree in Galilee, but also in the fig covered loins in Eden."

"Very interesting Rabbi. . .what of the reference to Ya'aqobe's[8] ladder?"

"While we could spend the day on this topic, the main point is that after Ya'aqobe's dream of angels ascending and descending on a ladder, he woke and said, "Surely the Lord is in this place." Polycarp responded excitedly.

"I understand Rabbi. Netan'el was acknowledging Yeshua as the Son of Man and King of Israel just as Ya'aqobe recognized Adonai!"

"Correct Saphar. Netan'el became the first one enlightened, seeing the divine light in the face of King Messiah. Can you make a connection with the ladder and Messiah?" Polycarp pondered this and then responded.

5. John 1:43–51
6. Proverbs 6:23. See also Dodd, *The Fourth Gospel*, 84–5
7. Genesis
8. Hebrew for Jacob

"I had been thinking about that during dictation. As Ya'aqobe's ladder represented the physical connection or access between 'heaven' and earth so Yeshua is our spiritual connection between these realms. He is the one that provides access to Adonai."

"Excellent my disciple."

7

Three Couplets

"Are you starting to see the pattern of the scroll of creation Saphar?

"Yes Rabbi. In the first couplet, Adonai's light of the first day revealed the glory of Adonai on the second day. In the second couplet, the baptism of the world on the third day provided the opportunity for land and physical light for the world on day four."

"Correct Saphar, it is the same with the Son. As the Word of Adonai, he revealed the spiritual understanding or light of Adonai, which helped us see His glory. Also, His baptism and anointing of the Spirit made it possible for Him to be the spiritual light of this world to help accomplish His mission of grace."

"What of the final period Rabbi, days five and six?"

"It is almost time for mid-day prayers Saphar, let us stretch, pray and prepare for a meal before we continue."

"Yes Rabbi."

After rising again from his cotton-padded chair, Yochanan reached upward in a prolonged stretch with his fingertips touching the ceiling of the adobe. He then moved toward the ladder that led to the pitched rooftop. Polycarp fixed his eye on his teacher and watched constantly, yet unobtrusively, as Yochanan rose to the roof rung by rung and clung to the latch of the hatch. He watched him open the hatch, rise above the rim and clear the opening until he heard footsteps above. He then, knelt, pivoted toward Jerusalem and recited his mid-day prayers.

Yochanan felt invigorated after prayer and stayed on the rooftop soaking in the midday sun. He glanced up at the fire in the sky and pondered the facts that this star provided light, warmth, growth, life and a center for this world. This pondering produced a thoughtful observation.

"Just like the bright morning star,[1] Yeshua, provides all the same dynamics spiritually." The most meaningful truth for this day and age, he supposed, was that Yeshua was the center around which all souls needed to focus.

Polycarp was setting out lunch when he heard the creaking of the rungs of the ladder. He stopped spreading the fruit he had purchased earlier and focused on the hatch and ladder as before. Yochanan knew why his young disciple was stark still while he ascended and descended the ladder but did not make it known that he noticed. While he appreciated his concern, he would never think to discourage his thoughtfulness. When Yochanan had stepped off the last rung, Polycarp poured water and wine for them both and turned again to the fruit. On the low, well-worn wooden table in the middle of the room were figs, pomegranates and grapes, which normally did not start to ripen until Shavuot.

The warm beginning to the year provided early planting and many of the foods typically harvested later in the festal cycle had come in early. The fruit, water and wine strengthened their body and mood. The two, Rabbi and disciple, ate in silence contemplating the project.

"Let us finish our introduction and then look toward continuing tomorrow," said Yochanan, breaking the silence. Polycarp took care of the necessary clean up and after finishing he again set up his amanuensis station in the main area. After visiting the aphedron,[2] they both took their usual places and reviewed where they had left off.

---

1. Song of Songs 6:10 ESV
2. Latrine

8

Life

"So Saphar I am ready for your next answer about the days of creation."

"The fifth day, Adonai created all the creatures of the sea and sky, and gave the command to multiply," replied Polycarp confidently.

"That is what happened my young disciple but what is the theme of the fifth day?" Polycarp thought for a moment and then responded in an interrogative manner.

"Since these creatures were created and brought to life on the fifth day the theme is . . . life?"

"Yes Saphar. While the command to be fruitful and multiply is linked to the theme of life, the fact remains that there were no nepheshim or souls on the earth before the fifth day."

"I can see that now Rabbi." Again, Yochanan chanted the blessing before quoting Torah and recited the fifth day passage from Genesis.

> And Elohim said, "Let the waters swarm abundantly with moving creatures with mature souls, and birds that may fly above the land across the visible extension of the sky." So, Elohim created the great sea creatures and every mature soul that moves, with which the waters swarm, according to their kinds, and every winged bird according to its kind and Elohim saw that it was good. And Elohim blessed them, saying, "Be fruitful and multiply and fill the waters in the seas, and let birds multiply on the land." And there was evening and there was morning, the fifth day.[1]

1. Genesis 1:20–23

"So Saphar, we see that the souls of creatures were created on the fifth day by the Father. Now some may argue whether or not the souls of creatures will arrive in Olam Habah[2] but we can discuss that topic another time. Answering this question is not necessary for our introduction. We have simply seen by the comparison of the days of creation and events of Messiah that what the Father started in the physical world, the Son finishes for the spiritual world. Do you remember the rabbinic literary device of Kal Vahomer popularized by Hillel?"

"Yes Rabbi. One uses Kal Vahomer to illustrate the concept of the light to the heavy. For example, the Master said, 'You have heard it said you shall not commit adultery. But I say to you, everyone who looks at a woman with lust has already committed adultery in his heart.'[3] The point is that what seemed heavy, not committing adultery, is now light compared to the heavy command of not looking at a woman lustfully."

"Well done my disciple. I will not ask why you chose this passage (Yochanan gave a sideways glance toward Polycarp) but Kal Vahomer also illustrates how souls created by the Father on the fifth day relate to what the Son has done. Just as the Father created physical life, so the Son would create spiritual life. Creating all the creatures' souls on the fifth day is no light task but it becomes light when compared to redeeming the souls of humanity. This is what the Father sent the Son to do, to make things spiritually new and bring as many souls as possible to the world to come, Olam Habah. The Master started this renewal, this creating of spiritual life, at a very fitting event, a wedding in Galilee. Let us finish the introduction with the final set of days.

>
> *Next, the third set, there was a wedding feast at Cana in Galilee, and the mother of Yeshua was there. Also invited to the wedding were Yeshua and his disciples. Then, being low on wine, the mother of Yeshua says to him, "They have no wine." Then Yeshua says to her, "What? Not for me or you mother, but because my hour has come."*[M] *His mother says to the servants, "Whatever, whenever he tells any of you, do it." Now there were six stone water jars placed for the cleansing of the Judeans having room for two or three metretas.*[4] *Yeshua says to the servants, "Fill the jars with water." And they filled them up to the brim. And he says to them, "Now draw some out and take it to the master of the feast." So they took it. Now when the master of the feast tasted the water having become wine,*

---

2. The world to come
3. Matthew 5:27–28 ESV
4. A liquid measure of 8 ¾ gallons

and did not know where it came from, but the servants who had drawn the water knew. The master of the feast calls the bridegroom and says to him, "Every man sets out the good wine first, and when they have drunk freely, the inferior. But you have kept the good wine until now." This act, the first miracle, Yeshua did at Cana in Galilee, and revealed his glory and his disciples believed in him.[5]

"I see several parallels here Rabbi," said Polycarp.

"Go on," Yochanan responded.

"The 'be fruitful and multiply' spoken by the Father is echoed here by the wine and the wedding. As Adonai produced life from the water of creation so the Master produced wine, a symbol of life, from the water jars. Also, as physical life was multiplied on the fifth day, the marriage is an example of, well. . .hem hem, multiplication." Yochanan smiled slightly, thoroughly enjoying his disciple's uncomfortable response. "Lastly, as you have said in the last phrase, as the Father created physical life, the Son's miracle prompted faith in the disciples creating spiritual life."

"Very good Saphar, let us move past the concept of multiplication and ponder Yeshua' s miracle. What he did, should not be confused with the ancient tricks of magicians. This was no sleight of hand or conjuring, but an exertion of creative power physically altering water into wine. Magicians may be able to change the color of water but not permanently change its characteristics so that it is the very best wine in every way we experience wine. Yeshua proved to everyone present that He could do things that no one else could do. His power would be revealed time and again with the ultimate proof being seen in his resurrection."

5. John 2:1–11

9

Adam in Eden

"This brings us to the last event in the introduction, Saphar. It was just before his last Passover after his triumphal entry."

"Are you referring to when Yeshua cleared the temple of the animals and money changers? The whole world knows of that event."

"Yes . . ." said Yochanan slowly, pausing as if he were suddenly on the temple steps again feeling the portico marble under his feet. He could still see, hear and smell the throng of beasts and men hastened from the crack of the whip. Wood chairs and tables snapped into pieces on the stone steps while the tarnished gold and silver iconic coins tapped from tread to tread of the temple steps, clinking down to the dirt road. Many muffled cries carried throughout the temple and droves of doves fluttered in the outer courtyard entryway as their dislodged feathers floated to the portico, guising the grey marble.

"Rabbi?" Polycarp asked gently after some time, interrupting his teacher's fixed vision of the past. Yochanan responded slowly.

"This was the last time Messiah would be in the temple. It is fitting that this event concludes our introduction because it complements the theme of the sixth day of creation." A ready connection did not leap into Polycarp's mind between the sixth day and the cleansing of the temple, so he stayed silent and waited for Yochanan to respond.

"Nothing my young disciple?" he asked with his usual emerald gleam returning to his eyes. Polycarp could only turn his head slowly from side to side, as his mind opened for instruction.

"What is a temple my disciple?"

Polycarp pondered and then said, "It is, or should be, a place for Elohim to dwell with adam[1] on earth," responded Polycarp.

"Well said disciple. If what we have in Jerusalem is the latest temple what was the first?" Polycarp thought deeply for a minute before responding while Yochanan silently poured some more wine and repositioned himself in his creaking chair, causing some of the cotton padding to float to the packed dirt floor. Polycarp finally responded.

"While there have been many temples such as Herod's, David's, Samuel's in Shilo, and the tabernacle, I suppose the first place anyone enjoyed the presence and glory of the Almighty was Eden."

"Again, well said Saphar, let us review the sixth day."

Then Elohim said, "Let us make adam in our semblance, according to our likeness. And let them have dominion over the fish of the sea and over the birds of the heavens and over the livestock and over all the land and over every creeping thing that creeps on the land." So, Elohim created adam in his own semblance, in the semblance of Elohim he created them; male and female he created them. Also, Elohim blessed them and Elohim said to them, "Be fruitful and multiply and fill the land and subdue it, and have dominion over the fish of the sea and over the birds of the sky and over every living thing that moves on the land." And Elohim said, "Behold, I have given you every plant bearing seed that is on the face of all the land, and every tree which has bearing seed in its fruit, they shall be food for you. And to every beast of the land and to every bird of the sky and to everything that creeps on the land, everything that has mature souls, I have also given every green plant for food." And it was so. And Elohim saw everything that he had made, and behold, it was very good. And there was evening and there was morning, the sixth day.[2]

Yochanan continued.

"The sixth day reveals Adam and Chavah[3] in Eden. This is where the Father walked with them in the cool of the day. Eden was the first tabernacle or temple and Elohim enjoyed spending time with Adam and Chavah within these Seraphim guarded borders. As you know Saphar, the first Adam sinned and plunged all adam into our current state. However, the second Adam, Yeshua, rescues us from our current state, and will deliver us

---

1. Mankind or humanity
2. Genesis 1:26–31
3. Eve

to Olam Habah. The sixth day of B'resheet and our sixth event illustrate the bookends of human redemption. Let us complete our introduction Saphar."

"I understand now Rabbi. Could you hand me another vial of ink?" asked Polycarp.

"Of course, Saphar, just a moment..." Staying seated, Yochanan reached to his left and stretched to grab one of the vials of ink on a crude set of shelves mounted to the wall and then slowly handed it to Polycarp.

The scribe quickly prepared the vial and closed the other tight. After stirring the ink, he dipped his dry quill and said, "Ready Rabbi."

10

Adam in Jerusalem

After this, he went down to Capernaum, with his mother and his brothers and his disciples, but they did not stay there many days. The Passover of the Judeans was near, and Yeshua went up to Jerusalem. Then he found in the temple those selling oxen and sheep and doves, and the moneychangers who were sitting. Now having made a whip of cords, he drove all the sheep and oxen out of the temple. Now with the moneychangers he poured out the coins and overthrew their tables. And to those selling doves he said, "Take these things from here; do not make my Father's house a house of trade." His disciples remembered that it was written, "Zeal for your house will consume me." Then the Judeans said to him, "What sign can you show us since you are doing these things?" Yeshua answered them, "Destroy this temple, and in three days I will raise it up." The Judeans then said, "It has taken forty-six years to build this temple, and will you raise it up in three days?" However, he spoke concerning the temple of his body. Then when he was raised from the dead, his disciples remembered that he had said this, and believed the Scripture and the word that Yeshua had spoken.[1]

"Saphar, in creation we see the first Adam in the first temple and in redemption we see the second Adam in the last temple. The first Adam's failure required the second Adam's sacrifice. The cleansing of the physical temple was the Master's last act before the spiritual cleansing of the cosmos

---

1. John 2:12–22

through the cross. Yeshua came to make all things new. There will be a new garden, city, earth, and cosmos. In addition, this third set of events also illustrates the difference in souls of the fifth and sixth days."

Polycarp looked at Yochanan intrigued and asked. "Could you elaborate on this illustration Rabbi?" Yochanan gladly answered.

"The first fruit of souls the Father created on the fifth day were much different than the souls of the sixth day; Adam and Chavah. Similarly, our souls are bound by this sinful world but those souls who believe in Yeshua will be so transformed that our previous state will seem beastly."

"I see the Son in a whole new light now Rabbi. All of the physical creation of the Father is in the process of spiritual redemption because of what Yeshua accomplished."

"Yes Saphar. I hope that our introduction will help others see that, first, as the Father created physical light and separated darkness from light, so Messiah is that spiritual light of Elohim that divides the spiritual darkness in this world. Second, as the Father created the physical universe, which declares His glory, so the Word became flesh and reflects that same glory. Third, as the pooling of the waters provided a baptism for the world, providing physical life, so the baptism of the Anointed One provided spiritual life. Fourth, as the Father provided physical luminaries for the world so the Son is the spiritual light for the tribes and the nations. Fifth, as Elohim created the first physical life on the fifth day so the first spiritual life of Yeshua's ministry occurred at the wedding. Finally, Saphar, I hope they see that the second Adam in the last temple completes what the first Adam in the original temple could not accomplish."

"It is a good introduction Rabbi."

"Thank you Saphar." Yochanan grasped the arms of the creaking wooden chair and straightened his arms while arching his back and bringing his shoulder blades closer together in a prolonged stretch. "That is enough for today Saphar," he said in a slow exhale as he raised himself from the chair and started toward the door. It was obvious that he was tired and needed food and rest. Polycarp carefully gathered the parchments, put them safely in a worn ridged leather binder, and set them in the cabinet with the rest of the scrolls. Yochanan tightened his wrinkled right hand around the top of his staff and stepped over the threshold of the adobe while grasping the doorjamb with his left. Simultaneously his faithful disciple busied himself with switching the amanuensis station with the low table and started gathering the leftover challah, fruit, water, and wine.

II

Disciple Servant

After a short, prayerful walk around a nearby field, Yochanan felt invigorated and returned to the adobe for the final meal of the day. Per usual Polycarp left nothing to add to the setting of the table. The two enjoyed their evening meal with conversation of local news and opportunities to help the villagers of their small enclave. The two climbed the ladder to the rooftop after the meal to share in prayer. Dusk provided a feeling of renewal as the sun slipped slowly away and gave way to another beginning with the darkness, reminding them of the first day of creation.[1] Climbing down the ladder Yochanan started toward the cabinet for some parchments. Polycarp stirred the coals of the fire and set atop the embers some more dry kindling, and soon the crackling wood provided light and warmth to the adobe.

Yochanan lowered a thick white candle to the flame, a yellow fire flicker licked the wick of the candle, and the wick shone bright. He then set the candle on his modest nightstand and situated himself on his mat with his back leaning against the wall to enjoy his nightly reading. Polycarp gathered most of the leftover food, moved toward the threshold and turned toward Yochanan.

"Shalom Rabbi" he said,

"Shalom Polycarp," responded Yochanan. The disciple closed the door of the adobe and started his nightly circuit walking toward Chavah' s home, which was his first stop.

---

1. Jews base the beginning of their day on the evening with the words from Genesis "then there was evening and morning. . ." Since the first day began in darkness so all days start with the evening.

Each night of the week, except on the Sabbath where he would make his rounds before sundown, he would visit the local widows. Stopping by to deliver food, he would also sit for a bit and converse with the woman leaders on the events of the day. He was careful to listen more than he talked and the widows looked forward to his visits more than the produce he would bring. Before returning to the adobe, he stopped by a fruit supplier who also welcomed his nightly visits. After visiting a short time, he picked up the produce set aside for himself and the Elder and returned to the adobe.

Opening the deteriorating door slowly he saw Yochanan asleep on his mat with the candle out and the parchments returned to the cabinet. He put some more wood on the low fire, wrapped the fruit in sackcloth, and gently climbed the ladder to the rooftop. He sat and stared at the celestial creations and spent considerable time looking through the concentrated wide band of stars nearest this sphere. Polycarp then climbed down the ladder, shut the hatch, settled on his matt for the night and pondered his amazing, loving Creator.

12

Apostle and Proselyte

Skipping every other stone tread Nicodemus climbed the narrow exterior stairs until he reached the heavy wooden door. He then thrust his full weight against it causing the top hinge to sever as the door opened and crashed against the interior wall.

"Yochanan, you have to go now! They have Ya'aqobe the Just and they are looking for you!" Inside, Yochanan was stuffing the last of the challah, dates, jerky, nuts and water skins in a cloth shoulder bag as he responded.

"Everything will change now Nicodemus."

"Everything has already changed, you know that!" Yochanan's steely eyes darted and fixed on Nicodemus' eyes.

"You know what I mean. This was the only city where the two coexisted. The balanced beacon to the diaspora splits today! Mark my words, Judah will revolt and the Christians will flee, confident in their interpretation of the prophecy."[1]

Nicodemus went to the door and whistled. Below, a boy barely of age wearing a small black yamika with two horses, signaled his readiness from the alley across the worn dirt road. The two men donned their hoods, left the adobe, and turned swiftly at the landing, their burnt umber cloaks catching the wind behind them as they descended the staircase. After reaching the horses, Nicodemus addressed Yochanan.

"This proselyte is committed to the Way and will help you get out of the city. There are others waiting for you in Ephesus, please go with him Yochanan." Nicodemus stared at Yochanan begging him with every crevasse

---

1. Durant, *The Story Of Civilization*, 576–7

of his face while he waited his response. Yochanan's stern gaze upon him softened, and he spoke to his old friend in a calm voice.

"Thank you Nicodemus. Perhaps Ephesus can be a new beacon. Keep me informed on your progress and send for me if things change."

After the two embraced quickly, the apostle and the proselyte mounted their horses and set out toward the north of Jerusalem. They slipped out of the city by the Water Gate on the east and moved north along the low area of the Kidron until they were able to move west to the road to Caesarea. At Mt. Gerizim, ten hours later, Yochanan, without looking, broke the silence between himself and his new traveling partner.

"We will camp here for the night and start early. Who will we be meeting in Ephesus?"

"His name is Ya'aqobe and he is a former Master Scribe."

Yochanan nodded and then responded while simultaneously fixing his eyes on his companion.

"What is your name proselyte?"

"Polycarp."

"Very well Polycarp, you may address me as Rabbi for now. Do you understand what that means?"

Polycarp nodded once, looked directly back at Yochanan with thankful eyes and said,

"Yes Rabbi."

Yochanan opened his eyes abruptly and the bright mid-month moonlight caused his iris' to close slightly. He breathed deeply and lay still on his mat contemplating what he had just experienced. His dreams were typically of fantasy or the future. This vision was of the past. The accuracy and detail of the vision was distracting but familiar. He had dreamed the past before but only rarely. However, when he did experience this phenomenon, it always meant a significant change was imminent. He glanced toward Polycarp who was still asleep with his amanuensis station ready for the morning dictation. Yochanan slowly closed his eyes and slowly drifted back in slumber, silently sifting through the secret specter.

13

Messiah Begins

Yom Shishi[1]

Daybreak broke through as yesterday. The two, habituated in their sleeping routine, rose in similar fashion with Yochanan out the door before the dawn interrupted Polycarp's sleep. Opening his eyes, his first thought was that today was preparation day and he became excited for the Sabbath tomorrow. Today they took their time on their morning stroll through the market and spent hours greeting and praying for those in the enclave. People needed to prepare themselves for worship by talking through the long week and the concerns of the times. As the Elder, Yochanan was comforting and encouraging people while challenging them to be diligent in their obedience to Torah and Messiah Yeshua. Returning to the adobe, Polycarp shifted the furniture as before and the two authors sat down to continue creating their enjoyable saga. Again excited, Polycarp asked,

"Now that the introduction paralleling the days of creation is complete Rabbi, what of the rest of the record?" Yochanan responded to his question.

"Perhaps you have noticed that after the six days of creation, the story of B'resheet[2] backs up a bit to restart with more specifics about creation. It records the life stories from Adam through Joseph culminating with Israel's redemption. We will also restart our account with the beginning of Yeshua's ministry and record specific events of Messiah's life. These events will not

---

1. Hebrew for Sixth Day—Friday
2. The book of Genesis

only culminate with the redemption of Israel, but also the nations and the entire cosmos."

"I have fresh ink, quills, and parchment ready Rabbi." Yochanan nodded in approval.

"Before we start Saphar, we will also pull one more guiding principle from the book of creation for our structure of this gospel. Do you recall the divisions of B'resheet?"

"There are many answers to that question Rabbi, however, I suppose the clearest sections can be seen by the word '*Toledot*.'"

"I share that belief," said Yochanan, "*Toledot*, as you know, means 'generations' or 'account of.' For example, at the end of the book of Adam it says,

This is the book owf the generations of Adam.
When Adonai created man, he made him in
the likeness of Adonai.[3]

"This word *Toledot*, or generations, is used at each narrative change of the patriarchs. Essentially, it is a literary call to the reader telling them that the record of the previous patriarch has ended, and the next record is beginning. Adam, Noach, Shem, Avraham, Yitzach, and Yaakov all have this postscript or colophon.[4] This word creates the continuity of structure for the entire book. It also provides transitions for each section, which some believe reveals the different authors of B'resheet.[5]"

"We will also use a word for our divisions, which is the word *Moed* or *Heorta*.[6] We will tell the story of Messiah by recording his presence in Jerusalem during the feasts of Adonai. While Yeshua celebrated all the feasts, every year, there were three cycles of feasts after his baptism that were significant. What Yeshua did during these three festal cycles reveals his mission of exposing the world to the wonders of the glory, grace, and goals of Adonai. The first cycle of feasts, especially at Passover, included many miracles and proved that he knew humanity better than they knew themselves. Write this as an introduction to the first cycle. . ."

---

3. Genesis 5:1 ESV

4. A note or emblem at the end of a work providing information regarding authorship

5. A theory that major figures in Genesis (Adam-Joseph), were the authors. See Taylor, *Who wrote Genesis*, 204–11

6. Feast (moed in Hebrew and heorta in Greek)

> *Now when he was in Jerusalem on the Passover at the feast, many believed in his name when they saw his miracles that he was doing. However, Yeshua himself did not believe in them; due to his full understanding of humanity. Also, He did not need anyone revealing anything concerning humanity because he fully knew the condition of humanity.*[7]

"The Master was present at the creation of humanity, which is hard to comprehend. However, he knows our desires, passions and intentions better than we do. He also knows the spiritual condition of every single soul. Can you imagine that my disciple?"

"It is unfathomable Rabbi."

"The others and I were his disciples for three and half years and he always knew each one of us better than we knew ourselves. He came to save us from our sinful condition and then sent us out with a similar mission. Just before he rose into the sky, we met with him on that familiar mountain. We were all sitting amidst the brown soil and sparse grass of the scorched hilltop listening to his last words. Yeshua commanded us, during this discipleship graduation, so to speak, to go and make disciples of our own. He said that we would be His living testimonies in Jerusalem, Judea, Samaria, and to all the earth. But first he would provide a living pattern or example of what he would commission us to do after his resurrection."

"Saphar, this is exactly how he started his ministry during that first Passover season! First, in Jerusalem, he revealed the need to be born anew to a leading Jew. Then, in Judea, a Judean proclaimed him as Messiah. After this, he offered living water to a woman in Samaria and finally, he healed the son of a Gentile official. In each of these instances, Yeshua and the Baptist made it clear that what humanity really needs is his saving grace. He communicated this same need in different ways depending on his audience. He knew the hearts of these four souls and approached them each with their own specific need. Let's start with Jerusalem and Nicodemus."

---

7. John 2:23–25

14

Born Anew

Now there was a man of the Pharisees, his name, Nicodemus, a ruler of the Judeans. He came to him by night and said to him, "Rabbi, we know that you are a teacher come from Adonai, for no one is able to do these miracles that you do, unless Adonai is with him." Yeshua answered and said to him, "Amen, amen, I say to you, if someone is not born anew they cannot experience the kingdom of Adonai." Nicodemus says to him, "How is a man able to be born existing as an old man? Is he able to enter into his mother's womb a second time and be born?"[1]

"Rabbi, could I please ask a question?"

"Of course, my young disciple, go ahead," replied Yochanan.

"Being born anew is a common saying among Rabbis, why was Nicodemus confused?" Yochanan responded.

"Being born anew is a common saying, however, it is typically used by Jews referring to a proselyte.[2] The non-Jew who realized the truth of Yahweh, and committed their life to him, was born anew or adopted into the family of Israel.[3] However, from Nicodemus' perspective, he was already in the family of Israel. The thought that he needed to be born anew was never in question. This is how the Master went straight to the nephesh[4] of

---

1. John 3:1–4
2. See *The Babylonian Talmud*, Yebamot, 22a
3. See Ezek. 47:21–3
4. Hebrew for Soul

Nicodemus. He used a concept familiar to Nicodemus to challenge ethnic differences while simultaneously revealing his spiritual need for renewal." Polycarp nodded his head, understanding Yochanan's point. "Let's continue Saphar."

> *Yeshua answered, "Amen, amen, I say to you, if anyone is not born of water and the Spirit, he cannot enter the kingdom of Adonai. That which is born of the flesh is flesh, and that which is born of the Spirit is spirit. Do not wonder that I said to you, 'It is necessary for you to be born anew.' The wind blows where it wishes, and you hear the sound of it, but you do not know where it comes from or where it goes. So, it is with everyone having been born of the Spirit." Nicodemus answered and said to him, "How are these things able to be?" Yeshua answered him, "You are the teacher of Israel and you do not know these things? Amen, amen, I say to you, that which we know we speak and that which we have seen we bear witness, but you do not receive our testimony. If I have told you earthly things and you do not believe, how will you believe if I tell you heavenly things? No one has ascended into the sky except he who descended from the sky, the Son of Man. And as Moses lifted up the serpent in the wilderness, so must the Son of Man be lifted up, so that whoever believes in him may have life eternal."[5]*

"Saphar, for 'anyone,' especially a non-Jew, to be able to be born of the Spirit of Yahweh was extremely hard for Nicodemus to understand. Even more difficult for him to comprehend was the possibility that a Jew not born of the Spirit would not see Olam Habah.[6] Nicodemus needed to understand that salvation was not limited to Israel alone, but was available for anyone through Israel. The Spirit would not show partiality. Having the Spirit is like the wind; you cannot see wind, but you see the effects of its power. The actions of those who have the Spirit will reveal the Father, not their position or heredity. Nicodemus also needed to believe that Yeshua was Messiah, the Anointed One chosen by the Father. Just as the bronze serpent was the focal point for physical life in the desert so Yeshua is the focal point for spiritual life in Olam Hazeh."[7]

---

5. John 3:5–15
6. The world to come
7. This present world

"Rabbi, is it valid to say that, as there was a protection from the physical serpents with Moses there is a protection from spiritual serpents with the Master?"

"Perhaps Saphar, that observation is something to think about indeed. Of course, Yeshua not only provides our protection but our redemption and salvation as well. He wanted Nicodemus to understand these truths. Ready your quill."

15

Burial Spices

For in this manner Adonai so loved the cosmos that he gave his one and only Son, that everyone believing in him should not perish but have life eternal. For Adonai did not send his Son into the world that he might separate [N] *the world, but that the world might be healed through him. The one believing in him is not separated. However, the one not believing has already been separated because he has not believed in the name of the one and only Son of Adonai. But this is the separation, that the light has come into the world, and humanity has loved the darkness rather than the light for their actions were evil. For everyone who does wicked things hates the light and does not come to the light, lest his works might be rebuked. However, the one practicing the truth comes to the light, that his actions might be clearly seen that they have been done for Adonai.*[1]

"The spiritual light of Messiah is more present and powerful than the light we wake up to Saphar." Yochanan paused, slowly rose from his padded chair while ignoring the familiar creaking. Turning toward the garden, he looked out the rear window of the adobe as if looking through a square viewing lens to the past. He recalled three specific times that he tangibly experienced this spiritual light. There was the corporeal light of the Spirit at Yeshua's baptism, his shining face and transformation on the mountain during Unleavened Bread,[2] and the misty light around Yeshua when he

---

1. John 3:16–21
2. During his second year of open ministry, see Matthew 17

departed. He had slowly lifted to the sky in a thick, heavy, soft, luminous cloud. Yochanan whispered quietly, "Baruch atah Meshiac."[3] After some time Polycarp broke the silence.

"Whatever happened to Nicodemus Rabbi?" Yochanan turned his head, set his emerald eyes on his disciples' eyes, smiled, and spoke.

"That day he believed in the light of Yeshua and he was born anew, and grew in the knowledge of the grace of the Father and his Messiah. Remaining in the Sanhedrin, he was able to help the Way from time to time. He also had the privilege of helping bury the Master. Imagine his delight when he saw Yeshua risen from the dead and smelled the faint fragrance of the burial spices he applied just three days prior." Yochanan laughed aloud as Polycarp smiled with delight.

"That powerful connection stays with him still and he tells of it often, proclaiming the truth of the Master's resurrection. You see my disciple; everyone must make a choice for good, which is selflessness, or for evil, which is selfishness. For the most part, every person you meet of every day has already made this choice. Our part is to encourage those who have chosen good and to look for divine opportunities to nudge those in the darkness toward the light."

"I understand Rabbi. So, Nicodemus is one example of the Master reaching Jerusalem, what about the greater area of Judea?" Just then, Yochanan heard a growl coming from near the front door.

"I hear your stomach Polycarp, let us stretch our legs on the way to the mikvah[4] and then eat some food."

"Thank you Rabbi, I am a bit hungry."

"A bit you say? I would not want to hear your stomach when you are starved!"

---

3. Hebrew for "Blessed are you Messiah"

4. Hebrew word for a local man-made pool of flowing water for cleansing by immersion; a baptismal

16

Irenaeus

Gathering their Sabbath clothes from the cabinet the two grasped their staffs and headed for the center of the enclave. In the center was the synagogue where Jews and Gentiles of the Way gathered for worship, reading of scripture, prayer, and immersion. Every preparation day and Sabbath, the synagogue hosted chanting and singing of Davidic psalms, the weekly Torah portion for instruction, and the recitation of the Amidah.[1] While the mikvah provided cleansing, most baptized themselves just before the Sabbath in order to enter into worship the following day with a rinsed body and a cleansed soul. Yochanan and Polycarp usually came early to miss the heavy crowds in the afternoon.

"Rabbi, do you mind if we call on Irenaeus to join us? I covered the principles and history of immersion last week and I would like to provide him the opportunity for immersion with this new understanding."

"Of course, how is the training of your young disciple Irenaeus advancing?"

"He is passionate about Yeshua and seems limitless in his desire to seek the Father...there he is now." Polycarp pointed to a thin, tall young man in brown sandals, wearing a linen tallit with Tzittzit[2], a tan cloak, and a black skullcap.

"I believe he was waiting for you Polycarp, an eager disciple indeed. It seems you have chosen well."

---

1. "Standing Prayer" of blessings
2. See Numbers 15:38

"Erev Shabbat[3] Irenaeus" said Polycarp.

"Erev Shabbat Rabbi, Elder Yochanan, it is wonderful to see you both."

"Shalom Irenaeus, I have been hearing good things about you," said Yochanan. "Tell me of your latest lesson as we make our way to the synagogue."

Irenaeus was bubbling with excitement at this opportunity to review his lesson with Polycarp and especially with the Elder. During his explanation, he was talking almost too fast to understand and he hardly took a breath during his recitation.

"Yes, Elder Yochanan, it was concerning the mikvah. I learned that after the overstepping of Yahweh's commands by Chavah and Adam the Father provided a cleansing sacrifice for their sin. He also clothed them with this sacrifice and instructed them in immersion for their physical cleansing. It is believed that our practice today is, most likely, very similar to our ancient parents." Polycarp nodded in agreement and encouraged him to describe the process.

"Since we are approaching the mikvah, young disciple, give us the main points of our practice of immersion today."

"Thank you, Rabbi. The first principle is, of course, one at a time." Young Irenaeus chuckled quickly at the thought picture of more than one person in the mikvah and said, "It would get crowded quickly and would be. . .awkward." Both Polycarp and Yochanan, unsuccessfully, tried to hold back smiles and waited for him to continue. "Second is to disrobe and prepare your heart as if before Yeshua himself. Third is to enter slowly confessing in your mind your sin and remembering his sacrifice on the cross. Fourth is to immerse yourself entirely including spreading your fingers and toes for complete immersion by the water like Yeshua was with the Spirit. Fifth is to recite the prayer '*Baruch ata Adonai eloheinu melech ha-olam asher kidshanu b'mitzvo-tav v'tzi-vanu al ha-tevilah*' which means; blessed are you, Adonai, ruler of the universe, who has sanctified us with the mitzvot[4] and commanded us concerning immersion. Lastly, exit slowly, dry off, and dress quickly in clothes appropriate for Shabbat." With this last principle, they had arrived at the preparation area just before the entrance to the mikvah.

"Very good my young disciple let the Elder go first and then you and I can follow."

---

3. Eve of the Sabbath—A Jewish greeting the day before Sabbath
4. Hebrew word for commands or good deeds

17

Wilderness Mikvah

Completing their immersion in the mikvah, they started back toward the adobe. Irenaeus wanted to continue with them but Polycarp had informed him before about the project. He understood that his Rabbi's time would be limited for a season. However, they did request that he go to the spring and bring some fresh water to the adobe. Irenaeus was very willing to perform this task and left immediately to get the water yoke.

Upon arriving at the adobe, Polycarp and Yochanan enjoyed a meal of Challah with honey, figs, dates, and water. Polycarp then gathered extra wood in preparation for the Sabbath while Yochanan gathered his thoughts. As the scribe settled in his chair with preparations complete, he asked a question.

"On to Judea Rabbi?" The wrinkles around Yochanan's eyes deepened as he smiled and nodded.

> *After these things Yeshua and his disciples went into the Judean region, and he stayed there with them and was baptizing. However, Yochanan was also baptizing at Aenon near Salim, because there was much water there. Now, they were coming and being baptized for Yochanan had not yet been put in prison. Then a debate arose between some of Yochanan's disciples and a Judean about purification. And they came to Yochanan and said to him, "Rabbi, he who was with you across the Jordan, to whom you bore witness; look, he baptizes, and all come to him." Yochanan answered and said, "Humanity is able to receive nothing, not one thing unless it is given to him from the sky. You yourselves bear my witness*

> that I said, 'I am not the Messiah, but I have been sent before him.' The one who has the bride is the bridegroom but the friend of the bridegroom, who stands and hears him, rejoices with gladness at the bridegroom's voice. Therefore, this joy of mine is now made full. It is inevitable for him to increase and for me to decrease."[1]

Yochanan had been slowly pacing about the adobe during this dictation but at this point, he stopped, turned to Polycarp and spoke.

"Some present during this time were very concerned that Yochanan ha Matbil[2] was losing his followers to Yeshua. However, the Baptist and Yeshua understood that this Judean initiated argument was not about numbers of followers. It concerned purification, expiation or atonement. The Judean was rightly concerned about his purification. Levitical law requires that the priests baptize several times before entering the temple. He wondered how this baptism in the wilderness of Judea, by an Essene Rabbi helped his purification. My suspicion was that the Judean genuinely and desperately wanted cleansing from his sin here in this present world. However, Yochanan ha Matbil knew that his physical immersion pointed to Messiah's spiritual immersion. Yeshua's baptism would not only physically cleanse in Olam Hazeh but also spiritually cleanse so one may be welcomed in Olam Habah. What the Judean wanted was atonement. The Baptist pointed him to Yeshua because he offers spiritual atonement and eternal life. There was a very stark difference between the Baptist and Messiah. Let us finish the words of Yochanan ha Matbil."

> The one arriving from the beginning is above all. The one existing out of the land is from the land and speaks as one from the land. The one arriving from the sky is above all. He testifies to what he has seen and heard, but no one accepts his testimony. The one having accepted the testimony he has sealed because Adonai is unconcealed. For the one Adonai sent speaks the words of Adonai, indeed he gives the Spirit without measure. The Father loves the Son and has given all things into his hand. The one believing in the Son has life eternal but those incredulous to the Son shall not see life, indeed the wrath of Adonai remains on him.[3]

Yochanan sat down at this point, causing some lint of the cotton cushion to drift in the afternoon sunlight coming through the window.

1. John 3:22–30
2. John the Immerser
3. John 3:31–36

"Saphar, Yeshua was with the Father at creation but his atonement is timeless. The Father sent him at this specific time to redeem all adam,[4] including those of the past, present, and future. Only the one who had been with the Father could testify and reveal the Father. He also revealed that the righteous path through this life, and the acceptance into the next, is through the Son. As he used physical birth to illustrate spiritual birth for Nicodemus in Jerusalem, so he used physical baptism to illustrate the spiritual baptism of the Spirit with the Judean. As you well know my disciple, he did not stop there."

"I understand Rabbi, on to Samaria."

---

4. Hebrew for Mankind or humanity

18

Ethos Not Geos

Now when Yeshua learned that the Pharisees had heard that Yeshua was making and baptizing more disciples than John, although Yeshua himself was not baptizing but his disciples, he left Judea and departed again into Galilee. Now it was necessary for him to pass through Samaria, so he comes to a city of Samaria called Sychar, near the piece of land that Ya'aqobe had given to his son Yoseph. Now the spring of Ya'aqobe was there so Yeshua, being wearied from the journey, sat in the manner upon the spring. It was about the sixth hour.[1]

Yochanan stopped and chuckled a bit and then said, "It is amazing how quickly news travels today Saphar. It was the next morning, only hours later, that Yeshua recognized that the Pharisees were trying to make something of this Judean argument. He immediately removed himself from the drama and, for a reason unknown to us, we marched straight to Ya'aqobe's[2] well. We traveled light with only one cloak and a few satchels of food, wine skins and...other necessities. I learned the importance of a good pair of sandals that day. After that trek I found a pair with double souls and extra thongs."

"The road was a mix of stone and dust with the topography changing often. Each of us followed him closely kicking up a collective murky cloud of earth around us. His intent on arriving at our destination as soon as possible was clear. Now, we were unclear exactly where we were going, but he was about to transform a town in Samaria while simultaneously challenging

1. John 4:1–6
2. Hebrew for Jacob

our perspective of who is worthy of eternal life. We arrived at Ya'aqobe's spring with the sun over our heads and our stomachs empty. While he sat at the spring, as if on the teaching seat of the synagogue, we went into the city for additional food. Do you have enough ink Saphar?"

"For now, Rabbi, please continue."

> *A woman from Samaria comes out to draw water. Yeshua says to her, "Give me a drink." For his disciples had gone away into the city that they might buy food. The Samaritan woman then says to him, "How do you, a Jew, ask a drink from me, a woman of Samaria?" For Jews ° do not associate with Samaritans. Yeshua answered her, "If you had remembered the free offer of Adonai, and the one who is saying to you, 'Give me a drink,' you would have perhaps asked him, and he would have perhaps given you living water."*[3]

Yochanan stopped here in anticipation of Polycarp's curiosity. Polycarp noticed the pause, set his quill aside carefully making sure to center the tip on the quill rest, and looked up at Yochanan.

"Rabbi, I know that most Samaritan's recognize the Gerizim temple instead of the Jerusalem temple as the chosen place for worship. In addition, they only recognize the Torah and not the Nevi'im or Ketuvim.[4] What did the twelve think of Yeshua purposely going to Samaria?" Yochanan chuckled softly and then responded.

"As slow as we were in comprehension at times, we were beginning to understand that his intent to reveal the Father concentrically from Jerusalem outward was not simply geographical. More importantly, was his desire for Israel to be a light of righteousness and eternal life to all people no matter their place, position or patrimony."

"What about the matron of the spring Rabbi? To see Yeshua openly talking with a woman must have been puzzling to the twelve."

At that moment there was a "knock, knock, knock" upon the door and the two looked at each other puzzled and then turned their heads quickly to the door, surprised at the interruption.

Irenaeus left the Rabbi and Elder after the request for water. He quickly ran to his adobe to harness the water yoke upon himself to retrieve water from the local spring. Arriving at the spring he sat crossed legged on

---

3. John 4:7–10
4. Torah—5 Books of Moses, Nevi'im—Prophets, Ketuvim—Writings

the outskirts and patiently waited his turn to draw water. The spring was a three-cubit wide hole in the limestone ground. Hewn by the patriarch's centuries before him, it provided water for families and flocks. Besides the water yoke, he also knew it was necessary to bring the one-hundred-cubit rope. He had twisted the strands himself and attached it to the leather bucket's iron handle made by his father.

As his turn arrived, he was thankful that he had come at an opportune time where few people were at the spring. Kneeling at the raised stone-rimmed curb that encircled the opening, Irenaeus was determined to carry as much fresh water as possible to his Rabbi and Elder to help sustain them. He also wanted to get the water to the adobe as soon as possible. He lowered the thick, long, twisted cord and bucket repeatedly to fill both larger buckets of the water yoke. After filling each of the buckets with the crisp, clear liquid, he wrapped the rope and lifting bucket around his waist and shoulders, crouched under the yoke, and lifted. He was careful to tame his usual hurried gate on the way to the Elder's adobe to spare what impatience would usually spill. Upon arriving at the adobe, he set the full buckets down at the threshold and knocked three times.

Polycarp, hearing the knocks on the door, rose from his amanuensis station and swung the door open wide, noticed the yoke and exclaimed, "Irenaeus, that was quick indeed."

As a wide smile of satisfaction came upon his face, Irenaeus exclaimed, "Here is you fresh water Rabbi, from the spring."

After lifting the buckets one after another to the cistern and filling it to the brim Polycarp replied, "Thank you, my young disciple, the Elder and I are in your debt and we will thrive with our project because of your provision."

"Thank you, Rabbi." replied Irenaeus. Fixing his eyes on Polycarp, he smiled with joy. Breaking eye contact, he reattached the buckets, lifted his water yoke to his shoulders, and went to fill the buckets again to provide for the widows before sundown.

"A worthy disciple indeed," said Yochanan.

19

Nephesh Not Genus

The two assumed their positions. Polycarp went to his station and Yochanan to his cotton-padded chair. "Now," said Yochanan, "about the woman at the well. She was surprised at Yeshua' s willingness of openly engaging her in conversation. As I discovered later, her surprise was more about him being Jewish rather than his gender. She readily pursued the conversation after realizing the Master was willing to talk to a Samaritan. It soon became clear that Yeshua was concerned about her nephesh, her soul, and not her sex. He reminded her of the covenant of Adonai and used the physical water of the well to introduce the concept of living water to the woman; which intrigued her greatly."

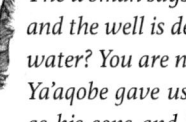
> *The woman says to him, "Sir, you have nothing to draw with, and the well is deep. From where then do you have this living water? You are not greater than our father Ya'aqobe, are you? Ya'aqobe gave us the well and drank from it himself, as well as his sons and his livestock" Yeshua said to her, "Everyone who is drinking of this water will thirst again but whoever, at any time, might drink of the water that I will give him, will not ever thirst in this present era* ^P*. Indeed, the water that I will give to him will become a well of water springing up into life eternal." The woman says to him, "Sir, give me this very water, that I might not thirst nor come here to draw."*[1]

Polycarp finished the last letter of this dictation and said, "Forgive me Rabbi I have another question."

1. John 4:11–15

"Yes disciple?" "

"It seems clear that the Master was talking of the Spirit so why did the woman think that if she received the living water she would never have to come to the well?" Yochanan paused, looked toward Samaria and answered.

"Saphar we have talked about those who call themselves 'Gnostic' and that they dismiss this material world and only consider special or spiritual knowledge, correct?"

"Yes Rabbi, I remember."

"The Samaritans, from her reaction, led us to believe that this local group was quite the opposite. It seemed hard for them to accept the spiritual or supernatural. It was almost impossible for the woman to think beyond the physical. Instead of a messiah coming to redeem all humanity unto Olam Habah, they were waiting for one who would physically restore the Father's kingdom here and now. The Samaritans had lost the wonder of the supernatural or spiritual power of the Almighty. However, they still thirsted for the miraculous, which is why Yeshua did what he did next."

> *He says to her, "Go, call your husband, and come here." The woman answered and said to him, "I do not have a husband." Yeshua says to her, "You have spoken nobly saying, 'I do not have a husband,' indeed you have had five husbands, and the one you now have is not your husband. You have spoken this truly." The woman says to him, "Sir, I perceive that you are a prophet. Our fathers worshiped on this mountain, but you say that the place where it is necessary to worship is in Jerusalem." Yeshua says to her, "Lady, believe me, a time is coming when neither on the mountain here nor in Jerusalem will you worship the Father. You worship what you do not know; we worship what we do know, for this salvation is from the Jews. However, a time is coming, indeed, it is now, when the true worshipers will worship the Father in spirit and truth, for the Father seeks such ones worshiping him. Adonai is spirit, it is necessary for those worshiping him to worship in spirit and truth." The woman says to him, "I know that Messiah is coming, the one they are calling Messiah. When he comes, he will disclose all things." Yeshua says to her, "I, whom am speaking to you, am he."*[2]

Yochanan paused here, stretched out his arms and legs simultaneously towards the door opposite the room, and groaned with the pleasant feeling of his muscles being stimulated. He then stood and looked down at Polycarp

---

2. John 4:16–26

without saying a word. Polycarp, instinctively knowing that his master had stopped for his many questions, spoke freely.

"It is clear now that Yeshua responded according to her needs as a Samaritan. However, instead of wondering how he was able to know those things, she wondered about the proper place to worship the Father. I am curious why she responded in this manner."

Yochanan's pleasant smile came to his face and the gleam in his eye brightened as he responded.

"There are many self-proclaimed prophets that could impress with similar abilities, although none with the true power of Yeshua!" Yochanan strongly clarified. "It is not a surprise that she was more concerned with the most important topic of the day; who is rightfully worshipping the Father. In other words, who is worthy of eternal life. She was expecting the typical exclusive answer given in the past. Instead Yeshua reminded her that the Father's plan for life eternal has its source in his chosen people and that this salvation is open to all who seek him."

"I understand Rabbi. His response did not repeat the standard arguments of where to worship, which had divided Jews and Samaritans for centuries. Instead, he focused on the Father's love for those who seek him and because of these things she suspected that he was the Messiah."

"Yes, my disciple. His supernatural insight into her life, and grace filled response of what the Father truly seeks, was appealing to her indeed."

"Rabbi, was this the first time the Master clearly revealed himself as Messiah?"

"It was the first time he spoke so plainly about it, and this Samaritan woman had that honor. We did not fully understand then, but he was purposefully crossing long held cultural barriers to reveal the Father's unbiased concern for all nepheshim, regardless of heredity or gender." Yochanan nodded toward the parchment on Polycarp's desk and he readied himself.

20

White For Harvest

Now at this time his disciples arrived, and they marveled that he was speaking with a woman, however, no one said, "What do you seek?" or, "Why do you speak with her?" Then, the woman left her water jar and went away into town and says to the people, "Come, see a man who told me all things, whatever I have done. Can this be the Messiah?" They went out of the town and came to him. In the meantime, his disciples were urging him, saying, "Rabbi, eat." But he said to them, "I have food to eat that you do not know." Therefore, the disciples said to one another, "No one brought him anything to eat." Yeshua says to them, "My food is that I should do the will of the one having sent me and to complete his work. Do you not say, 'There are yet four months, then the harvest comes'? Behold, I say to you, lift up your eyes, and see the fields that are white, already near harvest. The one reaping receives a reward and gathers fruit for life eternal, so that sower and reaper may rejoice together. Here indeed this saying is true that, 'This one is sowing so that one is reaping.' I sent you to reap what you did not labor for; others have labored, and you have participated in their labor."[1]

"We must always be looking for opportunities to spread the word of Messiah Saphar. Indeed, this is the reason we are in this room, providing this record.

---

1. John 4:27–38

"I agree and understand Rabbi. This is a major focus of my training with Irenaeus. Those who walk in darkness need to see the light of Messiah and drink of his living water." Polycarp pondered and then posed a question. "Rabbi, did she leave the water jar for Yeshua?"

"Yes disciple, after all, he told her to give him a drink. It is interesting that her first act of obedience was providing well water for the one who could provide living water. This scene at Sychar was a living example of the Son fulfilling the mission given by the Father. The Son completed the Father's work in preparing the Samaritans for this moment and used this awakening as a current example for our future mission. Throughout history, either the Father himself or the Father through other believers has been sowing seeds of faith in every type of person. We have the privilege of taking part in that work by revealing Messiah and watching that seed of belief blossom to the fruit of eternal life. Take up your quill Saphar and let us finish this section."

> *Then those of the town came out. Many of the Samaritans believed in him because of the account of the woman testifying, "Because he told me all that I ever did." So when the Samaritans came to him, they asked him to stay with them and he stayed there two days. And many others believed because of his word. Both groups said to the woman, "We no longer believe because of your account for we have heard for ourselves, and we know that this is indeed the Savior of the world." After the two days, he departed for Galilee. For Yeshua himself had testified that a prophet has no honor in his own hometown. So, when he came into Galilee, the Galileans welcomed him, having seen all the great things he had done in Jerusalem during the feast. Indeed, they themselves had also gone to the feast.[2]*

"It was clear, Saphar, that the Father had been keeping a spiritual curiosity alive in both the Samaritans and many of the Gentiles mixed among them for some time. The Father's timing is never coincidental, and it took very little time with the Son for them to realize that he was the Messiah. The miracles he performed were convincing to be sure, but more convincing was his presence. Spending time with Messiah changes a person and provides shimmer to our spiritual spark. It fuels the desire to put away your own darkness for his light."

"I understand Rabbi. He has corrected and comforted me many times, just as he came to those we have discussed. Like Nicodemus in Jerusalem,

---

2. John 4:39–45

the questioning Judean in Judea and the Samaritan woman. What of the rest of those on the earth, so to speak?"

Yochanan stepped back to sit once again in his chair. As he shifted his feet, there was a familiar creaking and kicking of dust that slowly speckled the waning sunlight. He then motioned to Polycarp with an upward movement of his index finger for him to ready his quill.

> *So, he came again to Cana of Galilee, where he had made the water wine. Now there was a certain government official whose son was sick in Capernaum. Having heard that Yeshua had come from Judea to Galilee, he went immediately to him and asked that he would come down and heal his son for he was about to die. So Yeshua said to him, "Unless you see signs and wonders will you not believe?" The government official says to him, "Sir, come down before my child dies." Yeshua says to him, "Go; your son lives." The man believed the word that Yeshua said to him and went away. Now after a while, as he is going down, his servants met him saying, "Your son lives." So, he asked them the hour when he got better, and they said to him, "Yesterday at the seventh hour the fever left him." So, the father knew that was the hour when Yeshua had said to him, "Your son lives," and he himself believed, and his whole household. This was now the second sign that Yeshua did when he had come from Judea to Galilee.*[3]

"This Gentile official," explained Yochanan, "had heard of the miracles performed by Yeshua' s during the Passover season and he believed this was his only chance to save his dying son. However, Yeshua wanted to test his belief in the Almighty, by questioning him about believing solely because of miracles. Yeshua' s question to him 'Unless you see signs and wonders will you not believe?' was direct, and challenged his faith. At first, the official only knew that Yeshua was his only hope for his son. However, after he heard Yeshua' s promise, this hope for his son turned to hope in Yahweh's Son. His faith did not require Yeshua to come down as he requested, because he had his promise. When the official heard the report sometime later, on his way to his son, his faith in that promise turned to a full commitment in Yeshua as Messiah. Then the official witnessed to his extended family and they also believed in Yeshua." As Yochanan finished he noticed his scribe deep in thought.

"Do you have another question Saphar?"

---

3. John 4:46–54

Polycarp paused while looking at his Rabbi and then asked, "What of Adonai's promises that have not yet come to pass?" Yochanan smiled and responded softly.

"The Father has given us many promises my disciple. You are right that many of those promises have not yet come to pass. While it has been quite a bit longer than the official had to wait for confirmation, the Father will make good on his promises. One clear example of his commitment to his promises is that he sent his Son. Yeshua not only fulfilled many of the Fathers promises but provides the hope for those promises not yet realized."

"Thank you, Rabbi. There is wisdom in the Master's teaching method. It is truly motivating that he led by example and reached out to Jerusalem, Judea, Samaria, and to all those on the earth before commissioning the eleven."

21

Junia

As dusk became more noticeable, the two locked eyes and without saying a word rearranged the room for the Sabbath. They centered the low, long table in the living area and Polycarp busied himself with food and comfort preparations for Sabbath guests. Yochanan ascended to the rooftop to watch the descending sun. As Polycarp finished his preparations there came a "knock, knock, knock" on the adobe door. Polycarp opened the tattered door and was greeted by Irenaeus and his mother Junia,

"Shabbat shalom!" They replied in unison, as they extended their arms with gifts of Challah and wine.

"Shabbat shalom" said Polycarp, as he welcomed them into the adobe.

Junia fixed her eyes on Polycarp and said, "Thank you for your invitation and your time with my young one Rabbi. His character is becoming strong and, in that, I can see your hand."

"I enjoy Irenaeus," replied Polycarp as he smiled at Irenaeus, "Thank you for loaning him to me from time to time. You have other children, are they around?"

"They are away with my sister getting some needed training in agriculture," said Junia. Just then, they all heard the latch of the hatch and Yochanan' s strong voice as the waning sunlight shone through the roof.

"Let us welcome the Sabbath from the roof. Polycarp, please bring up only the necessities."

Junia and Polycarp ascended the ladder with clay cups and plates while Irenaeus gathered the candles, flint, wine, and challah. Once on the roof their eyes traced the darkly pitched two-foot-high perimeter parapet, which was backlit by the opaque orange dusking skyline. They then moved toward a table and two benches constructed of sanded tree limbs set in the middle of the roof. Yochanan had made the table before his travels with Yeshua. The table frame and benches he honed out of cedar and was careful to select limbs of equal diameter for the legs as well as the supports and cross braces. The table was the size the Ark of the Covenant and was able to seat ten people comfortably. For the tabletop, he planed and joined three-inch-wide by two-inch-thick boards of yellow sandalwood. The fragrance and perception of the sandalwood top gave off a sweet golden impression and an ideal place to remember the Sabbath.

A traditional cloth runner, symbol laden with Stars of David, menorahs, and cherubim striped the table. Also placed on the table were candlesticks, cups and plates. The candles were at the center, the cups in between the candles and plates with the plates on the concentric fringe. A single, small loaf of braided challah adorned Yochanan's plate and the four positioned themselves around the table. As the sun hesitated to set, it drifted above the horizon. Irenaeus was waiting eagerly with the flint and striker in hand when he suddenly realized that he had not given the fire starter to his mother. He quickly passed the flint to her just as Yochanan turned and nodded toward Junia. She responded to Yochanan's prompting by striking the flint several times toward the oil-dipped wick of the first candle and the wick waxed to life. Irenaeus spoke first.

"We light the first candle to remember the Sabbath."

Junia then put the flame of the first candle to the top of the next candle, the second wick lit as the first, and Irenaeus spoke again.

"We light the second candle to remember to keep the Sabbath."

The four stood still and stared intensely into the flames of the candles for a moment. Junia broke the silence and the stillness by waving the heat of the candles over her head with both hands three times while chanting the Sabbath blessing.

"Barukh atah Adonai, Eloheinu, melekh ha'olam asher kidishanu b'mitz'votav v'tzivanu l'had'lik neir shel Shabbat."[1] Polycarp then recited the Kiddush.

> "And there was evening and there was morning, a sixth day. The heavens and the earth were finished, the whole host of them. And on the seventh day Adonai completed his work that he had done and he rested on the seventh day from all his work that he had done and Adonai blessed the seventh day, and sanctified it because in it he had rested from all his work

---

1. Blessed are you, Yahweh, our Adonai, sovereign of the universe Who has sanctified us with His commandments and commanded us to light the lights of Shabbat.

that Adonai had created to do. Blessed are you, Yahweh, our Adonai, sovereign of the universe."[2]

Yochanan then lifted his hands and looked upward and chanted.

"Baruch atah Adonai, Eloheinu, Asher qideshanu be'dam haMashiach."[3] All at the table responded,

"Amen." Irenaeus then poured wine into the four earthen cups that were on the sweet yellow table being careful not to spill a drop. When the cups were full, Yochanan spoke while looking upward and chanted the blessing for the wine

"Baruch atah Adonai Eloheinu, Melech haOlam, Borei pri haGafen."

Polycarp then translated, "Blessed are you, Adonai our Adonai, King of the universe, who creates the fruit of the vine."

Taking a small sip of the wine, they repositioned their cups as before and waited on Yochanan who had taken the challah from his plate. He broke the challah into four equal pieces and distributed them around the table each receiving their portion with head bowed. Again, looking upward he chanted the blessing for the bread,

"Baruch atah Adonai Eloheinu, Melech haOlam, HaMotzi lechem min haAretz Ve'noten lanu echem min haShamayim."

Again, Polycarp translated, "Blessed are you, Adonai, our Adonai, King of the universe, who brings forth bread from the earth, and gives us Bread from Heaven."

Each took a small bite of the bread before them and sat down at the branch-framed table staring into the flames of the candles.

Irenaeus broke everyone's focus from the flickering fire. He knew that after the blessings anyone was free to discuss the elements of the Sabbath, so he posed a question to Polycarp.

"Rabbi, at Passover we know that the wine represents the blood of Messiah and that the bread represents his body, which made the new covenant possible. Does this same significance apply to Shabbat?"

Polycarp responded, "While his blood and body are represented at the Passover Seder, what we do on the Sabbath is from another tradition." Yochanan and Junia looked on with enjoyment with the start of the conversation.

Polycarp continued, "The Master presented the proper Passover representation of body and blood during the cup of redemption at his last Seder. Let me ask you a question my disciple. What is different in the elements of

---

2. Genesis 1:31c-2:3

3. Blessed are you, Yahweh, our Adonai, who sanctified us by the blood of the Messiah.

that part of the Paschal Seder and the elements of what we do every Shabbat?" Irenaeus's eyes were wide with curiosity while his facial expression glowed with intrigue in the candle light. He thought for some time before responding.

"Rabbi, is it that at Passover we have unleavened bread and at Shabbat we have leavened challah?"

"Very good," Polycarp responded as Yochanan and Junia nodded with approval. "There is one other important difference my disciple, and the history behind these traditions reveals their purpose. The Sabbath tradition reminds us of the manna provided by Adonai in the wilderness and later, the showbread in the tabernacle. Shabbat is a weekly picture that Adonai will always provide for us, even in our sinful state. We remember this truth every Shabbat with the challah, while the wine reminds us if the sweetness of the Sabbath rest, Adonai ordained at creation." Polycarp paused and then continued.

"The Seder is very different in that we remember the covenant Adonai completed with the sacrifice of Yeshua. The unleavened bread and third cup of the Seder reflect his sinless sacrifice of body and blood for the new covenant, prophesied by Jeremiah. We only do this tradition once a year at the appointed time. To assign the covenant significance to the elements of the Sabbath would be misplaced. Is this clear my young disciple?"

"Yes Rabbi, I can see the difference now, thank you." Such was the conversation upon the rooftop well into the night. The guests left late and the Elder and Rabbi bedded down as usual, looking forward to the rest of the Sabbath.

The evening conversation left Irenaeus with unanswered questions swirling in his head. Certain comments made him realize that his mother had an eventful life before he was born. At that moment, during their walk home, he voiced his most pressing curiosity.

"Mother, what happened in Jerusalem, before you...we...came to Ephesus?"

Junia had expected this question, or something like it, for some time. Irenaeus was now old enough to feel comfortable to ask uncomfortable questions. She decided, finally, to talk plainly with him about the past, hoping it would prepare him for the future.

"Do you remember me telling you of your grandparent's conversion to Judaism?"

"Yes."

"Well, shortly after they died, when I was about your age, the Romans took their home and I was put in a holding area in the center of the city. I did not have rights as a Roman citizen so, most likely, I would have ended up as a slave in some Roman household. However, since your grandparents were faithful to the synagogue, one of the Jewish leaders ransomed me from the holding pen and brought me into his household. I learned many things from his wife and their other children. They treated me as if I was a blood member of their family. The Father truly poured forth his blessing on me during that time. Nero had just assumed the throne and, as we have studied, Jerusalem would see death and revolt during his reign."

Junia continued, "However, before those terrible days of revolution I met your father Andronicus, who was a member of the Way. We married shortly after we met and we had a small room in my Jewish benefactor's home where we contributed as best we could to the synagogue. It was a wonderful time of learning the Torah, and seeing how Yeshua lived the Father's commands. When I finally became pregnant with you, the Jewish revolt had begun and we decided to leave Jerusalem for Ephesus. As we have discussed before, your father gave his life so you and I could survive."

Junia paused and studied Irenaeus to see the effect this knowledge would have on her son. Irenaeus looked at this mother thankfully, appreciating the added information. They were approaching their adobe while Junia closed the discussion.

"You will meet your father in Olam Habah my son. Until then, learn and follow his passion for Messiah by bringing the truth of Adonai to the world." Irenaeus looked directly into his mother's eyes with understanding and pride and responded.

"I will mother, thank you for helping me understand our past." The two walked into their home and immediately went to bed.

22

Physical Atonement

Yom Shabbat[1]

As the Sabbath sun started to shine, the Elder and Rabbi nestled into their mats and slept well beyond their usual waking hour. Just before midday, they rose, prayed, ate, and made themselves ready for the Sabbath service at the synagogue.

"Saphar, do you mind bringing the ink, quill, and parchments to the synagogue?"

"Of course not Rabbi, I was wondering if you were going to feather in the continuation of the project with your Sabbath teaching. I will look for your usual cues."

"Thank you Saphar. It seemed good to me because the next events in our account happened during Yom Kippur.[2] Those events will be a fitting preparation as we continue to count the Omer to Shavuot,[3] looking forward to the fall feasts."

They quickly gathered all the necessary items for the service and the project. They would move an amanuensis station from the preparation room in the back of the synagogue to the main floor for Polycarp. They arrived at the synagogue in the early afternoon. After making the necessary preparations, they led the people in the appropriate prayers. Before the

1. Hebrew for Seventh Day—Saturday
2. Hebrew for The Day of Atonement
3. Hebrew for Pentecost

teaching time, Yochanan explained that this week he would be retelling certain accounts regarding Yeshua and commenting on their meaning. Polycarp positioned himself with his amanuensis tools to the right of the bema[4] and, after a quick summary introduction of previous events, Yochanan sat down and taught.

> *After this, there was the feast* [R] *of the Judeans, and Yeshua went up to Jerusalem. Now there is in the city of peace, by the Sheep Gate, a pool, which is called Bethesda,[5] in Aramaic, having five porches. In these were laying a multitude of those ailing; blind, lame, and paralyzed, awaiting the moving of the water. For an angel, at an appointed time, descended on the pool and stirred the water. Now he who entered first after the stirring of the water was made well at that moment from whatever disease held them. Indeed, there was a certain man there who had been there thirty-eight years, himself being an invalid. Yeshua, having seen him lying, and having known that he had already been there a long time says to him, "Do you desire to become well?" The invalid answered him, "Sir, I have no one to put me into the pool when the water has been stirred. Indeed, while I am going another descends before me." Yeshua says to him, "Arise, take up your mat, and walk." And immediately the man became well, and he took up his mat and walked.*[6]

Yochanan expounded to the assembly.

"On Yom Kippur, the day of covering, the Day of Atonement, Yeshua, the one who would atone for all our sins, goes to the pool and physically heals one who had no hope of being healed. I do not know if the angel ever visited the pool, however, Yeshua showed this man, and all those around, that he was the source of healing and the true water of life. His compassion for the lame man compelled him to provide a physical illustration of what he would do spiritually though the cross. Also, understand precious ones, that healing is not dependent on what we do, but on the power of the word of Messiah. Much could be said on this topic but let us continue to look at the actions of Messiah on this first Yom Kippur of his open ministry."

---

4. The elevated platform in a synagogue
5. House of mercy
6. John 5:1–9

> *However, on that day, it was the Sabbath so the Judeans said to the man having been healed, "It is the Sabbath, and it is not lawful for you to take up your mat." Then he answered them, "The one having made me well, that one said to me, 'Take up your mat, and walk.'" Then they asked him, "Who is the man having said to you, 'Take up your mat and walk'?" But the man having been healed did not know who it was, for Yeshua had moved on since there was a crowd in that place.*[7]

"Those of you from the line of Ya'aqobe, Yisrael, will have more understanding on this point, but let us all understand that Adonai has given us the Torah. However, there are also protective ordinances, or fences, for the Torah made by man. Leaders in all generations have created fences for the Torah. Often, these fences were well intentioned. However, eventually, in almost all circumstances, men enforced these fences as Torah. These fences, created another layer of protection for obeying Torah and, at times, encouraged obedience. While this may seem prudent, the fact remains that Adonai spoke the Torah. . .not the fences. Now, Yeshua did not call for rebellion and neither do I. In fact, his call was for quite the opposite. However, be careful to understand the difference between what Adonai requires and what man requires. Yeshua did transgress against many fences of the Torah, but never the Torah of Adonai. Therefore, Yeshua told the man to take up and carry his mat, which was a fence, a protective ordinance. It was not surprising that the leaders opposed this action. Yeshua, however, was concerned for the one healed. He also knew the man would go to the temple to worship, especially on Yom Kippur. Let's continue with the story."

> *After these things, Yeshua finds him in the temple and said to him, "Behold, you have become well! Have no part in sin so that something worse might not happen to you." The man went away and told the Judeans that it was Yeshua who had made him well. And because of this, the Judeans persecuted Yeshua, since he did these things on the Sabbath. But Yeshua answered them, "My Father is working until now, and I am working." Also, because of this statement the Judeans sought all the more to kill him, since he not only loosened the Sabbath,* [s] *but he also called Adonai his own Father, making himself equal with Adonai.*[8]

Yochanan glanced over at Polycarp and then turned to the congregation and said, "I am sure some of you may have this question going through

7. John 5:10–13
8. John 5:14–18

your mind. 'What did Yeshua mean by saying, have no part in sin so that something worse might not happen to you?'"

"I do not know how the man came to be lame, however, from the Master's caution regarding sin, there seemed to be at least two answers to this question. First, this man may have become an invalid due to an accident during an unrighteous act. Or, the caution was given because the man could now move about freely with more opportunity for sin. In any event, I would caution against the mystical belief that sin causes physical ailments. There are those who believe that sinning can cause someone to become sick in some way. For example, some believe that adultery causes leprosy. But what of the adulterer without leprosy and what of the leper who does mitzvot[9]?"

"My children, these conditions of the heart are not as simple as we would like them to be, which is why we should lay these wonderings at the feet of Messiah. He is the one who knows the inner most thoughts of every being. Only he can work all things for good, including infirmities. The Father and the Son search these things and they do not rest in this aspect, not even on Shabbat. However, this was hard for the Judeans to understand. What we see from this healing event is that Yeshua has power over our physical condition. He is the one who is able to atone and redeem any aspect of this physical creation. Let's continue with the account."

---

9. Good deeds

23

Spiritual Atonement

> So Yeshua answered and said to them, "Truly, truly, I say to you, the Son is not able to do anything of himself except whatever he might see the Father doing. For whatever possibility he does, these things the Son also does, likewise. For the Father loves the Son and shows him everything he himself does; and greater works than these will he show him, so that you might marvel. For even as the Father raises the dead and gives them life, so also the Son gives life to whom he will. For not even the Father judges anyone, but has given all judgment to the Son, in order that all may honor the Son, just as they honor the Father. Whoever does not honor the Son does not honor the Father who sent him. Truly, truly, I say to you the one hearing my word and believing in the one having sent me has life eternal and does not come into judgment, but has passed from the state of death to state of life."[1]

"Yeshua made it clear that he could only do what the Father would do. Conversely, any possible thing the Father can do he has given the power and possibility to the Son. He wants us to understand that he can only do what the Father would do, so we can trust that the Son's actions will absolutely mimic the Father's intentions. This is important to understand if we are to comprehend the depth of his physical and spiritual atonement. The Son has the power over life in this world and the next. Adonai has given him the

---

1. John 5:19–24

responsibility of personal judgement for every nephesh.² Let us make the most of our time and honor the Son by living his example in the hope that others will see the Father in our actions. Yeshua continued. . ."

>  "Truly, truly, I say to you that an hour is coming, and now is when the dead will hear the voice of the Son of Adonai, and those having heard will live. As the Father has life in himself, so also, he gave life to the Son to have in himself. And he gave to him authority to execute judgment because he is the Son of Man. Do not marvel at this, for an hour is coming when all those in the tombs will hear his voice. Those will come forth and those having accomplished good to the resurrection of life, and those having habituated evil to the resurrection of judgment."³

"Yeshua also made it clear that his spiritual atonement is not limited for those present today. His power reaches to those who have passed in the past as well as to those formed in the future. He knows the souls who are straining for good and those who have given themselves to evil. His judgement is true and he is the only one qualified to provide atonement because he has the greatest witness available in the cosmos, the Father. As Yeshua continued, remember, he was addressing the Judeans."

> "I am not able to do anything myself. As I hear, I judge, and my judgment is just, because I seek not my will but the will of him who sent me. If I bear witness concerning myself, my testimony is not true. There is another bearing witness concerning me, and I know that the witness that he bears concerning me is true. You verified with Yochanan, and he has borne witness to the truth. Indeed, the testimony I receive is not from man, but I say these things so that you might be saved. He was a burning and shining lamp, and you were willing to rejoice for a season in his light. But the testimony that I have is greater than that of Yochanan. For the works that the Father has given me to accomplish, the very works that I am doing bear witness concerning me that the Father has sent me. Also, the one having sent me, the Father himself, has borne witness concerning me. His voice you have never heard, his form you have never seen, and you do not have his word abiding in you, because you do not believe whom he sent."⁴

2. Hebrew for Soul
3. John 5:25–29
4. John 5:30–38

Spiritual Atonement

"Yeshua was completely dependent upon the Father. I am sure you all remember the Baptists testimony of Yeshua' s baptism. Ya'aqobe, you were there," Yochanan gestured to an elderly gray bearded man in the second row of the synagogue. "I have heard the same testimony from you. Adonai himself testified audibly and corporally of Yeshua Ha Mashiach.[5] The mitzvot[6] that he performed afterwards came by the power of the Most High. The Judeans, however, rejected him, his testimony, Adonai's witness, and the scriptures."

> "You search the scriptures because you think that in them you have eternal life; and these scriptures bear witness concerning me. However, you are not willing to come to me that you might have life. I do not receive glory from humanity, but I have known that you do not have the love of Adonai in yourselves. I have come in the name of my Father and you do not receive me. If another should come in his own name, you will receive him. How are you able to believe, when you receive glory from one another and do not seek the glory that comes from the only Adonai? Do not think that I will accuse you to the Father. There is one who accuses you: Moses, in whom you have hoped. For if you believed Moses, you would have somehow believed me; for he wrote concerning me. But if you do not believe his writings, how will you believe my words?"[7]

"From the time of Saul unto now, our nation is more apt to follow an earthly king rather than Adonai. We are more willing to receive a testimony we can explain, and that ensures we can maintain the illusion of control, rather than relinquishing control to the Creator. Yeshua came to make the Father known and that is exactly what he did. In his revealing of Adonai, he proved to be Messiah and understood the heart of all humanity. When he mentioned Moses, he also meant Torah. Torah, in part, intends to reveal our sin so we can see our need for Messiah. Yeshua revealed Adonai so we could see the way to life eternal, which is through belief in the Father's Anointed One."

"My precious ones Yeshua is the only one qualified to provide atonement. The testimony of Adonai, the scriptures, and his miracles prove that he will cover, redeem, and judge righteously. He provides physical and spiritual atonement for those before us, for us now, and for those who will be. This narrative of the invalid of Bethesda helps us to understand these

---

5. Jesus the Messiah
6. Hebrew for Commands or Good deeds
7. John 5:39–47

truths. As we look forward to Shavuot and Yom Kippur reveal your heart to Adonai, increase your mitzvot, and minimize your sins. Also, be thankful for our great Messiah Yeshua who provides all that we need for Olam Hazeh and Olam Habah."

The Elder and the Shamash closed the service with the singing of Psalms and prayer. Afterwards they all went their own way, to ponder the message and enjoy the Rest of the Sabbath.

24

Ya'aqobe

Yom Rishon[1]

Polycarp was unusually early in rising the next morning and crossed the threshold of the adobe before Yochanan was awake. Last night, after the synagogue service, Irenaeus had requested early morning prayer and Polycarp wanted to continue to engage his disciple during the project. This also provided an opportunity for him to gather some necessities for the week's events. The two met early in the field beyond Junia's adobe. Someone looking on would have thought the two were sneaking off for something more nefarious. After prayer, the two returned to Junia's adobe and Irenaeus' mother again offered her help in any way toward the project.

"I will ask the Elder again if there is anything that comes to mind," said Polycarp.

"One other thing Rabbi, please?" replied Junia. Polycarp nodded for her to continue. "Would the Elder be open to others quietly enjoying your sessions? If yesterday was a glimpse of what goes on every day with you and the Elder, you must feel very privileged. If this request is completely unacceptable, I fully understand Rabbi. If the answer is no it will be forgotten immediately with no ill will."

Polycarp responded, "I do consider myself blessed to be able to help the Elder in this important work. Let me ponder your request, Shavua tov.[2]"

1. Hebrew for First Day—Sunday
2. Hebrew for Good week

"Shavua tov Rabbi, thank you."

Polycarp then visited several places to gather the necessities for the week and arrived back at the adobe anxious for dictation. Yochanan was absent. Until his return, Polycarp focused on food storage, cleaning, and replenishing the water, wine, and supplies for his station.

Yochanan opened his eyes and slowly turned his head toward Polycarp's mat. Noticing his absence, he decided to visit Ya'aqobe. Seeing him at the synagogue yesterday sparked an idea related to the project. After his rooftop prayers, he quickly freshened up, wrapped himself in his tan linen cloak, grasped his staff, and lumbered toward the other side of the enclave. Winding through the small adobes on the wide dirt path, which was the main road, he arrived just as Ya'aqobe was climbing down from his morning prayers. His adobe was rectangular, connected to several other homes, and had an external stone staircase to access the rooftop.

"Good day Ya'aqobe," said Yochanan.

"Good day Elder, are you passing by or do I have the honor of an early visit just seeing you yesterday?"

"If you would do me the honor Ya'aqobe I have a request, if you have the time." Ya'aqobe's cheeks wrinkled a smile. He then nodded and gestured with his hand for Yochanan to cross the threshold of his adobe first. The two sat down in two armless wooden chairs at a small copper table, made by Ya'aqobe. Yochanan presented his request.

"What!" cried Ya'aqobe in a hushed tone due to the hour of the day, "You realize Yochanan this is extremely unorthodox, this request of yours."

"Do not let my seemingly unorthodox request allow you to slip in your etiquette my old friend."

"Yes, yes, of course, my apologies Elder, but what you are suggesting would shock our small community."

"I realize it may seem unorthodox Ya'aqobe but remember the many times the Master did something similar. Does it seem so unorthodox remembering his actions regarding these matters? The results were always more positive than negative. Indeed, the negative response was part of what he was trying to expose and rid of those around him."

"Yes, yes," replied Ya'aqobe, "but are you sure this decision, which will require days of training, will turn out as if the Master had commanded?"

"No, I do not Ya'aqobe, we both understand that I am not the Master. However, I am confident that I needed to come to you and request that you train them."

"Them!? You mean you want both of them to be trained and act in that capacity?"

"Ya'aqobe, first consider what the Master would do. Take some time to think and pray on this and if you still have reservations you may drop the matter entirely with no ill will."

Ya'aqobe struggled through his initial rejection and responded, "Alright Elder; I will think and pray. It seems I left the rooftop too soon."

As Yochanan approached the adobe, Polycarp greeted him from the rooftop. He had completed all of the preparations and was enjoying reflecting on Irenaeus' progress of discipleship. He opened the hatch and climbed down the ladder.

"You have been busy disciple, thank you for all the preparations."

"My pleasure Rabbi. Rabbi, may I pass along a request from Junia?"

"Of course, Polycarp, what is it?"

"She enjoyed your Sabbath teaching and was wondering if she could sit in on our sessions." Yochanan thought for a long moment before responding.

"Thank you for passing along her request. I will consider this later. This will be a busy week for us, so it was wise of you to prepare early. Shall we pick up where we left off?" Yochanan sat down in his chair as Polycarp nodded and took his position at his amanuensis station.

25

Physical Feeding

"In summary Saphar we have recorded three major events. First, we have our six-day introduction paralleling the days of creation. Second, we see Messiah revealing himself during Pesach[1], to the diverse, ethnic world starting with Jerusalem. Third, we learned about the healing of the invalid during Yom Kippur. This physical healing proved that Yeshua is the only one able to provide timeless physical and spiritual atonement. There are many more things that could be said of his first year of open ministry but let us move on to the second year."

> *After these things Yeshua went away to the other side of the Sea of Galilee; the Sea of Tiberius. Now a large crowd was following him, because they experienced the miracles that he performed on the sick. So Yeshua went up on the mountain, and sat there with his disciples. It was close to the Passover feast of the Judeans.*[2]

"By this time Yeshua had gained in popularity so that everyone, in one way or another, heard about his abilities. The amount of people who came to see him was staggering. It was necessary for all of us to withdraw and rest occasionally. The time alone helped clarify our perspective on the phenomenon we were experiencing over the years. He further revealed Adonai this second year and continued to perform miracles during the feasts." As Polycarp finished staining the parchment, he raised his feathered quill.

"Yes Saphar?"

1. Passover
2. John 6:1–4

Physical Feeding

"Did he perform miracles only on feast days?"

"An excellent question my disciple. While the number of miracles seemed greater during these times, it is hard to say if these miracles occurred only on the proper calendar dates of the feasts. Understand Saphar, that there is still no agreement on determining the first day of the first month. As you know, the first new moon after the tequphah[3] is what determines the first day of Nissan, the first month of the year. The dates of the entire festal cycle depend on this determination. Some judged the disappearance of the moon in its cycle as the first day, others conjunction,[4] others the day after conjunction and still others at the first sighting. This resulted in differing dates for the feasts throughout the regions. Due to the various groups differing in their determination, there was no uniform agreement on the specific dates of the feasts. Those groups, the Judeans, the remnants of the other eleven tribes, the Essenes, and the Samaritans rarely shared the same exact dates of the moedim.[5] However, since Judea was the largest remaining tribe, most followed what the Pharisees determined in judging the festal dates. Let us continue. . ."

> *Then Yeshua, having lifted up his eyes and having seen a large crowd coming to him, he says to Phillipus, "Where shall we buy bread, so that these people might eat?" Now he said this testing him, for he himself knew what he was about to do. Phillipus answered him, "Two hundred denarii of loaves would not be sufficient for each of them to get just a bite." One of his disciples, Andrewas, Shimon Kaypha's brother, says to him, "Here is a boy who has five barley loaves and two fish, but how can these be for so many?" Yeshua said, "Have the men recline." Now the grass was lush in that place so about five thousand men in number reclined. Then Yeshua took the loaves, and having given thanks, it was distributed to those reclining. Likewise, also with the fish, as much as they wanted.[6]*

Polycarp finished the scratching of the last word and looked up and said, "Rabbi, why did the Master test Phillipus, and were you able to gaze into the basket to see how the replication was happening?" Yochanan pushed on the creaking arms of his chair and stood at this point.

---

3. Te-Ku-Fa, Hebrew word used for the vernal equinox

4. When the earth, moon and sun are lined up producing a completely dark moon. The opposite event is a full moon.

5. Hebrew for Feasts

6. John 6:5–11

"If you remember Saphar, Phillipus was the first to seek the Master. Phillipus believed right away that he was Messiah. I believe Yeshua saw the greatest hope in Phillipus for one of us to think beyond the physical to the spiritual. All of us had seen so many things we could not explain. His challenge to Phillipus put our minds in motion on a different way to provide for the masses. However, not understanding his power we could not imagine beyond ourselves." Yochanan turned toward the rear wall, looked out the window into the sky, and then continued.

"As for the replication, as you put it, we were all serving the masses. All I know is that I never glimpsed the bottom of that basket. I did notice that every loaf and every fish he handed to me seemed to be different from the one before. I believe it was multiplication, not replication. The best I can guess is that he was creating loaves and fish at the bottom of the basket as we were grabbing them from the top. It was simultaneously inexplicable, amazing and gracious." He turned back toward Polycarp, smiled and finished his thought. "Now that I think about it, I never did see the bottom weaving and I have no idea where that basket is now."

"Do you think it would still produce loaves and fish if we could find it, Rabbi?"

Yochanan laughed.

"I am sure it would need the Master's touch, my wondering disciple." Yochanan gave his standard nod toward Polycarp, which was one of his nonverbal signs to continue.

> *Now when they were filled, he says to his disciples, "Gather together the leftover fragments, that nothing might be lost." So, they gathered together the fragments and filled twelve hand baskets from the five barley loaves left over by those who had eaten. Then the people, having seen the sign he had done, said, "This is indeed the Prophet who is coming for the world!" Then Yeshua perceived that they were about to come and seize him to make him king. So, Yeshua withdrew again to the mountain by himself.*[7]

"Five thousand men with their families is a lot of people Rabbi; how long did this feeding last?"

"The task took the rest of the day. The masses had plenty of time to see all twelve of us strategically strewn on the hillside bringing them armloads of bread and fish for them to prepare and cook. Our worn sandals made paths in the lush grass, making the hillside look like a patchwork quilt of families. Seeing this for hours convinced them that Yeshua was so different

---

7. John 6:12–15

from anyone in the current Judean leadership that they wanted to forcibly bring him back to Jerusalem and start their own revolt. None of us realized then that he came at this point in history to redeem instead of raze. So, he again slipped away, to let the food calm the mood of the masses."

"I know you have seen the pattern so far Saphar. The Master, most of the time, used the physical to illuminate the spiritual. Living in the physical is all too familiar to us. However, there is a spiritual capacity, diluted since Adam, that the second Adam came to restore. Since we are both physical and spiritual beings, he desires us to act in both realms. The challenge he continually set before us was to hone the awareness of our spiritual capabilities and use those to positively influence our physical world."

"I have seen the pattern Rabbi and thank you for helping me to strive toward the spiritual. Since you mentioned the word hone, allow me to sharpen my quill before we continue."

26

Physical Rescue

> *Now when evening came, his disciples went down to the sea, and having entered a boat, were going across the sea to Capernaum. Now it had already become dark and Yeshua had not yet come to them. The sea was agitated by both the wind and strong gusts. Then, having rowed about twenty-five or thirty stadia[1] they see Yeshua walking on the sea and coming near the boat, and they were frightened. But he says to them, "It is I; do not fear." When they were willing to receive him into the boat then the boat immediately came upon the land to which they were going.[2]*

Polycarp stopped his quill abruptly and looked up immediately toward Yochanan. "Rabbi, walking?! How did the boat travel? I mean. . .what exactly happened!" Yochanan chuckled as Polycarp collected himself. "My apologies Rabbi, could you please explain?" Polycarp's interjections interrupted Yochanan's usual pacing. He was standing in the middle of the dusty sunlit room as he turned his head and smiling eyes toward his excited disciple.

"I wish I could elaborate my young disciple but it is true that one moment we were mid-way in our tempestuous journey and the next we were at the calm shore of our destination. Before we left, Yeshua required time alone with the Father and sent us on our way across the sea. We had discussed, amongst ourselves, when and how he would follow but none of us could have predicted him walking on water. He could have used the other boats

---

1. Distance for one lap around a historical Grecian foot race track; about 607 feet
2. John 6:16–21

on the shore but because of our fear in the storm, he came right away to save us. Because of our fear, he came to rescue us from our terrible position. He dismissed the torrent surrounding us and delivered us to better shores. For those who have ears to hear, this was another example of the Master Teacher using the physical to illuminate the spiritual. He will rescue all in this tempestuous world that believe and deliver them to the better shores of Olam Habah."

"I am sure you will always remember that experience and lesson Rabbi."

"Too true Saphar, I wish the masses understood his lessons for them. Here is what happened on the other side."

> *On the next day, the crowd standing on the other side of the sea, saw that there was not another boat missing other than the one. They also saw that Yeshua had not entered the boat with his disciples, but his disciples went away alone. But other boats from Tiberius had come near the place where they had eaten the bread after the Master had given thanks. So, when the crowd saw that Yeshua was not there, nor his disciples, they themselves entered into the boats and went to Capernaum, seeking Yeshua.*

"Obviously, we were not there to see the masses scramble to find Yeshua or the subsequent boarding of the boats, but it must have been a sight. When they finally arrived at the Capernaum shore it was clear that they were more interested in another meal rather than recognizing Messiah."

> *Now, having found him on the other side of the sea, they said to him, "Rabbi, when did you come here?" Yeshua answered them, "Truly, truly, I say to you, you seek me, not because you saw signs, but because you ate of the loaves and were satisfied. Do not work for the food that is perishing, but for the food that endures to eternal life, which the Son of Man will give you. Indeed, even Adonai the Father has sealed him." Then they said to him, "What must we do, that we might do the works of Adonai?" Yeshua answered and said to them, "This is the work of Adonai, that you should believe in him whom he has sent."*[3]

"Rabbi, why was their first concern 'When' Yeshua arrived?"

"Do you remember the wilderness wanderings where Adonai led Israel by the pillars of fire and smoke?"

---

3. John 6:22–29

"Of course Rabbi, there was also manna or bread provided for the masses during those years."

"Correct, and what happened here should be seen through that lens of history. Did the pillars announce when they were moving on?"

"No Rabbi, they just moved, although I am sure some would have liked some notice."

"You are correct my disciple. Why was there no notice given by the pillars or the Master? Was Adonai or Yeshua being inconsiderate?" Yochanan paused with that familiar gleam in his eyes.

"With all due respect, you know my position on this Rabbi. Your last question was rhetorical correct?"

"For you, of course Saphar, but it would have been a good question for the masses. I believe their 'When' question revealed that they still had their own agenda. They had not fully committed to the Masters agenda. Their expectation was that he should not only provide for them but also provide at the times they saw fit. All of us would do well to put away our agenda and fully surrender to Messiah's agenda. Like all of us, they focused more on the physical than the spiritual. Yeshua wanted them to see the Father's work through him so they would believe on him. He provided the bread and loaves to help them to understand that he also offers spiritual nourishment. Unfortunately, they only wanted more of his physical provision." Again, Yochanan nodded toward the parchment.

> *Then they said to him, "What sign then will you do that we may see and believe you? What will you perform? Our fathers ate the manna in the wilderness; as it is written, 'He gave them bread from the sky to eat.'" Yeshua then said to them, "Truly, truly, I say to you, it was not Moses who gave you the bread from the sky, but my Father gives you the true bread from the sky. For the bread of Adonai is the one coming from the sky and gives life to the world." Then they said to him, "Sir, give us this bread always."*[4]

Polycarp raised one hand while finishing his scratching with the other causing Yochanan to pause and sit back in his chair.

"I am puzzled Rabbi, why did they not acknowledge the miracle of multiplication of the loaves and fishes?"

"They knew from the scriptures that Moses gave their fathers manna that came from the sky Saphar. Yeshua only provided bread and fish from a basket! How could he be equal to, or greater than Moses without producing manna? However, Yeshua rightly pointed out that it was the Father,

4. John 6:30–33

not Moses, who provided the physical manna. He used this opportunity to help push them toward the understanding that the Father is the one who provides all sustenance. Just as the Father provided physical life for their fathers with manna, the Father provides spiritual life for them with Yeshua. This was however, only the beginning of Yeshua's metaphor. This metaphor would get progressively harder for them to accept."

Suddenly there was a loud knuckled, 'knock, knock, knock' on the door that slightly startled them both as they both snapped their heads toward the tattered door. It was before midday and both looked back toward each other wondering who could be at the door.

27

Spiritual Feeding

As Polycarp moved toward the door, the first thing he experienced was the smell of freshly baked challah and aged wine. His stomach compelled him to open the door quickly giving the visitor, Ya'aqobe, the same start he had given them with his knuckled knock on the door.

"Polycarp! Are you trying to tear the leather hinges from the jamb?"

"My apologies Ya'aqobe, please forgive me."

"You are forgiven, young Rabbi. In fact I brought a mid-morning meal for you and the Elder."

"Please come in, Ya'aqobe," bellowed Yochanan from his padded chair, "I did not expect you so soon." He rose slowly to greet his old friend. Polycarp took some water as well as the bread, figs, and wine to the rooftop and quickly prepared the golden table for the mid-morning meal. On the rooftop, the three prayed with eyes toward the sky for the meal, the project and their small diaspora enclave.

The challah was sweet, the figs were tart, and the wine, the balance of the two. They mostly ate in silence only talking briefly about whom in the enclave needed help. However, at the end of the meal Yochanan and Ya'aqobe looked slyly at each other and then simultaneously glanced toward Polycarp. Polycarp saw the familiar playful gleam in both sets of eyes and stopped mid bite in a piece of challah, wondering what was about to happen. Yochanan started the banter.

"Well Ya'aqobe, it isn't every day you bring me a late morning meal, although every day would be good."

Ya'aqobe responded playfully. "I'm not sure that I have ever brought you a meal in the morning my friend. Indeed, I don't remember ever

Spiritual Feeding 81

bringing you a meal, regardless of the time of day! However, I am glad your expectations are such that I will not be doing this regularly." Yochanan chuckled as Ya'aqobe continued. "After your interruption. . .I mean request, earlier this morning, I went back to my rooftop to pray and think about what you asked." Polycarp swallowed his mouthful of challah and raised his index finger to interject to ask about the request but Ya'aqobe was speaking too quickly.

"I know, in part, why you did not ask me to perform such an honor. My skills are limited in the act but not in the ability of instruction. Adonai has impressed upon me the importance of what must be done and so the answer is not only yes, but I regret not proposing the idea to you." Polycarp's curiosity was piqued now and could not hold back a quick interjection.

"What request Rabbi?" He said very quickly. Yochanan answered Ya'aqobe as if Polycarp were absent from the rooftop.

"Your answer is more gracious than I expected." Yochanan then quickly tilted his head the opposite direction while simultaneously raising both palms toward Ya'aqobe. "Not that I have seen you as ungracious my friend."

"Elder, you know very well that my skin is thicker than that my old friend." Yochanan responded,

"Will you allow me to share the news? When should you start?"

Polycarp was thoroughly intrigued at this point, but he now understood that there was a coy game unfolding before him. He also knew that all would be clear soon, so he contained his excitement and interjections.

"Of course, it should come from you Elder; and 'when' is why I am here at midday. I suspect that the timing of the completion of my task should match with the completion of yours. If I start right away I believe the accomplishment of each goal will coincide."

"My thoughts exactly Ya'aqobe, the Father is indeed in this. The news of it will happen tonight and you will begin tomorrow morning?"

"Yes, that was my thought as well. Thank you for approaching me."

"Thank you Ya'aqobe."

The three cleared the table and descended the ladder of the rooftop. As Polycarp walked Ya'aqobe out of the adobe, Yochanan sat back in his chair and looked smiling at Polycarp. As Polycarp sat at his station, Yochanan said, "Now where were we. . .ah yes! We were about to cover the bread of life." The gleam was still in his eyes.

> *Yeshua said to them, "I am the bread of life; whoever comes to me shall never ever hunger, and whoever believes in me shall never ever thirst again. But I said to you that you have also seen me and yet do not believe. All that the Father gives*

> me will come to me, and whoever comes to me I will never ever cast out. For I have come down out of the sky, not that I should do my will but the will of the one who sent me. Indeed, this is the will of the one who sent me, that I should lose none of those he has given to me, but raise them up on the last day. For this is the will of my Father, that everyone beholding the Son and believing in him might have life eternal, and I will raise him up on the last day."[1]

"Yeshua continued his metaphor with the crowd that followed by saying that he is the bread, the manna, from heaven. As the manna sustained Israel in the wilderness until they arrived at the Promised Land, so Yeshua will sustain his people until Olam Habah. The physical manna perished overnight and appeared again the next morning. Yeshua, however, rose eternally after he perished and will eternally renew all those who believe in him. He was providing a picture for the crowds to see beyond the physical to the reality of the spiritual. It was difficult for many to accept because, even though they saw his miracles, they were unable to look beyond themselves and their own desires." Yochanan nodded toward Polycarp.

> So, the Judeans were grumbling about him, because he said, "I am the bread that has come down from the sky." They were saying, "Is not this Yeshua, the son of Joseph, whose father and mother we know? How does he now say, 'I have come down from the sky'?" Yeshua answered and said to them, "Do not grumble with one another. No one is able to come to me unless the Father who sent me draws him and then I will raise him up on the last day. It is written in the Prophets, 'And they will all be taught by Adonai.' Everyone who has heard and learned from the Father comes to me. Not that anyone has seen the Father; except he who is from Adonai; he has seen the Father. Truly, truly, I say to you, the one believing has life eternal.[2]

"Saphar, just as Israel in the wilderness, the Judeans grumbled in their hearts over what Adonai had sent. In the past, the Father used physical hunger to draw the Israelites to *What* would sustain them. With the living Manna, the Father is using spiritual hunger to draw souls to *Who* would sustain them. Those who believe in Messiah will enter Olam Habah and life eternal. This present world operates according to the flesh but the world to

---

1. John 6:34–40
2. John 6:41–47

come operates according to the spirit. What a wonder that we can taste the spiritual in this present world."

"Baruch atah Adonai" breathed Polycarp.

"Amen. It is close to mid-day Saphar, but let us push a bit further."

28

Spiritual Rescue

"I am the bread of life. Your fathers ate of the manna in the wilderness, and they died. Here is the bread that comes down from the sky so anyone might eat of it and not die. I am the living bread that came down from the sky. If anyone shall have eaten of this bread, he will live in the new era. Indeed, this bread that I will give is my flesh so that the cosmos will have life." Then the Judeans were arguing with one another saying, "How is he able to give us his flesh to eat?" Then Yeshua said to them, "Truly, truly, I say to you, if you shall not have eaten the flesh or drunk the blood of the Son of man you do not have life in yourselves. The one partaking of my flesh and drinking my blood has life eternal, and I will raise him up on the last day. Indeed, my flesh is real meat, and my blood is true drink. The one partaking of my flesh and drinking my blood abides in me, and I in him. The living Father sent me and I live because of the Father. Indeed, the ones partaking of me, they will live because of me. This is the bread having come down from the sky. Not like the bread the fathers ate and died, the one partaking of this bread will live to the new era."[1]

Yochanan paused at this point, stood slowly and turned toward Polycarp.

"Yes Rabbi?" asked Polycarp. Yochanan raised his head a bit and softened his look toward his disciple.

1. John 6:48–58

Spiritual Rescue

"I thought you might have a question Saphar."

"Not really Rabbi, I can see clearly that the Master meant for us to. . .partake of him. This statement reminds me of others we have already recorded. In the beginning of your record, you said Yeshua was the word of Adonai that had become flesh. In addition, with the Samaritan woman, Yeshua said that his food was to do the will of Adonai. In this instance, he said that he gives his flesh to redeem the world. This illustrates that the relationship and interaction of the corporeal with the non-corporeal is difficult to understand and language is insufficient for a comprehensive explanation. There is also a fundamental difference in material, if you will, between the physical and the spiritual. While hunger and satiation are possible for both states, how our mortal bodies consume needed physical sustenance is completely different from how our souls consume needed spiritual sustenance. It seems that Messiah's challenge, and now ours, was communicating spiritual realities when the audience only understood language relating to the physical. All physical creation exists by Adonai's power and if we do not partake of the food of physical creation, our biological life force dissipates. Likewise, all spiritual creation also exists by Adonai's power and if we do not partake of Messiah, our spiritual life force dissipates. This partaking or consumption of the soul is belief. Therefore, spiritual eating and drinking, is at least, faith in Adonai."

"You continue to impress me my growing disciple. It was very difficult for many to understand that the offering of his body, blood, and all of who he was, made it possible for him to sustain us in both realms. When we taste the glory in the world to come, it is only because we have believed what his sacrifice accomplished in this present world." Polycarp smiled and made himself ready as Yochanan spoke.

"Please make note that he was in their synagogue for this last discourse."

> *He said these things in the synagogue, while teaching in Capernaum.*[2]

"Ready Saphar?"
"Yes Rabbi."

> *Now having heard this, many of his disciples said, "This analogy is difficult, who is able to comprehend it?" However, Yeshua, knowing inwardly about his grumbling disciples said to them, "Does this cause you to stumble, what if you should*

---

2. John 6:59

> behold the Son of Man ascending in the past? The one giving life is the Spirit; the flesh does not benefit anything. The matters which I present to you they are spirit and life. But there are some of you who do not believe." (Yeshua knew indeed from the beginning those who were not believing and who it is who would betray him.) And he said, "This is why I mentioned to you that no one is able to come to me unless it shall be granted to him from the Father."[3]

Yochanan offered some explanation.

"The crowd, the Judeans, and the greater company of the disciples, were struggling with what he was saying. Yeshua seemed to be sifting through those pliable to the Father's calling and those hardened against the Spirit. He knew that there were many reasons why people followed him. However, he wanted those who followed to be convinced that it was the Father drawing them by his Spirit. The Son of Man reference was to illustrate that his form before his birth would have been harder for them to accept. He did not take on this fleshly existence to relate to us, but so we could relate to him and see the Father. His incarnation and his metaphors were to help us understand the connections between the physical and the spiritual. Let us finish this section and we will take a short break."

> From that time, many of his disciples withdrew from the others to the rear and no longer walked beside him. ᵀ Then Yeshua said to the twelve, "Are you not also wishing to depart?" Shimon Kaypha answered him, "Master, to whom will we go? You have the matters of life eternal and we have believed and have come to know that you are the Holy One of Adonai." Yeshua answered them, "Did I not choose the twelve of you? However, one of you is a slanderer." He spoke of Yehuda the son of Shimon Iscariot. Indeed, as one of the twelve he was about to betray him.[4]

Yochanan chuckled and spoke.

"Shimon[5] was always the first to talk and, most times, his words were appropriate. In this instance, no one could have responded better." Yochanan's speech drifted off and he again paused in reflection. His mind drifted until he was standing on a distant, rocky barren hillside with twelve other men. Polycarp knew the appropriate length of time to wait before asking his question.

3. John 6:60–65
4. John 6:66–71
5. Hebrew for Simon

"What is it Rabbi?"

"I'm sorry Saphar. I often wonder what was going through Yehuda's mind. I can never fully understand why he did what he did with so many opportunities for teshuvah.[6]"

"Perhaps it is good that you do not fully understand Rabbi." Yochanan tuned and looked at Polycarp.

"Well said my disciple. Should we take our break to take care of necessities?"

"As you wish Rabbi, where you go I follow." Yochanan smiled, rose from his chair and turned suddenly toward Polycarp.

"Polycarp."

"Yes Rabbi?"

"We will probably be having two guests tonight for the evening meal so please prepare something a bit more diverse than the usual."

"Of course, Rabbi."

---

6. Hebrew for repentance

29

Evening Meal Invitation

Polycarp ventured to the garden to gather loquat, early lettuce and almonds. While gathering the produce he was recalling the comments between Ya'aqobe and Yochanan earlier. He was confident that they related to the visitors this evening. He suspected that the two joining them would be Irenaeus and Junia but the purpose and specifics of what the two Elders had plotted still escaped him. The coy game played earlier had his thoughts racing to try to understand what Yochanan was planning. The Elder was always pondering how he could make Yeshua known to as many as possible, so, his scheme had to fit within this overall intention.

Gathering enough food for four, which would also provide a pleasing variety, Polycarp started making the necessary preparations.

"What of Ya'aqobe?" Polycarp was speaking his thoughts aloud now while he cleaned the food at the wooden basin inside the white plastered walls of the small adobe.

"How could Ya'aqobe be useful to the Elder? Was he planning the next project where he would play a part? Ya'aqobe is very old. I know there would be much to learn from him because he was a . . ." Just then, Polycarp stopped cleaning, raised his head quickly and looked out the window to the garden and the hanging fruit outside the rear of the adobe.

"That must be it!" Excitement rushed to every part within Polycarp's body. "Well, they wanted to help." He again said aloud. "They will be helping in a way they never considered!"

Yochanan visited the aphedron, washed, and started down the dirt road through the enclave. As he approached Junia's adobe, he noticed that she and Irenaeus were tending to their garden on the rooftop. Junia noticed the Elder and greeted him warmly from the roof.

"Good day Elder. What gives us the pleasure of seeing you this sunny afternoon? I will be down right away."

"No need Junia," Yochanan bellowed, "I only came by with an invitation." Irenaeus was lost in thought but once he heard the Elder's voice, he was quick to leave the garden and place his dirty hands on the pitch of the parapet and look over to greet the Elder.

"Good day Elder!"

"Good day Irenaeus." Junia then responded to Yochanan in her normal forthright but courteous fashion.

"Whatever the invitation, we accept." Yochanan smiled.

"There will be one day, Lady Junia, that your quick willingness will be rewarded with disappointment, however, today is not that day. Since you have already accepted I will say no more and see you both tonight at our adobe for the evening meal, good day."

Junia was initially puzzled at the invitation during the week but smiled down at Yochanan and responded, "Thank you Elder, we will see then. Good day."

After his preparations, Polycarp took care of his own necessities and then replenished the materials for his amanuensis station. Before the project, he had visited Hylinane, the glass smith, who provided twelve opaque vials, the perfect size and depth for his quills. The short, cubed bottles had some small bubbles throughout the walls but the round necks were perfect for quill dipping and the openings fit the corks used for wine skins. Hylinane's shop was always warm and Polycarp would replenish his supplies on occasion and watch him work. He would marvel at the artistry of blowing melted sand and nitrate into clay molds to produce glimmering glass objects of every shape and style.

Polycarp had carefully filled the delicate glistening gifts with black ink provided by Melan the ink maker. The enclave could always tell when Melan was making more ink. The burning wood and oil would waft through the adobes for stadia. Earlier, Polycarp had helped him add the acacia gum to his batch of burnt cypress wood, oil, and water. The sweet smell of the burnt resin stayed with the ink and opening a new bottle sparked his memory of Melan and his shop.

Yochanan, opening the door and letting in the afternoon sunlight, brought Polycarp's attention back to the adobe.

"Hello Saphar, making ready I see, excellent."

"Everything for the meal tonight is ready and covered Rabbi. Was your invitation well received?" Yochanan smiled thoughtfully and glanced sideways to look into Polycarp's eyes while he reached for his wooden water cup near the basin. Polycarp saw his gleaming glance and noticed again the wisdom in his eyes.

"I realize that evening meal invitations on a day other than the Sabbath is. . .unorthodox, but we will have two more for dinner tonight my disciple. Thank you for your efforts." Yochanan drank deeply from the round cup, wiped his beard clean of the droplets of water and moved across the room to sit in his familiar chair. Polycarp smiled at his response, took his place at his station and filled his freshly cut quill with the new ink from the newly blown glass jar.

30

Sermons of Sukkot

"So Saphar, we left off with Yeshua announcing that he is the actual bread of life with the closest of the disciples continuing to follow because they believed he was the Messiah. He made this known during Passover and you know how important bread is during this feast. It was especially meaningful because Passover bread is always without leaven just as the Master was without sin. The next events I would like to record were during Sukkot[1] of the same festal cycle."

> *After these things, Yeshua was walking about in Galilee for he did not desire to walk about in Judea, because the Judeans were seeking to kill him. Now the Judeans' Feast of Booths was at hand. His brothers then said to him, "Pass over from here and go into Judea, that your disciples will also see your deeds which you are doing. Indeed, no one does secret things while he seeks to be in public. Since you do these things, show yourself to the world." However, not even his brothers believed in him. Then Yeshua said to them, "The opportunity for me has not yet come, but your ready opportunity is always here. The world is powerless to hate you. However, it hates me because I bear witness concerning it, that its works are evil. You go up to the feast. I am not going up to this feast yet, for my opportunity has not yet approached." After saying these things to them, he remained in Galilee.[2]*

---

1. Hebrew for Booths or Tabernacles
2. John 7:1–9

"As you know Saphar, Sukkot is an eight day festival filled with prayer, celebration, teaching, and two very important themes. You know the major themes, correct?"

"Yes Rabbi. Daily water pouring services give thanks to Adonai for the harvest. These culminate on the final day with a temple wide water pouring ceremony. This celebration also incorporates the other major theme of Sukkot, which is light. In the court of women, the large golden menorahs, taller than myself, are lit and provide reflections of the temple light to every courtyard in Jerusalem."

"Correct Saphar, the sight and sounds of the light and water during Sukkot are truly unforgettable. Yeshua used these images to continue to convey his message to the masses. He waited until these images had been presented several times before going up to the temple."

"Rabbi, before we continue, could you elaborate on what Yeshua meant when he said, 'the world is powerless to hate you?'" Yochanan adjusted himself in his chair and leaned forward arching his back in a prolonged stretch. With his elbows on his thighs and hands clasped, he looked at Polycarp and responded.

"His brothers, just like you and I, are a part of this fallen world. We know that we are unrighteous. We also know that everyone else around us is unrighteous. Whether anyone realizes it or not, no one person in this world has the basis to judge anyone because all have sinned. To know that no one is perfect makes the worst of us feel better. It is almost impossible to hate someone who is in the same life situation. However, meeting someone who is wholly other and clearly filled with the Spirit of Adonai brings up emotions foreign to humanity. Yeshua was without sin, or evil, which was a stark spiritual contrast seen by all of creation. Because he was truly righteous, most would be offended because he reminded them of a purity they could never achieve on their own. He knew it was necessary to be strategic in his presentation to this present world, to help as many as possible to receive him."

"I understand Rabbi, thank you. I am ready when you are."

> But when his brothers had gone up to the feast, then he also went up, not publicly but secretly. Then the Judeans were seeking him at the feast, and said, "Where is he?" Indeed, there was much murmuring about him among the crowds. Truly, some said, "He is good," but others however said, "No, he deceives the people." No one, however, publicly preached about him because of the fear of the Judeans. Then later, midway through the feast Yeshua ascended into the temple and was teaching. Then the Judeans were marveling, saying,

> "How does this one know scripture, not having studied?" Then Yeshua answered them and said, "My teaching is not of myself, but of the one who sent me. If anyone desires to practice his will, he will understand whether the teaching is from Adonai or if I speak on my own. The one who speaks on his own seeks his own glory. However, the one seeking the glory of the one having sent him is true, and there is no unrighteousness in him."[3]

Polycarp finished this portion and asked a question.

"What would he teach on Rabbi?"

"Too many topics to cover now, Saphar, however, two things happened every time he taught. He revealed Adonai more fully, and helped refine our expectation of Messiah. He taught during these festal opportunities because people were more receptive during these gatherings. Everyone who came to Jerusalem during the feasts was looking for some sort of miracle or answered prayer. Adonai had done miracles in the past on these days and the hope was that he would reveal himself again during the feasts."

"He waited until the middle of the feast because the crowd was more focused on Adonai. What was unique about his teaching is that they could not deny the truth of what he was saying. They were amazed at his teaching because it was from the Father. He made it clear that everyone should discern for themselves if his teaching agreed with Torah and what they knew of Adonai. Here is the rest of what he said during this time."

> "Has not Moshe given you the Torah? However, none of you practices the Torah. Why do you seek to kill me?" The crowd answered, "You have a demon! Who seeks to kill you?" Yeshua answered and said to them, "I did one deed, and because of this you all wonder. Moses has given you circumcision, not that it is from Moses but from the fathers, and you circumcise a man on the Sabbath. If a man receives circumcision on the Sabbath, so that the Torah of Moses may not be broken, are you angry with me because I made an entire man's body well on the Sabbath? Do not judge according to appearance but judge with right judgment."[4]

"Rabbi, was the Master saying these things for the Priests and the Pharisees?"

"Yes Saphar, he was presenting a contradiction in their actions to try and dislodge their perspective. Circumcision is a sign of the covenant and

---

3. John 7:10–18
4. John 7:19–24

therefore new life in Israel. It is also a command, which does not have Sabbath restrictions. If they could make sense of the freedom of circumcising on the Sabbath, how much more should they be able to understand the freedom of healing an invalid on the Sabbath?"

Polycarp asked another question.

"So, was he then challenging the crowd to turn to Torah for judgement rather than the leader's rules?"

"I believe so disciple. While the leaders justified many of their own rules, many of those rules were not the Father's intention. Some leaders meant well by trying to provide fences for the Torah. They rationalized that additional rules would prevent anyone from getting to the point of being able to break a command. However, the leaders eventually treated these fences as Adonai's rules, which provided a prideful appearance of obedience. Indeed, some of these anthropological ordinances limited the opportunity of true obedience from those who truly desired to obey. Do you understand my disciple?"

"I believe so Rabbi. If other rules prevent the choice of obeying, or not obeying a command, then how can one receive the blessing of being obedient to the command?" Yochanan smiled and nodded.

"Wet your quill Saphar."

31

Water of Life

> *Then some of those from Jerusalem said, "Is this not whom they seek to kill and look, he speaks publicly and they never say anything to him. Have the rulers truly acknowledged that this is the Messiah? But we know where this man comes from and when Messiah comes no one will know where he comes from." Then Yeshua shouted while teaching in the temple saying, "You know me, and you know where I am from. However, I have not come of my own accord and the one having sent me is true but you do not know him. I know him, because I am with him and he sent me." Then they were seeking to arrest him, but no one laid a hand on him, because his hour had not yet come. But much of the crowd believed in him and said, "When the Messiah comes it is impossible that he will do more signs than this man has done."*[1]

Yochanan looked again at Polycarp and when he finished he said, "Time and again Yeshua knew what those around him were thinking. Even though he was in this present world, he maintained a deep connection with the Father. He would eventually provide a similar connection for all of us by sending the Ruach."[2] Polycarp raised his quill.

"I apologize for so many questions Rabbi."

"Go on disciple, there is always time for learning."

---

1. John 7:25–31
2. Hebrew for Spirit—Also see the record of Shavuot (Pentecost) in Acts 2

"We know that the Master was born in Bethlehem but lived in Nazareth fulfilling many prophecies. Why did these people from Jerusalem believe that they would not know Messiah's origin?"

"Not all understood the scriptures and the difference between his birthplace and where he grew up. Most knew that his family was from Nazareth which went against the popular belief, or myth, that Messiah would come from nowhere, suddenly." Yochanan locked eyes on Polycarp, feigned a serious look and ominously said, "A very common saying during this time was that there are three things that come wholly unexpected, Messiah, a godsend and a scorpion."[3] Polycarp laughed and repositioned himself at his station and made ready his quill.

The Pharisees heard the crowd murmuring these things about him, and the Chief Priests and Pharisees sent officers that they might arrest him. Then Yeshua said, "I am with you now for a short time and then I am going to the one who sent me. You will seek me and you will not find me and where I am then you cannot come." Then the Judeans said to one another, "Where is he about to go that we will not ever find him? Is he about to go to the Dispersion among the Greeks and teach the Greeks? What is this saying that he spoke that 'You will seek me and you will not find me,' and, 'Where I am then you cannot come'?"[4]

"Rabbi, did the Judeans not know that he would return to the Father because they did not believe he was from the Father?"

"In part Saphar, however, they also did not accept the limitation that he could go where they could not. Their understanding of life was limited to the physical. Keep in mind that there had not been a recorded miracle since the Maccabees.[5] Even though people hoped for the miraculous, their faith that something spiritual or supernatural would actually happen waned. Yeshua, however, changed that understanding in front of the entire known world."

Then on the last day of the feast, the great day, Yeshua stood up and shouted saying, "If anyone thirsts, let him come to me and drink. The one believing in me, as the Scripture has said, will have rivers of living water flow out from within him." Now this he said about the Spirit, whom those, having

---

3. Robertson, *Word Pictures*, 127

4. John 7:32–36

5. Before the Maccabees, arguably, the last recorded chronological miracle in the OT was in the book of Jonah

> *believed in him, were about to receive. Indeed, Spirit was not yet here because Yeshua was not yet glorified. Then from among the crowd, having heard these words, they said, "This truly is the prophet." Others said, "This is the Messiah." Others, however, said, "Indeed, the Messiah does not come from Galilee. Has not the Scripture said that from the offspring of David and from Bethlehem, David's village, is where Messiah comes from?" So, there was a division among the people because of him. Some of them wanted to arrest him, but no one laid hands on him.*[6]

Polycarp looked up quickly after finishing his quill scratching.

"With the sight and sounds of all the water surrounding him from the ceremonies this must have been an amazing experience Rabbi."

"The connection could not have been more obvious Saphar. It was clear that he was saying that as physical water provides physical life so he provides spiritual life. He did not state it as a comparison or figurative application, but as reality. The miracle of this Sukkot was Yeshua's proclamation as Messiah and offer of salvation to humanity. There were, however, many different expectations for the coming of Messiah and therefore many different reactions."

> *Then the officers came to the chief priests and Pharisees, who said to them, "Why did you not bring him?" The officers answered, "Never has a man spoken like this man speaks." Then the Pharisees answered them, "You have not been deceived, have you? Not one of the rulers or the Pharisees has believed in him. But this crowd, not understanding the Torah, are condemned." Nicodemus, who had gone to him before, and who was one of them, said to them, "Our Torah does not judge a man before hearing from him and understanding what he does." They answered and said to him, "Are you not also from Galilee? Search and see that no prophet arises from Galilee."*[7]

"Saphar, this was a day of days. Those with open minds could not deny the presence of Adonai upon Yeshua. The leaders, however, were convinced, due to their pride, that their ruling cohort was unaffected. Nicodemus was not alone in seeing the power of Adonai in Yeshua. He understood that the spiritually parched souls of all humanity needed the living water of Messiah. His presence, and later sacrifice, would renew spiritual wonder and reveal

6. John 7:37–44
7. John 7:45–52

the grace of the Father. Yeshua was rapping on the door of every heart at Sukkot. It was a joy to see many open up and receive him as the Living Water of Adonai."

"Knock, knock, knock."

32

A Spiritual Invitation

The rap on the wood entry door caused the whole door to move slightly on the leather hinges. The elder and disciple, startled by the knocking, suddenly realized that it was dusk and they had gone longer than usual with dictation. Polycarp quickly dried the ink on the parchments and stowed the sheets in the small cabinet by his station. Yochanan rose slowly and moved toward the door. They both paused and leaned their ear toward the entry as they detected murmuring on the other side of the door.

"You usually don't spill Irenaeus you must be careful."

"I'm sorry mother, but I was trying to keep up with you. I can tell you are excited."

"You are right my boy. I apologize for the quick pace but an invitation to the Elder's adobe during the week has to mean something out of the ordinary." The two stood in anticipation at the threshold staring at the listing entry door.

"You must attend to that soon," Junia whispered, casting an upward head nod toward the door while simultaneously making eye contact with Irenaeus. He nodded his head in agreement, as the door opened abruptly revealing Yochanan' s silhouette. He saw Junia with a basket of challah and Irenaeus with his yoke of two water jars on his shoulders to replenish their cistern. Flashes of the Jerusalem water pouring ceremony just discussed lit again before Yochanan' s mind and he smiled serendipitously.

"Welcome! I apologize for the wait. We were captivated by our task and completely lost track of the day."

"We can return later, or tomorrow Rabbi," offered Junia.

"Of course not, dear Lady, we had just come to a good stopping point when you knocked on the door, please come in."

Irenaeus looked at his teacher, "Good evening Polycarp."

"Good evening Irenaeus. It is good to see you disciple. Thank you for the water. Help me fill the cistern and then with the meal, will you?"

"Of course, Rabbi."

Polycarp, in usual fashion, with Irenaeus' help, lifted the previously prepared loquat, early lettuce, challah, and almonds to the rooftop and prepared the golden table. Junia nimbly managed the ladder to the rooftop with cups and a wineskin in one arm while Yochanan repositioned the living area and then slowly climbed the ladder to join his guests. Polycarp's menu set a delightful tone, and after a long day and a short prayer, they each realized their hunger. They all ate in silence for some time, enjoying the glowing lamp lit experience of the familiar company and rooftop. Then, Yochanan broke the silence.

"I suppose you have been wondering why I invited you both here during the week, which is, of course, a bit conspicuous," said Yochanan softly, dispelling the silence.

"Only since you invited us," replied Junia in a playful tone. Polycarp sat back to enjoy the unfolding conversation confident that he knew the purpose of the gathering. Yochanan saw Polycarp relax and noticed the suspicious smile that came to his bearded face. He was thankful of his disciple's ability to read the social cues of the previous conversations with Ya'aqobe. Junia looked at Polycarp and then Yochanan, sensing that Yochanan had enjoyed keeping everyone in the dark of the purpose of the meeting. Irenaeus' eyes quickly darted back and forth between the three elders trying desperately to hear the silent communication. He was about to emotionally explode when Yochanan spoke again.

"As you all know, the good news of Messiah must be proclaimed to all who will hear. You have heard me talk of the importance and urgency of this task. The project, Polycarp recording my eyewitness account of the Master, will be able to reach where we personally cannot. Adonai has called me to provide this account to as many synagogues and ecclesia as possible before Shavuot."[1] They all looked at each other in excitement at this revelation.

"Polycarp is a superior Scribe but even he cannot produce the amount of copies necessary in such a short time. Therefore, I have asked Ya'aqobe for a favor. Since he has accepted, I now must ask you both for a favor as well." Somehow, it appeared that Yochanan was looking at all three of his guests

---

1. Pentecost—Essentially fifty days after First fruits

simultaneously while he paused. All eyes were wide and fixed on Yochanan when Junia spoke during his purposeful pause.

"I know that Ya'aqobe was a prominent member and teacher of the Scribes. We all understand that his faith in Messiah resulted in excommunication, which is why he lives here in our small enclave. He is a good choice to help Polycarp but how can we assist?"

"The favor I have asked of Ya'aqobe is not that he picks up his quill. Indeed, his hands are limited for this task." Junia and Irenaeus were both puzzled and quiet while Yochanan continued.

"The favor and task that Ya'aqobe has agreed to perform. . .is to teach both of you according to the order of the scribes so you can assist Polycarp once we are finished with the project."

Irenaeus was again ready to explode emotionally while tears of honor welled up in his eyes. His mother, frozen by the suggestion, processed the privilege, responsibility, and danger that Yochanan had just offered. Her first response was somewhat terse from decades of patriarchal programming.

"A woman and a boy just recently of age are not allowed to train as scribes." Surprising herself, she could hardly believe the harsh words rolled off her tongue. She knew that Yeshua had personally called women for service despite cultural rejection. Yochanan, perceiving her internal struggle, responded calmly.

"It is true that the Halacha[2] of the Pharisees forbids this training, but the Torah does not. What do you say to your Elder's request?"

Junia paused and reflected a bit more on the many times the Master had involved women in his ministry and then gathered her response. "Of course, the answer is yes. It is an honor and responsibility beyond our dreams or capabilities, thank you."

Yochanan smiled deeply and responded, "Adonai has seen your dreams and he will fulfill them. As far as your capabilities, you should wait to thank me, for those I leave for Ya'aqobe to hone. Training starts tomorrow morning at his adobe. Do not be late, for if there is anything equal to his talent as a Scribe and Teacher it is his temper."

Irenaeus' excitement immediately turned to trepidation. While Ya'aqobe was well known in the community he was not known for his patience. Junia, feeling the tension emanating from her son, looked down and said, "Shalom my son, Adonai goes before us as he did with David before Goliath." Laughter lightened the mood of the glowing rooftop.

---

2. Hebrew to "walk" or "go" intended to communicate living one's life a certain way in every aspect of life.

After the laughter subsided, Yochanan, smiling, looked around the table and said, "I would like to tell you all a story." The three took this opportunity to refill their cups and nestle into their chairs.

"There was a man within the Judean leadership who was zealous for the Torah. He knew intimately the events surrounding Yeshua, studied the previous accounts, and knew of his claims. One bright spring morning he felt compelled by the Spirit to grasp the scroll of Isaiah from his shelf and open it randomly for his daily reading. The scroll rolled open to the part that describes the wise servant of Adonai. When he read that the servant would sprinkle the nations with living water, announce to kings what they had not heard, and illuminate to all what they had not seen, he was convicted into considering if Yeshua was the Messiah.[3] He paused and prayed to Adonai for illumination and then continued his reading. Now, though he had read this passage many times, his heart connected the truths of this scripture with the recent historical events like never before, making a profound impact. As he read that the servant was homely, despised, rejected, pierced, and crushed for our sin as a lamb to the slaughter, he became spiritually broken. As he read that Adonai accepted the servant's sacrifice as payment for our sins, he felt his brokenness start to heal like never before. Each newly illuminated truth forced him into the simultaneous realization of the fear and mercy of Adonai. After weeping all night in sackcloth and ashes he arose to the morning light. He shaved, bathed, and went immediately to the Sanhedrin. How do you think this revelation of his epiphany that Yeshua was the Messiah was received by the council?"

Everyone around the table was transfixed on Yochanan and slowly turned their heads from side to side, silently answering his rhetorical question. He continued his story.

"While he was given the chance to renounce his statements before the Sanhedrin, he did not repent of his new belief. Then, after a scourging, scribes locked him in stocks among the northern adobes of the city as a discouraging message for those still supporting the Way. However, after they locked the stocks they simply left him there to die, confident no one would release him. After the scribes left, sometime later, he tells of a young woman who walked calmly up to the stocks, pulled the pin on the latches and calmly walked away. At dusk the former leader struggled free of the stocks and went to the only person he could trust. Nicodemus provided a horse, supplies and said one word to the man."

Junia whispered aloud, "Ephesus."

---

3. See Isaiah 52:15 especially the Masoretic text translation

A Spiritual Invitation

Everyone at the table turned their gaze to her and nodded slowly as Yochanan looked at Junia and Irenaeus directly and finished.

"Yes, the word was Ephesus, and what I have shared with you is part of Ya'aqobe's story. He would probably never tell you these things himself but I thought you should know a bit more about your new teacher. He is committed to Messiah and making him known. He is also committed to train you two as scribes to help proclaim Messiah to the known world."

With the story ended, the three smiled, brimming with spiritual confidence. Over the next hour they all discussed scribal principles, ink, perfect quills, and writing techniques. The hour passed quickly. Then the new scribes in training made their way home looking forward to the morning.

33

Light of the World

Yom Sheini[1]

As the spring sun started to shine, the translucent sky allowed the clarity of the star's brilliance to be particularly defining. Morning seemed more surreal than real and the definition of the things of reality were especially acute. It was one of those lifelong memorable mornings presenting life as hyper-realized, stitching together the joy of being alive with the intensity of the moment. Junia and Irenaeus had made their preparations the night before and woke early, excited about what the day would bring.

The Elder and Disciple rose early to avoid the crowds at the bathhouse and were already returning.

"Rabbi, what happened after Yeshua shouted that he was the water of life?" Yochanan chuckled, looked toward the sky, raised his hands above his head and responded.

"He shouted that he was the light of the world. Is your station ready?"

"Yes Rabbi."

The two arrived at the adobe, opened the door that was now scratching into the dirt floor, and put their things away before settling in their usual places. When Polycarp was ready, Yochanan began the day's dictation.

---

1. Hebrew for Second Day—Monday

> [2] Additionally, Yeshua spoke to them, saying, "I am the light of the world. The one accompanying me will never walk in the darkness, but will have the light of life." Then the Pharisees said to him, "You are bearing witness about yourself; your witness is not true." Yeshua answered and said to them, "Even if I am bearing witness about myself, my witness is true, for I know where I came from and where I am going. However, you do not know where I came from or where I am going. You judge according to the flesh; I am not judging anyone. However, even if I do judge, my judgment is true, for it is myself and my father who sent me, I am not alone. Now even in your law it is written that the testimony of two men is true. I am the one bearing witness about myself, and the Father who sent me bears witness about me." Then they said to him, "Where is your Father?" Yeshua answered, "You know neither me nor my Father. If you would have known me, you would have known my Father also." These words he spoke in the treasury, teaching in the temple. However, no one arrested him, because his hour had not yet come.[3]

Polycarp finished and then closed his eyes as he said, "I can picture it Rabbi. I can see him shouting that he is the water of life at the water pouring ceremony and then shouting that he is the light of the world while the menorahs are blazing in the temple."

"Yes Saphar, those who were open to belief started to understand that spiritual light was something completely different from physical light. What he offered was more than sunshine, understanding, or wisdom from the Sages. He was offering to see Adonai through him. Our star shines and our eyes allow us to perceive the light. Just as our eyes allow us to see the radiance of the sun, so Yeshua allows us to see the glory of the Father. The one who is without sight and yet believes sees clearer than the one who does not believe even though they have sight."

"Rabbi, when Yeshua said 'the Father who sent me bears witness about me,' was he referring to his baptism when the Spirit came and the voice of Adonai spoke over him?"

"Yes, this event and the miracles he had performed. The leadership, however, quickly forgot, or rationalized away, the miraculous and continued to only focus on the physical." Yochanan started again.

---

2. 7:53–8:11 do not appear in any manuscripts until the 5th century—Robertson, *Word Pictures*, 135

3. John 8:12–20

>
> *Then he said to them again, "I am leaving, and you will desire to see me, but you will die within your sinful state. Where I am going, you cannot now come." Then the Judeans said, "Will he kill himself, since he says, 'Where I am going, you cannot now come'?" Then he said to them, "You are from that which is below; I am from that which is above. You are of this cosmos; I am not of this cosmos. This is why I said to you that you would die by your sinful actions. For if you do not believe that I am, you will die by your sinful actions." Then they said to him, "Who are you?" Yeshua said to them, "Just what I have been telling you from the beginning. I have many things to report and decide about you but the one having sent me is true and what I have heard from him I declare to the world." They did not understand that he had been speaking to them about the Father. Then Yeshua said to them, "When you have lifted up the Son of Man, then you will know that I am and that I do nothing of myself but speak just as the Father taught me. Also, the one having sent me is with me. He has not left me alone, for I always do the things that are pleasing to him."*[4]

"The Master made so many references to eternal life Saphar. His focus was explaining the difference between this present physical state and our state in the world to come. When the Father spoke and the Spirit descended on him, Yeshua prepared for his departure. He knew then that the next three cycles of the feasts were his last in Olam Hazeh. He also knew that he needed to complete his mission before returning to the Father so he could retrieve us at the appointed time. After his crucifixion and resurrection, many of the Judeans and Pharisees, as well as Gentiles, sought him. Even though they did not find him physically, they will be with us in Olam Habah."

"A wonderful thought indeed Rabbi." Yochanan nodded and they continued.

> *While saying these things, many believed on him. Then Yeshua said to the Judeans who had believed him, "If you abide in my word, you are truly my disciples and you will know the truth, and the truth will set you free." They answered him, "We are Abraham's offspring and have never been enslaved to anyone. How is it that you say, 'You will become free'?"*[5]

---

4. John 8:21–29
5. John 8:30–33

"Rabbi, you are always very specific in your words." Polycarp read back a portion he had just written. "'Many believed on him' and some Judeans 'had believed him.'" Were there at least two groups of believers here?"

"Yes Saphar, the Greek as you have it written is sufficient for this distinction. There were those present that believed he was of Adonai in their innermost being. Then there were those who had believed his messianic argument but could not accept that their heritage meant nothing regarding eternal life. They were relying on the legacy of Abraham to save them. Yeshua, however, was about to make it clear that the Son is the only way to obtain life eternal."

> *Yeshua answered them, "Truly, truly, I say to you, everyone who practices sin is a slave to sin. But the slave does not remain in the dwelling to the next era, however, the Son remains to the next era. So, if the Son sets you free, you will be free indeed. I know that you are Abraham's offspring, yet you seek to kill me because you do not receive my word. What I have beheld in the presence of my Father I proclaim. Now, what you have heard in the presence of your father you do."*[6]

Yochanan paused, looked at Polycarp and waited for him to finish his strokes. The scribe felt the gaze and paused immediately.

"What are your thoughts on these words Saphar?" The quill scratched the last letter into the parchment and then Polycarp responded.

"Rabbi. . ." he said in a coy voice, while he slowly raised his tall torso and leaned back into the backrest of his chair, which caused Yochanan to smile. "This cosmos, this world, fell away from the constant presence of the Father due to the first rebellion. We are born into this sinful world as slaves to sin and therefore cannot escape to the world to come on our own. Instead of seeing Adonai's majesty directly, we only hear the distant murmuring of the evil one repeating his twisted message of rebellion. The Son however, endured this world, sacrificed himself, and defeated all evil providing hope for those left behind. It seems to me that the need of the Judeans is what we all need to understand. Only the Son had been in the direct presence of Adonai, and so, was the only one who could reveal the Father to our earthly enslaved souls. Yeshua came and gave himself as a sacrifice to provide the way of freedom from sin and rebellion. Those who believe he is the Messiah will do the deeds of Messiah and move on to Olam Habah."

"I wish that they had understood as you do disciple. Let's continue."

---

6. John 8:34:38

34

Rejection of the Light

So, they answered and said to him, "Abraham is our father." Yeshua says to them, "If you were Abraham's children, you would do the works of Abraham. However, now you seek to kill me, a man who has spoken the truth to you which I heard from Adonai. This is not what Abraham did. You are doing the works of your present father." They said to him, "We were not born of sexual immorality. We have one Father; Adonai." Yeshua said to them, "If Adonai were your Father, you would have somehow loved me, for I came from Adonai and I am here. Indeed, I have not come by my own initiative, but he sent me."[1]

"Rabbi, earlier Yeshua agreed that the Judeans were of Abraham and now it seems like he is saying they are not of Abraham. Could you please explain?"

"Turn back a page Saphar and you will see that you wrote the word 'offspring' before. Indeed, the Judeans are of the lineage of Abraham. That is without question. The word you just wrote in this section is 'children', which does not have a necessary link to lineage. A general truth is that children act like their parents. These Judeans were seeking an opportunity to kill the Messiah. Their heritage may have been from Abraham but their actions were from the evil one.

"I see now Rabbi, thank you for the clarification. What was stopping these Judeans from truly believing?"

---

1. John 8:39–42

"Yeshua was still talking to those who had not yet become fully convinced in their innermost being that he was the Messiah. They were still entrenched in their thinking that lineage is what makes one acceptable to Adonai. Their desire was power, influence, and control rather than truth. They perceived Yeshua as a threat to all those desires. He knew they were only thinking of themselves just like the Accuser. The simple logic that if Adonai sent Messiah, then Messiah would have the message of Adonai, was difficult for them to hear."

Polycarp drained his quill and pulled out his knife quickly to sharpen the edge. Yochanan took this opportunity to stand and stretch. He also went to the water pitcher and refilled their cups. After taking a drink, he sat back in his chair. When Polycarp was ready, he continued.

> *"Why do you not understand through my words. . .because you are not able to hear my word. You are of your father the accuser, and you desire to do what your father desires. He was a murderer from the beginning, and does not stand in the truth, because there is no truth in him. Whenever he speaks falsehood he speaks from his own character, for he is a deceiver and the father of deception. But because I speak the truth, you do not believe me. Which of you convicts me of sin? If I speak the truth, why do you not believe me? He who is of Adonai hears the words of Adonai. Therefore, you do not hear them because you are not of Adonai."*[2]

"These Judeans were not able to look beyond their own preconceived conclusions about salvation. The evil one had so influenced their desire for power and importance of their own bloodline that they did not remember the bloodline of Messiah. At first they wanted him to conform to their own notion of Messiah, however, once Yeshua likened them to the accuser they lashed back in complete rejection."

> *The Judeans said to him, "Are we not rightly saying that you are a Samaritan and have a demon?" Yeshua answered, "I do not have a demon, but I honor my Father, and you dishonor me. Also, I do not seek my own honor. The One is seeking and judging it. Truly, truly, I say to you, if anyone keeps my word, he will never see death in the next era." The Judeans said to him, "Now we know that you have a demon! Abraham died, and also the prophets, yet you say, 'If anyone keeps my word, he will never taste death in the next era.' You are not greater than our father Abraham who died or the prophets who died.*

---

2. John 8:43–47

Who do you make yourself out to be?" Yeshua answered, "If I glorify myself, my glory is nothing. It is my Father glorifying me, of whom you say, 'He is our Adonai.' But you have not known him. However, I know him. If I were to say that I do not know him, I would be a liar like you, but I do know him and I keep his word. Your father Abraham rejoiced that he would see my day. He saw it and was glad." Then the Judeans said to him, "You are not yet fifty years old, and have you seen Abraham?" Yeshua said to them, "Truly, truly, I say to you, before Abraham was, I am." Then they picked up stones to throw at him, but Yeshua concealed himself and went out of the temple.[3]

Polycarp looked at Yochanan and said, "This must have been impossible for them to understand." Yochanan responded.

"They had seen so much and still they were rejecting Yeshua as Messiah. The Father spoke confirming him and the Spirit came upon him for all to see. He did miracles in their midst and they knew of his healing power. When he spoke plainly, they only searched for ways to accuse him. Yeshua was correct when he said that they could not hear his words. They had made Adonai into their own image and could not imagine beyond themselves or this present world. Yeshua had been in the presence of Adonai since the beginning and was the spiritual light of Adonai, but their blindness stopped them from seeing this shimmer."

"Rabbi, I do not mean to be disrespectful but it seems they were blind in every way imaginable. Am I wrong?"

"No Saphar you are not wrong. I pray you never understand this blindness. However, we must always be careful to not think too much of ourselves. We should be thankful that Adonai has pried a sliver of our own stubborn eyelid open while he works on the eyes of others. On this great day, the last day of Sukkot, Yeshua clearly announced that he was the Anointed One of Adonai. He proclaimed to be the spiritual water of life and the spiritual light of the world. Everyone who heard what he said, and saw what he had done had a clear choice before them. Then, because he is so gracious, he provided a timely example of his teaching which also substantiated his proclamation. This example was another attempt to dislodge the Judeans mistaken perspective."

---

3. John 8:48–59

35

The Blind Receive Sight

> *Then passing by, he saw a man blind from birth and some of his disciples asked him saying, "Rabbi, who sinned, this man or his parents, that he should be born blind?" Yeshua answered, "Neither this man sinned nor his parents, but that the works of Adonai might be displayed in him. It is proper that we labor in the deeds of him who sent me while it is day; night is coming, when no one can labor. While I am in the cosmos I am the light of the cosmos." Having said these things, he spit on the ground and made clay with the saliva. Then he applied the clay to his eyes and said to him, "Go, wash in the pool, the one of Siloam," which means "Sanctified,"" so he went and washed and came back seeing.*[1]

Yochanan again paused at this point and waited for his disciple. Polycarp finished his strokes, paused also, and gave a slight snicker of disgust and spoke.

"It is interesting that those without infirmities believe those with infirmities have sinned. This kind of thinking seems illogical. It does not follow that specific ailments come from specific sins any more than specific virtues come from specific mitzvot.[2] There are too many counter examples in life to say that sin causes infirmities. We enter this world tainted because of the overstepping[3] by Adam and Chavah. Their moral disobedience affected

---

1. John 9:1–7
2. Hebrew for Commands or Good Deeds
3. See Genesis 31:36 and עָשָׂה

the physical and the spiritual life for this world. It is unfortunate that humanity cannot see past physical deformities to the precious spirit within."

"I believe you are correct Saphar. The spiritual blindness in the world is certainly because of our sinful state. Physical blindness or infirmities are those biological anomalies, which cover too many factors to comprehend completely. However, as Yeshua proved, those anomalies are opportunities for Adonai to reveal his glory. Yeshua also took this opportunity, with the blind man, to provide a living illustration of the spiritual truth he was trying to communicate to the Judeans. Remember, he had just proclaimed to be the water of life and the light of the world. His unique actions with the blind man were part of this illustration. Yeshua, the Water of Life, mixed his saliva with the dust of creation. He then applied the mixture on "adam," the man, and sent him to cleanse himself in the sanctified pool. Truly a physical representation of what Messiah offers us today in order to begin to see the Light of the world."

"How did the man react?" said Polycarp. Yochanan lifted his hand and motioned toward his quill.

> *Then their neighbors and those who had seen him before when he was a beggar were saying, "Is this not the man who was sitting and begging?" Some said, "It is he." Others said, "No, but he is like him." He kept saying, "It is me." Then they said to him, "How then were your eyes opened?" He answered, "The man called Yeshua made clay and anointed my eyes and said to me, 'Go to Siloam and wash.' Then, having gone and washed I received sight." They said to him, "Where is he?" He says, "I do not know." They brought who once was blind to the Pharisees. But it was on the Sabbath day when Yeshua had made the clay and opened his eyes. Then the Pharisees again asked him how he had received sight. Then he said to them, "He put clay on my eyes, and I washed, and I see." Then some of the Pharisees said, "This man is not from Adonai, for he does not keep the Sabbath." However, others said, "How is a sinful man able to do such signs?" Then there was a division among them. Then they say again to the blind man, "What do you say about him, since he has opened your eyes?" He said, "He is a prophet."*[4]

"We have talked about fences for the Torah before Saphar. The Torah does not forbid or encourage mixing or healing as Yeshua did with this man. This manmade prohibition of mixing and healing on the Sabbath reveals

---

4. John 9:8–17

how any of us can be so fixed in our own perspective that we miss the truth around us."

"Rabbi, I understand how transgressing Torah is sin because Adonai has made that clear. However, I do not understand how the Pharisees can decree that transgressing a fence is sin."

"As we have talked about before disciple, it is under the guise of ensuring that the people do not come close to transgressing Torah. As you stated earlier, 'If other rules prevent the choice of obeying, or not obeying a command, then how can one receive the blessing of being obedient to the command?'"

"It is unfortunate that the leaders refused to acknowledge the power of Adonai," said Polycarp.

"Indeed, it seemed like they rejected this teaching completely. Let's finish the account."

36

Those Seeing are Blind

The Judeans, however, did not believe about him who had been blind and had received his sight. Even when they summoned the parents, of him having received sight, and asked them saying, "Is this your son, who you say was born blind, how then does he now see?" Then his parents answered and said, "We know that this is our son and that he was born blind. But how he now sees we do not know, nor do we know who opened his eyes. Ask him; he is of age. He will speak for himself." His parents said these things because they feared the Judeans. Indeed, the Judeans had already agreed that if anyone should confess him to be Messiah, he was to be put out of the synagogue. [v] *Because of this his parents said, "He is of age; ask him." Then they called the man who had been blind out a second time and said to him, "Give glory to Adonai for we know this, that other man is a sinner." Then this one answered, "Whether he is a sinner I do not know. One thing I do know, that though I was blind, now I see." Then they said to him, "What did he do to you? How did he open your eyes?" He answered them, "I told you already and you did not listen. Why do you want to hear it again? You do not want to become his disciples." Then they reviled him and said, "You are a disciple of that one, but we are the disciples of Moses. We know that Adonai has spoken to Moses, however, we do not know from where this one comes from." The man responded and said to them, "Indeed, this is an amazing thing! That you do not know where he comes from, and yet he opened my eyes.*

> We know that Adonai does not hear sinners, but if anyone is god-fearing and does his will he hears him. Never in this age has it been heard that anyone opened the eyes of a man born blind. If this man were not from Adonai, he could do nothing like this." They answered and said to him, "You were born in sin entirely and would you teach us?" Then they cast him out.[1]

"Rabbi, why were the Judeans going to such great lengths to discredit this man's account?"

"It seemed to me that these men had one thing in the forefront of their minds. They refused to believe that Adonai could work through someone other than themselves to help, heal, or reveal his glory."

"What of the prophets and judges, Rabbi, surely they knew of these?"

"It is true disciple that Adonai used many different people throughout this age to work miracles and reveal his glory. However, remember that the Judean leaders desire to trace their authority back to Moses to establish a valid Sanhedrin. If someone out of their control was able to do the miraculous, they viewed them as a threat to their legacy, instead of seeing the glory of Adonai."

"Why did the man not explain how Yeshua had healed him when asked?"

"Tuflos,[2] the blind man, knew the culture better than most, even though he could not see. All those years he gleaned knowledge where he could and understood the intentions of those around him. Many times, what we see distracts from what we could hear and understand through our other senses. He understood that, to many, Yeshua' s unorthodox method would be confusing. To them it would not be a reminder of the Water of Life using the dust of adam to provide the ability to see the light of the world. They would see the method as some conjuring that they could use to convince themselves, and others, that Yeshua was something other than Messiah. Let us finish what happened at Sukkot Saphar and then we will break for a meal."

> Yeshua heard that they had cast him out, and having found him said, "Do you believe in the Son of Man?" He answered and said, "And who is he, Master, that I might believe in him?" Yeshua said to him, "You have seen him, and is he the one speaking with you." He said, "I believe Master," and he worshiped him. Yeshua said, "I came into this world for

---

1. John 9:18–34
2. From the Greek τυφλός, meaning blind

judgment, in order that those not seeing might see, and those who see might become blind." Some of the Pharisees who were with him heard these things, and they said to him, "We are not blind also." Yeshua said to them, "If you were blind, you would not have any sin; however, since you say, 'We see,' your sin remains.[3]

"Saphar, Yeshua was able to provide judgment, or conviction, simply by his presence. He simultaneously revealed the Father and forced personal confrontation with what one truly believed. Tuflos was both an example of physical sight and spiritual sight. Not only could his eyes now perform as designed but his soul was properly focused on the Father because of the Son of Man. Our *soul* focus is one of the *sole* concerns that Yeshua passed on to the Spirit. Yeshua has risen, but the Spirit still convicts us of the sin we cannot see or are unwilling to admit. Turning to Messiah during these times gives our sight clarity or maturity."

Yochanan turned toward Polycarp, smiled and said, "Let us leave the shadows of the adobe and step back into the mid-day light and prepare for a meal and the afternoon dictation."

"Yes Rabbi...I wonder how our two scribes in training faired with Ya'aqobe."

---

3. John 9:35–41

37

The Light of Ya'aqobe

Junia and Irenaeus woke to the crisp feeling of the day. They finished their early morning prayers on the rooftop of their adobe and made their way down to the street. "Did you remember your writing samples Irenaeus?"

"Yes mother," responded Irenaeus as he stepped down from the threshold, latching the door. The clank of the catch of the latch brought back the memory of the chore he still needed to accomplish for the Elder at his adobe. He had gathered some metal yesterday for the hinges and was waiting for an opportune time when both the Elder and Polycarp would be absent. He desired to surprise them with a proper fitting front door soon.

For now, however, he was eyeing the front door of Ya'aqobe's adobe and had mixed feelings about what he would experience in the next few hours. Junia knocked on the door, turned toward her growing son and smiled softly at Irenaeus. She noticed that lately, the angle of her head was rising when she looked at him. Just then, the door latch fell and the door swung open to reveal their host.

"Good morning scribes," bellowed Ya'aqobe as some birds sitting on the parapets above flew away startled. He motioned for them to come across the threshold and into the front room.

"Good morning Ya'aqobe," they said in unison as Junia followed with another thank you.

"Again, thank you for your willingness to teach us. There is no value we could place on the privilege of learning from you."

"I have done much thinking through the night," said Ya'aqobe." I view this to be a privilege to help in the spreading of the good news of Messiah.

Thank you both for your willingness to help the Elder." Irenaeus, surprised by the good nature of Ya'aqobe, turned to close the door.

"Please leave the door open Irenaeus; wide open. The air is brisk but manageable and I'll make every effort to communicate honor and virtue while a woman is in my house."

"Yes Elder," replied Irenaeus. Junia thought this to be unwise, but kept her silence.

"For the next several days you will address me as Rabbi and I will address you both as Talmidim.[1] Is that clear Talmadim?" Junia and Irenaeus looked at each other with excitement and again softly replied in unison.

"Yes Rabbi."

The front room of Ya'aqobe's adobe was unadorned but spacious with windows on the same wall of the doorway. The shutters were open and the light revealed a large desk toward the back of the room with a padded chair. Two smaller amanuensis stations with well-worn desktops and wooden chairs stood close to the door and windows.

"Please have a seat at your stations and I will go over what we will be coving for your training." Junia and Irenaeus quickly moved to their individual stations, set their provisions next to their chairs, and sat down to begin their anticipated scribal training.

Ya'aqobe opened his weathered teaching scroll, looked at them both and spoke in a clear, surprisingly soft tone.

"There has been a long debate over the centuries on who was the first scribe. Some argue Ezra, others Moshe,[2] and some say Ya'aqobe, or perhaps Avraham. However, it is my opinion that the first amanuensis was Adonai's amanuensis. This was of course Adam, who, possibly, recorded the beginning of the creation account of B'resheet.[3]" Ya'aqobe paused briefly and then continued. "What is an amanuensis, but someone trusted to give an accurate account? There are some that think that Adam could not have known how to write but how could he not have known? My suspicion is that we lost more of our first parent's knowledge due to their sin than we care to admit. Besides, who else was around to be Adonai's scribe? Who else was there to record the account of creation and then hand down the scroll for the next to record their part in history?" Ya'aqobe noticed the surprise on his students faces.

"I realize this opinion is different than what we assume happened on the mountaintop of Saini with Adonai and Moshe. However, the divisions of

---

1. Hebrew for Disciples
2. Hebrew for Moses
3. Hebrew for In the Beginning—i.e. the book of Genesis

B'resheet, I believe, provide a different view of its authorship. Furthermore, each scribe of the sections in B'resheet prefers a certain name of Adonai, which is fascinating.ᵂ Now, I am telling you this because you have now become a part of a long and trusted tradition of becoming Sapharim."

Ya'aqobe motioned with his hand toward the finely crafted wooden boxes on their desks. Junia and Irenaeus opened their boxes to find a formal scribal set of tools containing a quill, reed, knife, ink, and bottles. They set up their tools, removed a piece of parchment from under their box and started to take notes as Ya'aqobe continued.

"We will first cover abecedaries of both Hebrew and Greek and review the formation of both languages with vocabulary. Thank you both for bringing your writing samples, I will review those and provide suggestions. Then we will cover size, style, spacing, uncials, and general orthography with special attention to Greek prose and poetry. After this, we will focus on scribal signs and the strict guidelines for ruled lines, guide dots and spacing. You will then be ready for learning the proper strokes for both Hebrew and Greek letters. We will then review several Hebrew works, genres, and how these could affect the recording of events. These will also provide examples of the necessity of the precision in copying while identifying mistakes such as minuses, pluses, changes, and differences in sequence. After this we will look to the importance of the m'koriy[4] with special attention to what the Elder and Polycarp are producing."

"Lastly, we will cover the scribal tools and how they are made. You will be gathering material for various types of papyrus, other writing surfaces, and will make the sheets yourselves. Melan will be your instructor for ink and we will visit Hylinane to learn some of his trade. I will also instruct you on how to find and create the very best quills and reeds for you to apply your new craft." Ya'aqobe was pacing around the room and weaving through his students while speaking. After this introduction, he stepped back to his desk and peered toward his pupils. Junia and Irenaeus had outlined his introduction perfectly and they were both smiling with excitement. Ya'aqobe felt joy welling from within. He smiled with his lips and eyes, paused slightly, and said, "Let's begin."

---

4. Mi-kor-ee—The volarge or original

38

Living Psalm 23

With necessities and preparations complete, the Elder and Scribe went to the rooftop for midday prayer. Lengthy prayer surrendered to a short nap due to the wonder of the day and the strong sunshine. Polycarp was the first to stir. He stepped down the ladder, and made sure everything was ready for the evening. Yochanan followed shortly.

"You should have woken me Saphar, I was deep in my dreams."

"I wanted to let you sleep Rabbi, we have been very busy for days now." Both of them took their usual seats and prepared for the long afternoon.

"Thank you Saphar. Now, let us finish Yeshua's second year of revealing Adonai. We left off with his sermons at Sukkot. Let us move on to when he came to the Feast of Hanukah[1] that same year." While saying these words Yochanan nodded toward Polycarp, who readied his quill.

 "Truly, truly, I say to you, the one not entering the sheepfold by the door but is climbing in by another way, that man is a thief and a robber. However, the one entering by the door is the shepherd of the sheep. To him the gatekeeper opens and the sheep hear his voice. Then he calls his own sheep by name and leads them out. When he has brought out all his own, he goes before them, and the sheep follow him, for they know his voice. They will never ever follow another but they will flee from him because they do not recognize the voice of others." Yeshua spoke this allegory to them, however, they did not know what he was saying to them.[2]

1. Hebrew for Dedication
2. John 10:1–6

Polycarp looked a bit puzzled and said, "Was Yeshua still addressing the Judeans?"

"Yes. Many of the same people that were at Sukkot came to the Feast of Dedication. The Judeans still believed that Yeshua was a sinner for breaking their fences for the Torah. The healing of the blind man and the living allegory it served for the Judeans was still fresh in everyone's mind. He also knew that the leadership felt threatened because the people, the sheep, were listening to his voice. The people could hear the Father's truth in his words and it was a stark contrast to the controlling attempts of the Judean leadership. This Hanukkah message had the same theme of 'you hear but do not understand' but put in a different allegorical context."

"Again, Yeshua was drawing on the practices of our culture and what was in the forefront of people's minds. Since it was winter, there was limited pasture for food and limited oil for light and healing. Shepherds had switched from pasturing their flocks to keeping them penned and feeding the flocks themselves. The Master's allegory of the sheep had deep, relevant significance and reminded those present of one of David's most famous Psalms."

"Yahweh is my shepherd; I shall not want. He makes me lie down in green pastures. He leads me beside still waters. He restores my soul. He leads me in paths of righteousness for his name's sake. Even though I walk through the valley of the shadow of death, I will fear no evil, for you are with me; your rod and your staff, they comfort me. You prepare a table before me in the presence of my enemies; you anoint my head with oil; my cup overflows. Surely, goodness and mercy shall follow me all the days of my life, and I shall dwell in the house of Yahweh forever."[3]

"Here is the rest of the allegory he proclaimed on that winter day in the temple."

Then Yeshua again said to them, "Truly, truly, I say to you, I am the door for the sheep. All who ever came before me are thieves and robbers, but the sheep did not listen to them. I am the door, if anyone enters in through me, he will be saved and will go in and out and find pasture. The thief does not come unless there is a possibility to steal and kill and destroy. I came that they have the possibility for life and have it abundantly. I am the good shepherd. The good shepherd lays down his life for the sheep. However, the hired hand, not being a

---

3. Psalm 23 ESV

> *shepherd, or who does not own the sheep, sees the wolf coming and leaves the sheep and flees. Then the wolf snatches and scatters them. Because he is a hired hand, he cares nothing for the sheep. I am the good shepherd and I know those who are my own and my own know me. Just as the Father perceives me, I also perceive the Father and I lay down my life for the sheep. I also have other sheep that are not of this courtyard. It is necessary for me to bring those also and they will listen to my voice. Then there will be one flock, one shepherd. For this reason, the Father loves me, because I give up my soul that I might receive it back. No one lifts it from me, but I give it up of my own accord. I have authority to give it up, and I have authority to take it back. This commandment I received from my Father."*[4]

"Saphar, he is the shepherd sent by Adonai who spiritually feeds us and will bring us to the blessed pastures of Olam Habah. He is also the Anointed One of Adonai who protects us in this world while preparing a place for us in the world to come."

"Rabbi, are the 'sheep not of this courtyard' gentiles?" Yochanan smiled again and turned his gleaming eyes to his disciple.

"If I remember correctly we were all in the temple standing in the courtyard of Israel which is an unmistakable reference to the Jewish people. However, as you know there are other courtyards in the temple including the courtyard of the Gentiles. As he said those words he motioned all around with both arms suggesting that the other sheep were the other courtyards; essentially all the souls of the world." Polycarp angled his head slightly as a puzzled look came upon his face.

"Rabbi, did the people understand how these words spoke of David's Psalm?" Yochanan responded,

"The Psalm is very popular, so I believe there was a ready connection in most people's minds. However, as before during Sukkot, the crowds had a mixed devotion regarding Yeshua. Not everyone thought of Yeshua as the Good Shepherd." Yochanan raised his finger toward Polycarp.

> *There was again a division among the Judeans because of these words. Indeed, many of them said, "He has a demon, and is insane; why do you listen to him?" Others said, "These are not the sayings of one possessed by a demon. A demon is not able to open the eyes of the blind."*[5]

---

4. John 10:7–18
5. John 10:19–21

"Saphar, make it clear that these things, and what follows, took place during Dedication"

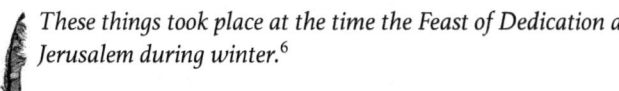
These things took place at the time the Feast of Dedication at Jerusalem during winter.[6]

"I am ready Rabbi, please continue."

---

6. John 10:22

39

Who is Elohim?

Then Yeshua was walking in the temple, in the colonnade of Solomon. So, the Judeans encircled him and said to him, "How long until you lighten our souls, if you are the Messiah, tell us plainly." Yeshua answered them, "I told you, and you do not believe. These deeds that I do in the name of my Father give evidence concerning me. However, you do not believe because you are not my sheep. My sheep hear my voice, and I perceive them, and they follow me. I also give them life eternal, and they will never ever perish in this era and no one will take them from my hand. My Father, who has given them to me, is greater than all, and no one has power to take them from my Father's hand. I and the Father are one."[1]

Yochanan again paused expecting a comment from Polycarp and waited for his disciple to finish. Polycarp knew of this statement of Yeshua being one with the Father. He also knew that it was a stumbling block for many Jews from considering Yeshua as Messiah.

"Rabbi, I understand that you wish me to respond to the last statement, but this topic does not have an easy answer." There was an awkward pause in their interchange for some time. Yochanan was comfortable with long awkward pauses. Polycarp was still learning the internal peace of this teaching tactic. Finally, Yochanan leaned forward in his chair, the creaking cross braces breaking the stilted silence.

---

1. John 10:23–30

Who is Elohim?

He looked into Polycarp's thoughtful eyes and said, "This is true young Rabbi, but how will you guide Irenaeus on this topic?" Polycarp paused, gathered his thoughts and responded cautiously.

"Adonai and Yeshua have provided the same promise of salvation to those who believe in Messiah. Therefore, they share the authority and responsibility to keep those who accept the truth of Yeshua. However, the Father gave this authority to the Son not the other way around. While Yeshua acknowledged that no one is more powerful than the Father, he also has divine power not seen in any other person." Polycarp paused for a moment and then continued.

"Yeshua is the Son of Adonai and the Son of Adam.[2] The oneness between an earthly father and son is powerful but the spiritual oneness of the one true Adonai of the Shema[3] and his son is something beyond our limited understanding. Adonai is wholly different from his creation and his son shares that same quality. A Greek anthropomorphism of polytheism for this unique situation is a simplification that does not consider the limitations of our understanding. The tension of the Shema and the oneness of Messiah and Adonai may exist with us, but it is clearly not an issue with the Father and the Son."

Yochanan nodded toward his disciple with kind eyes and slowly breathed, "Baruch atah Adonai." Then his demeanor stiffened as the memories of the temple during that season of Hanukkah flooded his mind. He recalled the righteous robed Judean vultures circling around Yeshua.

"Your delicate explanation, Saphar, is not how the Judeans received this bold statement."

> *Then the Judeans picked up stones again that they might stone him. Yeshua responded to them, "I have shown you many good deeds from the Father; for which of these deeds do you stone me?" The Judeans answered him, "For a good deed we do not stone you but for blasphemy, because you, being a man, make yourself Elohim." Yeshua answered them, "Is it not written in your law, 'I said, you are elohim'? If he called them elohim to whom the word of Elohim came, and scripture cannot be broken, why do you say of him whom the Father set apart and sent into the world, 'You are blaspheming,' because I said, 'I am the Son of Elohim'? If I am not doing the deeds of my Father, then do not believe me. If, however, I do them, even though you do not believe me, believe the deeds, that you may know and understand that the Father is in me and I am*

---

2. Son of Man—A messianic reference
3. Hear O Israel; Yahweh is our Adonai; Yahweh is one—Deuteronomy 6:4

in the Father." Then they, again, sought to seize him, but he escaped from their hands. Then he departed again beyond the Jordan to the place where Yochanan had been first baptizing and he abided there. Then many came to him. And they said, "Yochanan did no signs, however, everything that Yochanan said about this man was true." Then many believed in him there.[4]

"Yeshua knew from their circling that they wanted him to declare that he was Messiah in order that they might have an accusation against him. Instead, he pressed them to consider his miracles and their origin. However, these pharisaical vultures were only considering their own thoughts and desires. Graciously, the Master was continually trying to shake them from this perspective, so they could start to see the truth. He even pulled from the Psalms once again to try to open their understanding. Can you recite the Psalm the Master quoted from my disciple?"

"Yes Rabbi, it uses the word elohim for human rulers."

 *Elohim has taken his place in the divine council; in the midst of the elohim he holds judgment: "How long will you judge unjustly and show partiality to the wicked? Selah. Give justice to the weak and the fatherless; maintain the right of the afflicted and the destitute. Rescue the weak and the needy; deliver them from the hand of the wicked." They have neither knowledge nor understanding, they walk about in darkness; all the foundations of the earth are shaken. I said, "You are elohim, sons of the Most High, all of you; nevertheless, like men you shall die, and fall like any prince." Arise, O Elohim, judge the earth; for you shall inherit all the nations!*[5]

"This seems to aptly apply to that current situation, Rabbi."

"Go on Saphar."

"In the Psalm, Adonai is as the prophets of old contending against those power-hungry chieftains of the nation of Israel during David's time. Asaph, the author of the Psalm, describes these unjust judges as elohim because of the authority they have obtained. Likewise, Yeshua was in the midst of the ruling Judeans who were the present chieftains of Israel lording over the people with their own selfish, power-hungry desires. They were the current elohim of the masses. Also, just as Yeshua went first to the Jews and

---

4. John 10:31–42

5. Psalm 82—ESV

then to the Gentiles, so the Psalm ends with the salvation of the nations. Just like your last line states, 'many believed in him there.'"[6]

"I agree with your correlations my disciple. In addition, the Master again used Kol Vahomer[7], which seemed to elude to the Judeans. After all, if the scriptures could use 'sons of elohim' for those who were corrupt how much more fitting for one that is not corrupt?"

The Rabbi and Scribe repositioned themselves as Polycarp replenished his ink and switched quills.

"Before we break for the evening meal Saphar there is one more account during the days of Dedication that needs to be included in our record. Then we will move on to the Master's third and last year in Olam Hazeh. It is the account of Yeshua raising El'azar."[8] Polycarp's eyes widened a bit and he smiled as he stretched his back and readied his quill.

---

6. See Delitzsch, *Psalms*, 400–402
7. The light to the heavy
8. Hebrew for Lazarus

40

Lazarus in Languish

Now a certain man was languishing; El'azar of Bethany from the village of Miryam and Marah[1] her sister. Now it was Miryam who anointed the Master with ointment and wiped his feet with her hair, whose brother El'azar was ill. Then the sisters sent to him, saying, "Master, he whom you love languishes." Now when Yeshua heard this he said, "The end result of this languish is not death but it is for the glory of Adonai, so that the Son of Adonai may be glorified through it." Now Yeshua loved Marah and her sister and El'azar. However, when he heard of his languish he remained in that place where he was for two days. Then after this he says to the disciples, "Let us go to Judea again." The disciples say to him, "Rabbi, just now the Judeans were seeking to stone you, and are you going there again?" Yeshua answered, "Are there not twelve hours in the day? If anyone walks in the day, he does not stumble, because he sees the light of this world. However, if anyone walks in the night, he stumbles, because the light is not on him." After he said these things, he says to them, "El'azar, our friend has fallen asleep, but I go to awaken him." Then the disciples said to him, "Master, if he has fallen asleep, he will recover." However, Yeshua had spoken of his death, but they thought that he was speaking of the rest of sleep. Then at that time Yeshua said to them plainly, "El'azar has died. Now, I rejoice I was not there for your sake in order that

---

1. Hebrew for Mary and Martha

you might believe. But let us go to him." So Tauma,[2] referring to the twin, said to his fellow disciples, "Let us also go, that we may die with him."[3]

Yochanan looked toward the ceiling, stretching his neck, and stroked the bottom half of his beard with his right hand after this part of dictation. He then turned toward Polycarp and commented.

"This was an interesting interchange indeed. The messenger from the sisters delivered their note to Yeshua privately and we did not know the Master's response to the messenger until later. His reply about the situation not resulting in death explains why the messenger did not delay and went straight back to Myriam and Marah."

"But why did Yeshua wait two days Rabbi? Didn't the sisters expect him to come immediately?"

"Yes, they did Saphar. My suspicion is that he waited two days because he wanted to raise El'azar on a specific day." Yochanan rose from his chair to move about while Polycarp set his quill in its rest, sat back in his station and looked forward to the teaching moment.

"Remember that it was still the Hanukah season, which is the celebration for the dedication of the temple after the Maccabean revolt. This, of course, happened on the twenty-fifth of Kislev. Tell me young Rabbi, what would be the preparation day for this feast?"

"Preparation day would be the day before, the twenty fourth of Kislev."

"Quite right and if you look in the scroll of Haggai, you will find this date as a day of dedication for the rebuilding of the Zerubbabel temple. Yochanan raised both his hands and said,

"Consider from this day onward, from the twenty-fourth day of the ninth month. Since the day that the foundation of Yahweh's temple was laid, consider: Is the seed yet in the barn? Indeed, the vine, the fig tree, the pomegranate, and the olive tree have yielded nothing. But from this day on I will bless you."[4]

Polycarp responded, "So, the Maccabean and Zerubbabel temples share a dedication date?"

"Yes Saphar, and what is interesting concerning the dates is that although Hanukkah was declared during the Maccabees; Haggai made his

---

2. Hebrew for Thomas
3. John 11:1–16
4. Haggai 2:18–19 ESV

dedication over four hundred and fifty years earlier." Polycarp paused and then asked another question.

"Rabbi, If the Maccabean dedication happened on the anniversary of the Zerubbabel dedication, what about Solomon's temple?"

"Good question my disciple. The King's scroll records the completion of Solomon's temple in the eighth month. My opinion is that the dedication of Solomon's temple occurred on the same date. Afterward, they completed the furnishings and placed those and the ark inside the temple the following Rosh Hashanah.[5] It was then that Adonai's glory filled the temple which is also recorded in the King's scroll." Polycarp tried to veil his questioning visage and then looked at Yochanan and asked a question.

"While the temple dedications happening on the same date throughout history are amazing, how does this relate to El'azar?" A slight sly smile came to Yochanan's face as he continued.

"What are these bodies except temples of the Ruach HaKodesh?"[6] The glory of Adonai filled the earthly temples and his Spirit now fills us, his spiritual temples. The anniversary date for the dedications of the temples and the raising of El'azar happened on the same day. It is my suspicion that Yeshua waited until the last day of the Feast of Dedication to raise El'azar to provide this stunning correlation. Since this feast is a time to celebrate temple renewal it is fitting that Yeshua renewed El'azar's temple during Dedication."

"What a powerful picture indeed!" exclaimed Polycarp.

After a moment of spiritual pondering the two continued.

> *So, when Yeshua was coming he found he had already been four days in the tomb. Now Bethany was near Jerusalem, about fifteen stadia away. So many of the Judeans had come to Marah and Miryam that they might console them concerning their brother. Then when Marah heard of Yeshua's coming, she accosted him, however Miryam was sitting in the house. Then Marah said to Yeshua, "Master, if you had been here, it would not have been possible for my brother to have died. But even now I know that whatever possibility you ask Adonai, Adonai will give you." Yeshua says to her, "Your brother will rise again." Marah said to him, "I know that he will rise again in the resurrection on the last day." Yeshua said to her, "I am the resurrection and the life. The one believing in me will live even if he happens to die. Also, everyone living and believing in me shall never perish in the new era. Do you*

---

5. Hebrew for Head of the Year—The Jewish New Year
6. Hebrew for Holy Spirit

believe this?" She says to him, "Yes, Master; I have believed that you are the Messiah, the Son of Adonai, who is expected for the cosmos."[7]

"Marah seemed to be a woman of great faith Rabbi"

"She was Saphar. She was the most attentive, whenever there was opportunity for her to hear the Master speak. She also knew to be specific with her questions of Yeshua, which many of us did not learn until later."

"Rabbi, her response reminds me that there are many references in your record of the Master mentioning the new era or Olam Habbah. What will the new heavens and earth look like?" Yochanan readjusted himself in his chair, looked longing out the window and responded.

"All of what you see, the earth, the stars, the cosmos, and all who believe in Yeshua will be renewed. It is as Isaiah said:

"For behold, I create new heavens and a new earth, and the former things shall not be remembered or come into mind. But be glad and rejoice forever in that which I create; for behold, I create Jerusalem to be a joy, and her people to be a gladness. I will rejoice in Jerusalem and be glad in my people; no more shall be heard in it the sound of weeping and the cry of distress."[8]

"I only know what the scriptures say Saphar. However, I suppose it will be very similar to what we see now but without the pull of sin on our hearts. It will be, at the very least, a new perfected garden, earth, and cosmos with the full realization of Jeremiah's prophesy. His commands will be written on our hearts." Yochanan nodded toward Polycarp and he again dipped his quill.

---

7. John 11:17–27
8. Isaiah 65:17–19 ESV

41

Lazarus Lifted

> *Now having said these things she went away and secretly called her sister Miryam. She said, "The Teacher is come and calls for you." Then when she heard it, she rose quickly and came to him. Now Yeshua had not yet come into the village, but was still in the place where Marah had met him. When the Judeans who were consoling her in the house saw Miryam rise quickly and go out, they followed her, having supposed that she was going to the tomb to weep there. Now when Miryam came to where Yeshua was and saw him, she fell at his feet, saying to him, "Master, if you had been here, it would not have been possible for my brother to have died." Then when Yeshua saw her weeping, and the Judeans who had come with her also weeping, his spirit was deeply moved and stirred within. Then he said to them, "Where have you laid him?" They say to him, "Master, come and see." Yeshua wept. Therefore, the Judeans said, "See how he loved him!" However, some of them said, "Could not he who opened the eyes of the blind man also have kept this man from dying?"*[1]

Polycarp looked up at Yochanan, who noticed and paused for his question.

"Why did Yeshua weep Rabbi? He knew that he was going to raise El'azar."

"I believe it was, at least, a combination of two deep emotions Saphar. First, his empathy for us does not change with his knowledge of the future.

1. John 11:28–37

He felt the depth of grief that the others were experiencing in a way we cannot fathom. The intensity at which he feels other people's emotions matches his strength of character and self-control. Second, it is my suspicion that he was grieved that no one else around him had the capacity to imagine beyond this world of physical restraints. Even Marah, who had the greatest faith among them, could not imagine what was about to happen."

> *Then Yeshua, being again deeply moved inside, comes to the tomb. Now it was a cave, and a stone was lying against it. Yeshua says, "Take away the stone." Marah, the sister of the one having died, says to him, "Master, it is four days already he reeks." Yeshua says to her, "Did I not say to you that if you would believe you would see the glory of Adonai?" Then they took away the stone and Yeshua lifted up his eyes upward and said, "Father, I thank you that you have heard me. I have known that you always hear me, but I said this for those standing here that they might believe that you sent me." Then, having said these things he cried out with a loud voice, "El'azar, come forth." The one who died came out, his hands and feet bound with wrappings and his face wrapped with a cloth. Yeshua said to them, "Unbind him, and let him go." Then many of the Judeans who had come with Miryam and having seen what he did, believed in him. However, some of them went to the Pharisees and told them what Yeshua had done.*[2]

"Rabbi, did those who went to the Pharisees refuse to believe that El'azar was lifted back to life?"

"It is hard to know anyone's true heart Saphar. These few were genuinely concerned for Miryam but also fiercely loyal to the Pharisees. What is unfortunate is that they seemingly missed the purpose of this miracle. Yeshua wanted them to see this miraculous harkening of Hanukkah and the glory of Adonai so they could start to believe that Adonai sent Yeshua. I can only report their actions in that, instead of pondering the power of Messiah they reported to their rulers."

> *Then the chief priests and the Pharisees gathered the Sanhedrin and said, "What are we to do, for this man does many miracles. So, if we leave him alone everyone will believe in him, and the Romans will come and take away both this place and our nation." However, a certain one of them, Caiaphas, who was high priest that year, said to them, "You know*

---

2. John 11:38–46

> *nothing at all nor do you consider that it is profitable for us that one man should die for the people and all of the nation should perish." Now he did not say this of his own accord, but being high priest that year he prophesied that Yeshua was about to die for the nation. Now not only for the nation but also that he might gather into one, the children of Adonai who are scattered abroad. Then from that day they resolved that they would kill him. Therefore, Yeshua no longer walked openly among the Judeans, but went from there to the region near the wilderness, to a town called Ephraim, and he stayed there with his disciples.*[3]

After Polycarp finished his strokes, he responded to these verses.

"It is amazing how the Father weaves his will and plan within this reality through the lives of his children. He could do whatever he wanted to accomplish his goals, but he chooses to involve us in every detail of his redemption of this world."

"How true my disciple. Just like now, for us in this moment, my prayer is that he uses this project to bring souls into his kingdom. Now, since we have completed the events during the Feast of Dedication and Yeshua's second year revealing Adonai, let us wash and prepare for the evening meal. Tomorrow we will start the record of his final year in Olam Hazeh."[4]

"Yes Rabbi."

---

3. John 11:47–54
4. This present world

42

Recollections and Repairs

Late in the afternoon, Ya'aqobe looked up from his parchments strewn on the old wooden desk and gazed at his students, active in their transcription. He watched carefully and knew when each had completed the assignment.

"That is enough for today my scribes. I will review your work this evening," said Ya'aqobe as he carefully rolled up his teaching scroll.

"Thank you again Rabbi," said Junia as she and Irenaeus neatly packed their tools away in their scribal boxes.

"Please come an hour later tomorrow morning and we will continue. Both of you did well and we have covered much ground due to your attentiveness. Shalom my Scribes."

Each gathered their belongings, crossed the threshold of the doorway and started toward their adobe. Irenaeus stopped suddenly and turned toward Junia.

"Mother, there is an errand I would like to perform before meal time."

"How long will this errand take my son?"

"Only about an hour if. . ." Irenaeus looked at his mother pleadingly instead of finishing his sentence. Junia looked at her son and could tell he wanted the stealthy errand concealed for now. "Very well, go your way and I will see you in an hour or so."

Junia made her way back to the adobe with her thoughts and emotions divided. She was thankful for the opportunity provided by Yochanan and Ya'aqobe. However, she also knew that training a woman to be a scribe, to most, was sacrilegious. Her real fear was that, if the local Pharisees noticed this training, persecution would quickly follow. She thought back to the time when she and Andronicus were newly married. They both thought it counter intuitive for there to be more than one god so they supported the synagogue. The Jews held them in high regard for their commitment but they found only rejection from their Greek circle of friends and family.

Over the years, the couple had seen some of the horrors that occurred in Jerusalem from time to time. Junia had experienced more frightening things than a simple argument over respect for women. The Father had protected them and blessed them over the years. Later in life, just before Andronicus died during those oppressions, Adonai provided Irenaeus. The thought of her son experiencing something similar to those past persecutions brought all the bloody memories to the forefront of her mind. She remembered her promises to Andronicus while his broken body lay in her arms. She vowed to follow Adonai whether he gives or takes away. She also promised to raise Irenaeus in the admonition of Adonai and Messiah Yeshua. These vows had been her faith anchors over the years and they would help her stand firm now. As she approached her adobe, she was thankful that Irenaeus was on his errand. This allowed her time to return to the rooftop and pray, alone.

Irenaeus was bouncing down the southern path to the Elder's adobe hoping to go unnoticed. He was carrying his bag of tools and three special hinges for Yochanan' s front door. He put his blacksmith training to good use and made the perfect size hinges for the entry door. No longer would they have to lift the door onto the threshold or have it scrape on the ground inside the adobe. While forging the hinges he had an idea for the nails. All the Roman hardware and hinges he had seen had straight shank nails. These nails needed replacing often because, over time, they would simply slide out of their holes from supporting a heavy wooden door.

Earlier that year he had seen the planters in the fields using pointed, twisted poles to drill holes in the ground for their planting. After the workers made the holes, if they tried to pull the stick straight out without twisting, they would pull up clumps of earth instead of providing a planting hole. This gave him an idea for the nails that would fasten the hinges. He had made nails before, but this time he twisted the shanks while they were still glowing red and experimented with them when they were cool. While he could easily pull a straight-shanked nail out of a block of wood with a lever, this spiral modification made it extremely hard to remove the same nail. He was excited to use this invention to help Yochanan and Polycarp.

Irenaeus arrived at the field of Yochanan's adobe and moved slowly toward the entrance to hear for any dictation inside. Hearing nothing, he then circled the house while carefully stepping away from the house in order to spy the rooftop. Convinced that the Elder and Rabbi had left for evening preparations he went again to the threshold and opened the door. Confirming that no one was inside, he took out a metal marking tool and marked the top and the bottom of the leather hinges on the edge of the door and the jamb. With one hand, he gripped the top of the door and with the other, he grasped the rusting metal latch. He then ripped the door and the hinges from the jamb in one strong jerk.

After the dust cleared, he laid the door gently on the floor and removed the old hinges from the edge of the door and the jamb. Reaching into his tool bag, he grasped the hinges, twisted nails, a block of wood and his hammer. On a previous visit, he had taken the opportunity to measure the hinge dimensions and height of the door to bring the proper thickness board to set under the door for installation. Centering the hinges on his marks on the door slab, while lining up the pins of the hinges to the interior side of the door, he nailed eight twisted nails through the holes of the three hinges and into the edge of the door. He then placed the block of wood by the jamb opposite the strike and set the door atop the board. He then lined up the exterior edge of the door with the interior edge of the jamb. The hinges landed centered on his marks and he again lined up their placement and hammered the companion twenty-four nails into place. He removed the block of wood and the door floated motionless half open in the room.

Irenaeus then gave a slight push on the door toward the jamb. The door swung silently into the opening until it reached the catch of the latch and latched perfectly. He checked the reveals of the door to the jamb and they were roughly parallel without interference. Opening the door, he placed one hand on the top of the door and one hand on the latch as he did before and gave the door a softer but similar jerk. This time the door did not move. He smiled, cleaned up the old hinges, placed his tools in his bag, and skipped over the threshold hearing the catch of the latch behind him.

43

Anointing the Son

Yom Shlishi[1]

The long day stretched into evening with Yochanan and Polycarp arriving at the adobe later than expected. As Yochanan opened the door, the ease of its swing surprised them both. They looked at each other and simultaneously said, 'Irenaeus!" After putting their things away, they set out food for the evening meal. Exhausted, they ate and collapsed on their mats looking forward to the events of tomorrow.

In unusual fashion both the Elder and Scribe woke at the same time. Polycarp, who slept by the door, sat up, looked at the door, turned to Yochanan and spoke.

"Nice door."

Yochanan chuckled, rose and stretched his whole body upward with his hands touching the rafters of the adobe. He then turned to Polycarp to set the morning agenda.

"After prayer take some food with you to curb your stomach on the way to wash. I will make ready the rest of the morning meal and your station. Please make your way to Junia's adobe and try to catch them before they venture to Ya'aqobe's. Thank Irenaeus for the door and invite them both for the evening meal."

"Of course, Rabbi."

---

1. Hebrew for Third Day—Tuesday

Anointing the Son

After prayer, Polycarp gathered some challah, figs and water and moved toward the door.

"Oh, one other thing Polycarp..." Polycarp stopped suddenly and turned waiting for Yochanan to speak.

"Tell Junia she is free to invite Ya'aqobe for the evening meal...if she can stand a few more hours of his company."

Polycarp chuckled, "Yes Rabbi."

Yochanan made the necessary preparations and Polycarp was able to extend the invitation to the scribes. Upon returning to the adobe, Polycarp grasped the entry door as usual to let himself in and it swung wildly into the cabinet behind the door jostling some scrolls to the ground.

"My apologies Rabbi!" exclaimed Polycarp.

Yochanan, sitting calmly in his chair, responded in an even and quite tone, "That's the second time that has happened this morning." Polycarp smiled and took his place at his station.

"What of the invitation Saphar?"

"It was well received, and the new Scribes looked as if they had enjoyed themselves yesterday. Junia said that she would definitely extend the invitation to 'her Rabbi.'" Yochanan's face revealed that he was pleasantly surprised and at the same time puzzled that the day had seemingly gone so well.

"Perhaps Ya'aqobe is learning as much from his scribes as they are learning from him." The two finished their meal and took their usual places for dictation.

"Alright Saphar, I summarized the major events of the Master's first year of revealing Adonai, please summarize his second year."

"Yes Rabbi." Polycarp sifted through his leaves and took his time to remind himself of all that he had written and then answered carefully. "During the Pesach season the Master miraculously provided bread and fish for over five thousand people. Afterward he rescued the disciples from the storm as they were crossing the sea. On the other shore, Yeshua challenged the people spiritually by revealing that he is the spiritual manna or matzah provided by Adonai. While he made it clear that Adonai sent him to provide eternal life, many of the Judeans struggled with his graphic metaphors."

"Then, during Sukkot, he offered to quench spiritually parched souls. He proclaimed that he was the water of life during the great water pouring ceremony. In addition, during that same time, in the evening, he proclaimed to be the light of the world. He did this against the backdrop of the great menorahs illuminating every corner of Jerusalem. Numerous people believed in him during this feast. However, many of the Judeans and Pharisees still desired to kill him because of their lust for power. He then graciously provided one last example for the Judeans and Pharisees. He caused a blind man to regain his physical sight, hoping they would see the need for spiritual sight and salvation."

"Finally, during the Feast of Dedication, Yeshua compared himself to the Good Shepherd spoken of by King David. He used this analogy to show that the Father has given him authority to pasture all the souls that believe in him to the new tabernacle of Olam Habah. He also referred to himself as the door or the way of salvation." They both paused, and, having the same thought come to mind peered at Irenaeus' handiwork. Polycarp continued.

"His authority to make all of these claims was unmistakably proven by his powerful and compassionate raising of El'azar from the dead. He communicated his promise of spiritual resurrection by providing a physical resurrection. He also made it clear that since he is the one having power over life in this world, he also has power over life for the world to come."

"Very good Saphar, are you ready to record the Master's last year?"
"I am ready Rabbi."

> Then six days before the Passover, Yeshua came to Bethany, where Yeshua had raised El'azar from the dead. So, they made a dinner for him there and Marah served, El'azar being one of those reclining with him. Then Miryam, having taken a litra of expensive ointment of pure nard, anointed the feet of Yeshua and wiped his feet with her hair. The house was filled with the fragrance of the perfume. However, Yehuda Iscariot, one of his disciples who was about to betray him said, "Why was this ointment not sold for three hundred denarii and given to the poor?" However, he said this, not because he was caring for the poor, but because he was a thief, and had pilfered the moneybag. Then Yeshua said, "Leave her alone, so that she may keep it for the day of my burial. The poor you always have with you, but you do not always have me." Then when a great multitude of the Judeans knew that he was there, they came, not only for Yeshua but also that they might see El'azar, whom he had raised from the dead. Then the chief priests planned together that they might kill El'azar also because on account of him many of the Judeans were leaving and believing in Yeshua.[2]

"It was fitting Saphar that, ten days before his resurrection, the Master would have a meal with the one he raised from the dead."

---

2. John 12:1-11

"Rabbi, it must have been peculiar that the women who prepared El'azar for burial after his death had started to prepare Yeshua for burial before his death." Yochanan nodded and responded.

"What was also peculiar was that so many saw the truth of Messiah while others were desperate to hold on to their illusion of power. I suppose it is difficult to understand that the only way to experience true power is to aligning ourselves with Adonai for his glory. However, I still struggle to understand Yehuda's motivation, or the Judeans attempt to thwart the plan of Adonai. The only thing that provides a glimmer of understanding is that they were acting in their complete unbelief. What is encouraging, though, is that many more acted on their faith and belief in Yeshua."

44

Glorifying Adonai

"Rabbi, you said the house was filled with the fragrance of the perfume. What did it smell like?" Yochanan smiled at Polycarp and then closed his eyes as he sometimes did when scrolling through the catalogue of scripture in his mind. Finally, he opened his eyes and quoted from the scroll of Exodus.

 *Yahweh said to Moshe, "Take the finest spices: of liquid myrrh five hundred shekels, and of sweet-smelling cinnamon half as much, and the same of aromatic cane, and five hundred of cassia, according to the shekel of the sanctuary, and a hin of olive oil. Make of these a sacred anointing oil blended as by the perfumer; it shall be a holy anointing oil. With it you shall anoint the tent of meeting, the ark, the table and utensils, lampstand, the altars, the basin and Aaron and his sons. You shall say to the people of Israel, 'This shall be my holy anointing oil throughout your generations. It shall not be poured on the body of an ordinary person, and you shall make no other like it in composition. It is holy, and it shall be holy to you."*[1]

"When Yeshua entered the great city the next day he smelled of the tabernacle and the glory of Adonai." Yochanan nodded toward the amanuensis station.

---

1. Exodus 30:22–32 ESV Abridged

> *The next day the great crowd, the one having come to the feast, heard that Yeshua was coming to Jerusalem. They took branches of palm trees and went out to meet him and they were shouting, "Hosanna! Blessed is the one who comes in the name of the Master, even the King of Israel!" Then, having found a young donkey, Yeshua sat on it, just as it is written, "Fear not, daughter of Zion; behold, your king is coming, sitting on the colt of a donkey." His disciples did not understand these things at first, but when Yeshua was glorified, then they remembered that these things were written about him and they had done these things to him. Then the crowd that was with him, when he called El'azar out of the tomb and raised him from the dead, gave testimony. Due to this, other people also met him because they heard he had done this sign. Therefore, the Pharisees said among themselves, "Do you see that you are gaining nothing. Look, the world has gone after him."*[2]

"I remember when I heard of the raising of El'azar Rabbi. Everyone who knew of it was filled with excitement and anticipation that the Messiah might actually have come in our lifetime."

"Indeed Saphar, Jews and Gentiles from almost every nation were present at this time to see if what they hoped was true. However, as their cry of Hosanna suggests, the crowd wanted Yeshua to deliver them immediately. Most were ready to follow him instantly in overthrowing the current leadership, but this was not his intention."

"Still, it must have been amazing to see those who saw the resurrection give their testimonies."

"Yes, Saphar, it was amazing and revealing. The contrast between those who believed and those who did not was stark indeed." Yochanan rose from his chair to walk about the room as he continued the dictation.

> *There were also certain Greeks who went up that they might worship at the feast. So, these came to Phillipus, who was from Bethsaida in Galilee, and asked him, "Master we desire to see Yeshua." Then Phillipus brings them and tells Andrewas; Andrewas and Phillipus bring them and tell Yeshua and Yeshua responds to them, "The hour has come that the Son of Man should be glorified. Truly, truly, I say to you, if the grain of wheat does not fall onto the ground and perish, it remains alone; but if it perishes, it bears much fruit. Whoever loves his life loses it and whoever hates his life in this world will keep it*

---

2. John 12:12–19

> unto life eternal. If anyone serves me, let him follow me; and where I am, there will my servant be also. If anyone serves me, the Father will honor him.³

"Rabbi, were the Greeks surprised by his invitation?"

"Yeshua' s invitation to the Greeks was a surprise to many. However, those who traveled with him over the years knew of his greater mission. Most were convinced that the Messiah was coming only for the house of Israel. However, his gracious offer extended beyond Israel to all souls. We saw this earlier with the Samaritan woman and the Greek official. This offer was particularly interesting because he was introducing the concept of Halacha⁴ to these very interested Greeks." Yochanan paused here and slowly stroked his greying brindle beard to provide a chance for his disciple to respond.

Polycarp arched his back and stretched his shoulders backward causing several 'pops' between his should blades. He then relaxed, looked at his teacher and responded.

"I understand Rabbi. He was calling them to follow his path of obedience to Adonai's commands. But how could Greeks start to do this without knowing Torah?"

"Good question Saphar. His offer was the first and most important step in Halacha. He called them to deny themselves and follow him. The rest of the Torah they would learn as they listened in the synagogue and studied with the Jews of the Way. Following Adonai is a lifelong learning for all of us regardless of ancestry. Even Yeshua had to grow in the wisdom of Adonai." The familiar reed scratching against the parchment began again.

> *"Now my soul has been stirred but what shall I say, 'Father, save me from this hour'? However, it is because of this stirring that I have come to this hour. Father, glorify your name." Then a voice came from heaven. "I have now glorified it, and I will glorify it again." Then the crowd having stood there and heard it said it was thunder. Others said, "An angel has spoken to him." Yeshua answered, "This voice has not come for me but for you. The judgment of this world is now. The prince of this world will be cast out now. When I am raised upon the earth I will draw everyone to myself." Now he said this signifying what kind of death he was going to die. Then the crowd answered him, "We have heard from the Law that the Messiah remains unto the new era. Why do you say that*

---

3. John 12:2—26

4. Hebrew to "walk" or "go" intended to communicate living one's life a certain way in every aspect of life.

it is necessary that the Son of Man be lifted up? Who is this Son of Man?" Then Yeshua said to them, "This light is among you for a short season. Walk while you have the light in order that the darkness might not overtake you. Now the one walking in the darkness does not know where he is going. While you have the light, believe in the light, that you might become sons of light."[5]

---

5. John 12:27–36a

45

Proclaiming Adonai

"Saphar, this stirring inside Yeshua was because of his excitement for others who genuinely desired the truth. These determined Greeks helped encourage his prayer to Adonai. Yeshua' s life had already revealed the Father in so many unique and wonderful ways. However, the most powerful revelation would be at the cross, where he would not only reveal Adonai's depth of redemption but also remove the evil one; the obstacle for sanctification."

"Rabbi, why did Yeshua not respond to them plainly?" Yochanan' s eyes brightened with that familiar gleam when the Spirit stirred within. He turned his gaze toward Polycarp, smiled and responded a bit mischievously.

"Do you suppose, my young Rabbi that, answering them plainly regarding the Son of Man would have provided a better picture than his light metaphor?" Polycarp chuckled as he responded,

"I see Elder. Again, Yeshua was providing the answer they needed instead of the answer to their question."

"Correct Polycarp, they needed the Father to draw them and then to believe in Messiah until he sent the Holy Spirit. Only then, would they begin to understand. Remember, most in this Pesach crowd were also at Sukkot and heard him claim to be the light of the world with all Jerusalem ablaze. Unfortunately, many had not yet believed." Yochanan smiled and after few seconds nodded toward his quill.

> *Yeshua spoke these things and having departed, hid himself from them. Though he had done so many signs before them, they still did not believe in him in order that the word of Isaiah the prophet might be fulfilled. Which said, "Adonai, who has believed our report? Also, to whom has the strength*

of Adonai been revealed?" Because of this they did not have power to believe. For again Isaiah said, "He has blinded their eyes and hardened their heart, that they might not see with their eyes, and understand with their heart, and turn, and be healed." Isaiah said these things because he saw his glory and spoke of him. Yet indeed, even from the rulers, many believed in him. However, because of the Pharisees they did not confess him, in order that they might not be put out of the synagogue. For they loved the honor that comes from man more than the honor that comes from Adonai.[1]

"The Father knew that some would not believe no matter what they might see. However, in his grace, as Isaiah recorded, there would be a sprinkling of the nations. This sprinkling of the Spirit happened during Shavuot to convict the world of sin, righteousness and judgment. The event provided even more opportunity for the hard of heart to repent and the soft heart to experience Adonai like never before."

Then Yeshua cried out and said, "Those believing in me, believe not in me but on him who sent me, and those seeing me see him who sent me. I am the light that had come into the cosmos, in order that everyone believing in me might not remain in darkness. Now, if anyone hears my teachings and does not keep them, I do not judge him; for I did not come in order to judge the world but in order to save the world. The one rejecting me and not accepting my teachings has one judge. The word that I spoke, that will judge him on the last day. For I have not spoken on my own authority, but the Father, having sent me, has himself given me an injunction [x] *of what I should command and what I should say. Now, I know that his injunction is eternal life. Therefore, I say just what the Father has told me to say."*[2]

"Rabbi, was he referring to the light of the first day of creation?"

"Very good Saphar, Yeshua not only came to reveal Adonai, but he was the pure glory, the 'Ur' of creation. He is spiritual light. Just as our physical bodies experience physical light so our souls can experience his spiritual light. His teachings introduce his light and illuminate us toward a deeper understanding of Adonai. Those who believe in him have the privilege of reflecting his light in order to help others repent of their rejection of Adonai."

1. John 12:36b-43
2. John 12:44–50

"That is my passion also Rabbi. I am so thankful for his mission to provide life eternal and Olam Habah."

Yochanan sat down at this point and rubbed his eyes and temples with his left thumb and middle finger.

"Should we break for the mid-day Rabbi?"

"I believe so, if you do not mind please prepare the meal as I rest on the rooftop.

Polycarp stowed his tools, parchments and rose from his station. As Yochanan rose from his chair, he made his way to the ladder to the roof. Just before he started ascending, Polycarp commented.

"I wonder how day two went for our scribes."

"I am anxious to find that out as well," responded Yochanan as he climbed toward the hatch.

46

Pharisees and Scribes

After finishing installing the new hinges on the door, Irenaeus returned home excited to share his idea and errand with his mother. He found her on the rooftop and told her what had happened and explained every detail. His sleep that night went undisturbed, however, Junia had a restlessness in her spirit for the coming day. She eventually drifted off to sleep thankful for the extra hour Ya'aqobe had mentioned earlier.

Ya'aqobe arose a bit later than usual, quickly took care of necessities, and placed early figs, challah and grapes on a small wooden plate to take to the rooftop. Placing his wrinkled hand on the catch of the latch, he went to open the door as a grape rolled off the plate onto the floor. Kneeling slowly to pick up the grape, he noticed, through the window boards, two Pharisees on the opposite side of the burnt umber dirt road. He picked up the grape, examined it for cleanliness and popped it in his mouth as he stood upright. It had been a long time since any of his order had desired to visit, and much longer for any Pharisee. With the Way gathering followers in the outlying communities, he concluded that these two were here to investigate the enclave.

He grasped the catch again and this time opened the door, being careful not to spill any more grapes, and crossed the threshold. Without giving attention to the Pharisees, he turned and walked toward the stairs to ascend to the rooftop for morning prayers. As he did, the Pharisees shouted,

"Shalom!"

Turning toward the men Ya'aqobe responded, "Shalom."

He then turned toward the stairs when one of the Pharisees said, "Are you the Master Scribe Ya'aqobe? Are you expecting visitors today?"

Ya'aqobe kept moving slowly and deliberately toward the stairs and once on the first tread turned toward the men and said, "Since when are two noble Pharisees such as yourselves interested in the visitors of an old coppersmith? Now, being pious men, I am sure you will not interrupt an Elder's time of prayer."

Ya'aqobe continued to ascend until he reached the rooftop and started his normal morning prayer routine. The Pharisees glanced at one another and then sat crossed leg in the opening of the alley across the road.

Junia and Irenaeus departed after prayer and started toward Ya'aqobe's adobe. Junia decided to go through the marketplace first to pick up some items for their mid-day meal. This decision took them to the middle of the enclave instead of their typical direct route to their lessons. After selecting some fresh flat bread, dates, and grapes, they started toward the alley that would lead to Ya'aqobe's adobe.

Not long after sitting in the alley, the Pharisees started stirring becoming uncomfortable and hungry. The two argued briefly.

"Even if the report is true how could it make a difference?"

"It is not a question of making a difference but appropriateness, you should understand these things."

"Well, he will be up there for some time, let's get some food and come back. After all, if it the old scribe, where else could he go to teach his trade?"

"Very well, I suppose we will follow your stomach for now." The Pharisees stood, backed further into the alley and turned toward the market.

Junia and Irenaeus reached the opposite opening of the alley just before the Pharisees stood to leave. Irenaeus was the first to look down the row of adobes through the long alley and saw the men sitting with their backs against the ally walls.

"Mother, look! There are men across the road from Ya'aqobe's adobe." Junia looked up and pushed the panic away from her face.

"So there are my son, let us go around, we would not want to disturb them."

As they went north to go around the other adobes to the main road, the men rose, turned, and started down the alley. Junia and Irenaeus came to the road and Junia peered slowly around the corner and saw Ya'aqobe on the rooftop. After a few seconds, he saw her and motioned for her to come to the adobe. As the two made their way, Ya'aqobe bounced down the stairs, as best he could, to meet them.

"Come with me and hurry," said Ya'aqobe.

The three hustled inside and gathered up their tools, supplies and food. Once they had everything in their bags, Ya'aqobe peered out the door and eyed the alley. He closed all of the windows and crossed the threshold as the others followed with Junia making sure that the door latched. The three took a quick pace, kicking up the brown dust with their sandals. Weaving through the enclave, they headed away from the market to the outskirts of town. High stepping down a steep incline with high rock formations, they came to some hanging clematis, which concealed a small entrance to a cave. Disappearing into the foliage, after their eyes adjusted, they saw that the cave was about the size of the front room of where they had left their desks. There were oil lamps on the walls, scrolls on shelves and several older desks for transcription at the rear of the cave.

They all set their belongings down, lit the lamps and situated themselves in a similar fashion as the training room. While this type of drama was not foreign to Junia or Ya'aqobe, Irenaeus was thoroughly puzzled and panicked. Ya'aqobe noticed his distress.

"Irenaeus, I know that this is a bit concerning but there are those who would try to control others under the guise of religion. They would have others follow them instead of following Adonai. Who would you follow if you met such men?"

"I would follow Adonai of course Rabbi."

"Of course you would, my young Scribe!" Irenaeus smiled and Ya'aqobe continued.

"Now, sometimes, in order to be obedient to Adonai, we must distance ourselves from those who choose not to listen to Adonai. Do you understand Irenaeus?"

"I do Rabbi."

"Good. Some time ago, several of us from the Way knew that we would need safe places to gather. This cave has provided sanctuary in the past. This will be our new training area and we will vary our hours now considering our new audience. Now, where did we leave off?"

47

Patience and Passover

As Yochanan rested, Polycarp wound through the enclave visiting his widows to make sure all was well. He also stopped by the market for some items for the mid-day meal and then determined to walk by Ya'aqobe's to say shalom. As he turned the same corner Junia peered around a few hours prior, he noticed the closed windows and door of Ya'aqobe's adobe. He slowed his pace and then noticed two Pharisees talking with one of Ya'aqobe's neighbors. He knew the neighbor but did not recognize the Pharisees so he slowly stopped and flattened himself against the wall near the corner. The three were engaged in their conversation and did not notice Polycarp by the far corner. He was close enough to overhear.

"I don't know where they are, but they were here yesterday. I have put up with much from that old Scribe but now I fear he has lost his mind to farm out our trade to a Gentile boy and woman! They are also collaborating with Yochanan one of the leaders of the Way," said the neighbor to the Pharisees without caring who overheard.

"Rest assured Yehuda we will investigate and make sure that your scribal practices and honor remains intact. After all that is why we are here, to protect what Adonai has given to the Jews."

Polycarp slowly stepped back to the corner and around to the other side unnoticed. As he made his way back through the market he looked down the dusty brown alley walls and saw the three men still engaged in conversation. Taking a more direct route back to the adobe he arrived in time to see Yochanan starting to climb down from the rooftop. Polycarp explained what happened and the two returned to the rooftop to pray. After a short time, both were back in the main room with Polycarp preparing the meal and Yochanan pondering the events.

"The good news is that the Pharisees did not know where they were correct Rabbi?"

"My thoughts also Polycarp, let us be patient. We still have a standing invitation for all of them to meet here tonight so we shall continue."

"The meal is ready Rabbi."

"Thank you, my disciple." Again, Yochanan raised some of the challah, looked upward and chanted the blessing.

"Baruch atah Adonai Eloheinu, Melech haOlam, HaMotzi lechem min haAretz Ve'noten lanu echem min haShamayim." The two ate in silence, both in constant prayer for their friends.

After clearing the meal, they both returned to their seats to continue dictation.

"So Saphar, Yeshua, enjoyed a meal with the one he raised from the dead six days before his last Passover. He then entered Jerusalem the next day to a great welcoming crowd. During that day, he preached to the Greeks who had come to the feast. He also preached to the unbelieving Judeans telling them that he was the light sent by the Father that would provide life eternal. He would soon accomplish this mission. We will continue the chronology with the events of the Seder before his crucifixion."

 *Now before the Paschal Feast, knowing that his time had come to leave this cosmos to go to the Father, Yeshua, having loved his own who were in the world, loved them to the end. While supper was taking place, the Slanderer, had already put it into the heart of Yehuda Iscariot, Shimon's son, that he should betray him. Knowing that the Father had given all things into his hands, and that he had come from Adonai and was going to Adonai, he rises from supper, lays aside his tallit[1], grasps a towel and girds himself. Then he pours water into a basin and began to wash the disciples' feet and to wipe them with the towel he was girded with. Then he comes to Shimon Kaypha, who said to him, "Master, why do you wash my feet?" Yeshua answered and said to him, "What I am doing now you do not understand but you, all of you, will understand." Kaypha says to him, "May you never wash my feet in this present era." Yeshua answered him, "If I do not wash you, you have no portion with me." Shimon Kaypha says to him, "Then Master, not my feet only but also my hands and the head!"*

---

1. Jewish outer garment with tassels

> *Yeshua says to him, "The one washed does not have that need, except to wash his feet and he is completely clean.* ᵞ *Indeed, you are clean, but not every one of you." For he knew who was betraying him; that was why he said, "Not all of you are clean."*[2]

"Amazing, what was going through your mind Rabbi?"

Yochanan seemed frozen in time as he finished this last dictation. In his mind, he was sitting on the dirt floor leaning at that same rough wooden Seder table experiencing again his surprise, confusion, delight and sinfulness simultaneously. His fixed emerald eyes, surrounded by deep wrinkles, were peering well beyond the dusty room. As he blinked twice he broke the silence with a response to Polycarp's question.

"I thought of Avraham washing the feet of his visitors before Sara gave birth. I thought of Aharon washing his son's feet before the Levitical service. However, what I had finally realized at that moment was that he was providing a picture of the mission Adonai had given him. He was physically bathing our feet before spiritually bathing us by his sacrifice, so we could draw near to Adonai. He was doing what no one else could; cleansing us both physically and spiritually. He was preparing to perform the functions of both the Levitical and Melchizedekian Priesthoods simultaneously."

The gleam in Yochanan' s eye grew bright as he looked at Polycarp's wide curious eyes and continued.

"As you know Saphar the Levitical sacrifices provided cleansing so the worshiper was able to draw near to Adonai in this present world. Those sacrifices enabled the worshiper to get close to his glory residing in the earthly tabernacle and temple.[3] However, the Melchizedekian sacrifice of Messiah cleanses believers to be able to come near to Adonai in the world to come. Messiah's sacrifice enables believers to experience his glory in all of Olam Habah."[4]

"I see that now Rabbi. There has been much confusion in the past about the Aaronic and Levitical Priesthood sacrifices. Some confused their

---

2. John 13:1–11

3. "Moses was not able to enter the tent of meeting because the cloud settled on it, and the glory of the LORD filled the tabernacle." Ex 40:35, ESV. How was anyone in the nation going to get close to the glory of Adonai? The Aaronic and Levitical Priesthoods provided the way through sacrifice as detailed in the next scroll, Leviticus.

4. The Aaronic and Levitical Priesthoods provided the way to get close to Adonai on earth. The Melchizedekian Priesthood provides the avenue for souls to get close to Adonai in the world to come. "We have a High Priest who fulfills his office in royal dignity, not as the Priests on earth; and the scene of his ministry is heaven." See Westcott, *Hebrews*, 213.

application for eternal salvation or the world to come. They were the gracious means that provided a way for the people to draw near to the presence of Adonai in this world. Again, another earthly picture of the spiritual truth of what Messiah's sacrifice accomplishes."

"Well said Saphar, dip your quill."

48

Betrayal and Honor

> *Then when he had washed their feet and put on his tallit and reclined again, he said to them, "Do you understand what I have done to you? You call me Teacher and Master, which you rightly say. Indeed I am. If therefore, I am your Master and Teacher and I have washed your feet, you also ought to wash one another's feet. Indeed, I gave you a pattern that as I did to you, you should also do. Truly, truly, I say to you, a servant is not greater than his master, nor is an apostle greater than the one who sent him. If you know these things, blessed are you if you do them. I speak not of all of you; I know whom I have chosen. But the Scripture might be fulfilled, 'The one eating my bread lifted his heel against me.' I am telling you this now, before it comes to pass, that when it does come to pass you might believe that I am. Truly, truly, I say to you, whoever receives whoever I send in any way receives me, and moreover, whoever receives me receives the one who sent me."*[1]

Polycarp finished his last stroke for this section and raised his head while looking at Yochanan.

"Yes Saphar?"

"Rabbi, clearly Yeshua was giving them an example of servanthood but was there something else he was communicating?"

"Yes Saphar, and like much of this record we cannot expound on all that happened. However, this was the first of many rites of passage in preparation of the twelve becoming the new Sanhedrin, his Sanhedrin. The

---

1. John 13:12–20

first rite of passage for anyone who desires to follow is to serve and not be served. This rite sparked a self-sacrificial perspective in all of us so we could properly serve all those around us. He would also provide a special portion of the Ruach HaKodesh and commission us to go and make disciples as he had done."

"Thank you, Rabbi." Yochanan continued.

> *Having said these things, Yeshua was troubled in his spirit, and testified and said, "Truly, truly, I say to you, one of you will betray me." The disciples looked upon one another, being uncertain about whom he was speaking. Of his disciples, there was one reclining on the chest of Yeshua, which he loved. Then Shimon Kypha motioned and told him to ask of whom he is speaking. Then since he was leaning on Yeshua's chest he whispered to him, "Master, who is it?" Then Yeshua answers, "It is he to whom I will dip and give this piece of bread." Then, Yeshua, having dipped the piece of bread, lifts it and gives it to Yehuda, the son of Shimon Iscariot. Upon finishing the piece of bread, the Slanderer entered into him. Then Yeshua says to him, "What you do, do quickly." Now no one there reclining knew why he said this to him. Although some thought since Yehuda had the moneybag, Yeshua was telling him to buy what was needed for the feast or that he should give something to the poor. So, after receiving the piece of bread, he went out immediately and by then it was evening.*[2]

Yochanan leaned forward, grasping the arms of the chair with his strong wrinkled hands and pushed up as he stood. He then turned toward the window and spoke.

"The Master knew better than any of us that, the prophecies of David[3] and Zechariah,[4] needed to be fulfilled. However, Yeshua still grieved for Yehuda, again revealing his divine love. I was the one Shimon motioned to. Only Shimon and I caught a glimpse of what was unfolding. We were all going to have a very long night and Yeshua did not want Yehuda around for his last teachings." Yochanan paused while Polycarp selected another parchment and readied his quill.

"Ready Rabbi."

---

2. John 13:21–30

3. Psalm 41:8–10

4. Zechariah 11:12–13

> Then when he had gone out, Yeshua says, "Now the Son of Man has been honored, and Adonai is honored by him. If Adonai is honored by him, Adonai will also honor him alone, and he will honor him soon. Little children, I am with you only a short while. You will seek me, and as I said to the Judeans, so now I say to you, where I go you are not able to come. A new commandment I give to you, that you love one another as I have loved you. You also are to love one another. By this all will know that you are my disciples, if you have love among one another." Shimon Kaypha says to him, "Master, where are you going?" Yeshua answered him, "Where I am going you are not able to follow me now, however, afterward you will follow." Kaypha says to him, "Master, why am I not able to follow you now? I will lay down my life for you." Yeshua answered, "Will you lay down your life for me? Truly, truly, I say to you no. The Crier will not shout[5] until you have denied me three times.[6]

"Rabbi, when did you realize that the honor he was speaking of was his crucifixion?"

"I am still realizing it today Saphar! I saw dimly then and only now am I seeing small things clearly. Indeed, it seems that as my physical sight loses clarity my spiritual sight begins to become enlightened because of Messiah. I did not fully understand at the time that Yeshua considered it an honor to die for all of humanity. The Father honored him with this burden, and Messiah's obedience to the mission honored the Father. We all wanted to continue to follow him but this was his mission to accomplish and he could only accomplish it alone. Unclear to Shimon, or to any of us, was that we could do nothing to help him in his task. How does one steeped in sin and trapped in the physical even begin to glimpse the spiritual? The Master knew our limitations and he graciously consoled us by revealing another aspect of the salvation he would provide."

> "Let not your hearts be troubled, you believe in Adonai; believe also in me. In my Father's house, there are many rooms. If not, I would not have told you that I go to prepare a place for you. Also, if I go and prepare a place for you I am coming again and will receive you myself, that where I am you may be also. Now, you know the way to where I am going." Tauma says to him, "Master, we do not know where you are going. How can we know the way?" Yeshua says to him, "I am the

---

5. Levitical temple crier who called Israel to the start of the temple sacrifices
6. John 13:31–38

way, and the truth, and the life. No one comes to the Father except through me. If you had known me, you would have somehow also known my Father. From now on you know him and have seen him."[7]

"Even though he was the one about to suffer he was encouraging us. We would not only see him again, but he would also have a room ready for us in his Father's house. He also promised to welcome us personally into Olam Habah. What a wonderful sight and experience that will be Saphar."

"Rabbi, I know Yeshua said he was the Way, but the way to Olam Habah is also through death is it not?"

"Not just death Saphar but also resurrection. These two rites of passages are inseparable for any soul. However, Messiah not only reveals the way, and provides the way, but also brings the powerless along the way. After all, who among humanity is righteous enough to enter Olam Habah on their own?"

"Did you see the Father in him?" asked Polycarp.

Yochanan had been slowly pacing about the dirt floor during this dictation. With this question, he abruptly stopped and slowly looked skyward.

"Yes, I did. He revealed many truths about the Father and helped us understand the abundant life in this present world. However, over time it has become clear that I have experienced his truth more, and understood life deeper, since he departed."

"Although Yeshua revealed the Father, we were all slow to understand how to see the Father in the Son, especially Phillipus." Yochanan sat down in his chair and waved his hand toward Polycarp.

---

7. John 14:1–7

49

Love and Peace

Phillipus says to him, "Master, show us the Father, and it is enough for us." Yeshua says to him, "I have been with you quite some time and you still do not know me, Phillipus? Whoever has seen me has seen the Father. How can you say, 'Show us the Father'? Do you not believe that I abide with the Father and the Father abides with me? The words that I say to you I do not speak for myself, but the Father abiding in me accomplishes his deeds. Believe me that I am among the Father and the Father is among me. If not this, then believe on account of the deeds themselves. "Truly, truly, I say to you, the one believing in me will also do the deeds that I do. He will also do greater works than these because I am going to the Father. Whatever you might possibly request in my name, this I will do, that the Father might be glorified in the Son. If you request anything of me in my name, I will do it.[1]

"Yeshua had told us in the past that he had revealed the Father's name. Even Phillipus knew that revealing someone's name meant living out their character. However, Phillipus wanted to see what even Moshe could not see."

Polycarp looked down at the parchment on his table and asked another question. "Rabbi, is the description that the Father and the Son 'abide with each other' the best way we can express their spiritual connection?"

"By words, yes Saphar. However, this description can also help us understand the spiritual connection we can have with Yeshua. The Father was

---

1. John 14:8–14

always present for Yeshua and he was simultaneously communing with the Father in this physical world. Every believer has the same opportunity to commune with Messiah while simultaneously making the most of our lives in this physical world."

"Rabbi, what about doing greater works than Yeshua and his promise to do whatever is asked? Can every believer expect those...abilities?"

Yochanan looked at Polycarp, smiled, and said, "That would be wonderful Saphar. However, Yeshua only breathed a special portion of the Spirit on the eleven. As Yeshua was given the honor and burden to provide the sacrifice for redemption, the eleven were given the honor and burden to initiate making disciples of the known world. There was no possible way that this new Sanhedrin could have accomplished what it has without the supernatural power of the Spirit."

> "If you love me, you will guard my commandments and I will ask the Father and he will give you another advocate that he might be with you unto the new era. This is the Spirit of truth, whom the world is not able to receive, because it does not see him or know him. However, you know him, for he abides with you and will be among you. "I will not leave you as orphans; I will come to you. Yet a little while and the world will perceive me no more, but you perceive me because I live. So also, you will live. In that day, you will know that I am among my Father and you are among me and I am among you. The one having my commandments and guarding them is the one loving me. Moreover, the one loving me will be loved by my Father and I will love him and reveal myself to him." Yehuda (not Iscariot) says to him, "Master, how is it that you will reveal yourself to us, and not to the world?" Yeshua answered and said to him, "If anyone loves me, he will guard my word, and my Father will love him, and we will come to him and make our home with him. The one not loving me does not guard my words. Now, this message that you hear is not mine but the Fathers who sent me.[2]

Polycarp looked up again after finishing this section and asked another question.

"Rabbi, I know from the Tanakh[3] that the Spirit was given in a special way to only certain people, temporarily. Was the Spirit given directly to the apostles and then to the entire world at Shavuot?"

---

2. John 14:15–24

3. The three divisions of the OT or Hebrew scriptures—Torah—Nevi'im—Ketuvim—TNK, hence Tanakh.

"I believe that to be the truth Saphar. For the apostles, the Spirit was, in part, a special empowering for their task. For the world, it was as the Master prophesied. The Spirit would restrain evil, convict of sin, righteousness, judgement, and reveal the truth of Adonai. Yeshua accomplished his work of atonement and sent the Spirit as a pledge of future redemption. Messiah and the Spirit are the connection point between the physical and the spiritual. He is the one that provided the ability to experience the spiritual while simultaneously living in the physical. Let us finish this section and break for the evening meal."

"Yes Rabbi."

> *"These things I have said to you while abiding with you. However, the advocate, the Spirit, the Holy One, whom the Father will send in my name, he will instruct you and bring to your recollection all the things I have said to you. Peace I release to you; it is my peace I offer to you. What I offer is not as this cosmos offers. Do not be troubled or let your heart fear. You heard that I said to you, 'I am going away, and I am coming to you.' If you loved me, you would have somehow rejoiced that I am going to the Father, for the Father is greater than I. Also, I have told you now before this comes to pass that when it shall come to pass you might believe. I will no longer speak with you as often, for the ruler of this cosmos is coming, though against me he is nothing. However, that the cosmos might know that I love the Father I do exactly as the Father commands me. Stand up, let us go from here."*[4]

Polycarp was very interested in the first part of this dictation.

"Do you remember all of Yeshua's words Rabbi?" he said excitedly.

"Not all at once Saphar, but for any appropriate moment, yes. The connection with the Spirit that Messiah gave to us was unique indeed. However, what thrilled me more was the giving of the Spirit at Shavuot so all who believed could taste what he had provided for us. Of course, these things were necessary to offset the power of the Slanderer. Messiah will return one day and those of us left in this present world benefit spiritually by carrying on the mission of discipleship. It is part of Adonai's plan that we partake not only in the Spirit but in the worldwide mission of turning and training souls for Adonai."

"I understand Rabbi. . .Where did you go after the Seder?"

"He led us to Gethsemane. It was fitting that the redemption of the cosmos would start and culminate in a garden."

---

4. John 14:25–31

"From Eden to Gethsemane Rabbi?"

"Yes Saphar, however, like I mentioned before, it would be a very long evening and morning. For now, we have our own interesting evening before us, so let us prepare for our guests."

50

Plans and Perseverance

"Can you see anyone?" said Junia, as Irenaeus peered through the thick green clematis covering the cave opening. He looked, for some time, in all directions for any movement or difference in the landscape. Confident that no one was around he slowly pulled his head back through the clematis, the hanging pine colored vines were a green sea swallowing his face from the outside.

"I don't see anyone or any movement, it should be safe." Ya'aqobe looked at them both and said, "We have covered much today despite our. . .relocation. You two loop to the north and I will loop to the south. Be quick about what you need to take care of and we will meet at the Elder's adobe." Junia and her son nodded in agreement. The three penetrated the clematis slowly, stepped up the rocks to the surface, and went their own ways.

Twilight was upon the Elder and Rabbi as they finished preparations for their expected guests and the evening meal. Lamps lit the rooftop and the golden table was set with challah, fruit, nuts, and goat chops. Dark clouds to the west covered the Icarian but the winds were keeping the mists over the sea, which would provide a pleasant evening for their small enclave. Polycarp glanced over the parapet and saw three dark figures approaching the adobe. They stopped just shy of the threshold and looked up to see Polycarp's silhouette backlit with the lamps of the rooftop. He motioned for them to come in and they opened the newly hinged door and climbed the ladder to the roof.

Once upon the roof Yochanan called the five to form a circle. They held hands while he prayed.

Plans and Perseverance

"Baruch ata Adonai Eloheinu veilohei avoseinu, shetolicheinu leshalom, vesatzideinu leshalom, vesadricheinu leshalom, vesismecheinu leshalom, vesagi'einu limechoz cheftzeinu lechaim ulesimchah uleshalom"[1]

"Thank you, Rabbi," said Junia.

Yochanan responded, "Let us sit down, eat, and hear of all the exciting details of the events of today."

"How do you know that today was anything but a boring day of training?" said Ya'aqobe. Yochanan laughed, grateful for his friend's perspective on the situation. He then responded.

"My Saphar went to check on your Sapharim during mid-day and found your adobe empty. However, don't worry my friend, he found it well-guarded." Everyone laughed.

As the mood became light hearted, everyone reported every detail they could remember. After this, they established new training times for the coming days. Then Yochanan spoke plainly.

"The Pharisees are not to be underestimated but they do not seem to be an immediate threat. The project will go on. However, everyone should stay focused to finish as quickly as possible. Once the m'koriy[2] is complete we will set up the synagogue with all the proper furniture and materials to make the copies." Ya'aqobe spoke again.

"Obviously not on Shabbat, perhaps preparation day would be best." Yochanan looked at his friend and nodded in agreement.

The subject changed to Irenaeus recounting his stealth mission of re-placing the hinges on the door and everyone enjoyed the story and the meal. The five spent the rest of the evening talking of training, the m'koriy, and the dissemination of the copies of Yochanan' s account of Messiah. Every major city in Asia Minor would need a copy delivered to the synagogue or main house of the Way congregation. This would require extensive logistics and communication for five people. The next Sabbath would provide opportunity to enlist those willing to deliver this message to the two corners of the known world.

Before the Master Scribe and his pupils departed, they sat around the golden table for a dessert of fresh fruit and wine.

"The word 'fruit' has many meanings," said Yochanan. "We eat and drink the fruit of the vine and simultaneously we are the spiritual fruit of our Vine; Messiah. We have faith in him and we the fruit of his faithfulness. In addition, he has empowered every believer to spread the good news of the

---

1. The traveler's prayer-Blessed are you Yahweh our Adonai that You should lead us in peace, and direct our steps in peace, and guide us in peace, and support us in peace, and cause us to reach our destination in life, joy, and peace.

2. Mi-kor-ee—The volarge or original

new covenant spoken of by Jeremiah.[3] When someone responds positively to your words about this good news, that soul also becomes fruit. When this happens, you become partakers of the fruit of Messiah. As Yeshua sent the Spirit to abide with us, you abide in him and he will make your efforts in spreading his good news echo throughout eternity."

After pondering Yochanan's words in silence for a short time, everyone made their way to their own adobe. Ya'aqobe made it home without noticing any Pharisaical guards and Junia and Irenaeus made it to their adobe soon after. Sleep came later than desired but the fellowship was well worth the time. The coming days would see a renewed fervor of completing the project, which would be a blessing for the world. Polycarp cleaned up after dinner and the two Rabbi's drifted away as soon as they laid on their mats.

---

3. Jeremiah 31

51

The Vine and the Advocate

Yom Rivee-ee[1]

A "knock...knock...knock" sounded softly on Ya'aqobe's door. He stirred in his creaking wood framed bed unsure if what he heard was real since he was still half-asleep. As soon as he decided to dismiss the sound, it came again softly against his door.

"Knock...knock...knock."

This time he rose quickly threw his tallit around him and shuffled across the dirt floor into the front room. Looking through the cracks of the door, he saw Chavah, a neighboring widow, hooded, and waiting at the door. Ya'aqobe had taken her under his protection. He helped her to provide for herself since the murdering of her husband during the early persecutions of the Way. He lifted the rusty door latch, opened the door, invited her in, and closed the door quietly. She was trembling.

"Good morning Chavah. How can I help you?" He said caringly, bending slightly toward Chavah to hear her whispers.

"I apologize for the early intrusion but unfortunately it is I who can help you Master Scribe. You know about the Pharisees perched across the street yesterday correct?"

"Yes...and I know that Yehuda provided them some information."

---

1. Hebrew for Fourth Day—Wednesday

"Yes, but what you do not know is that the Pharisees know about who you are training and the Elder's project. They are going to find Domitian officers to bring back with them."

Ya'aqobe stood upright, paused for a moment and looked beyond Chavah to the Northwest, toward Rome. He stroked his grey beard several times with his right hand. His left hand was still on the latch of the door.

Slowly returning his gaze toward Chavah he said, "Thank you Chavah, is there anything else?" Still trembling slightly, she moved her head from left to right waiting on Ya'aqobe. He opened the door, put his right hand on her shoulder and calmly said, "Shalom alekem Chavah.[2] Adonai works all things for his glory. Please pray for us and again thank you for this news." Chavah smiled, thankful for the blessing, and then went her way. Ya'aqobe closed the door and started preparation for the days training.

The clouds from the Icarian drifted their way Eastward and the two Rabbi's awoke to an overcast morning. They hurried to take care of necessities and meal preparation and were soon ready to begin dictation. Yochanan stood, leaning up against the rough wooden roof ladder, which was made of debarked, whole branches. Polycarp was poised at his amanuensis station.

"Where did we leave off Saphar?"

"The master and the eleven had just left the last Seder and were on their way to Gethsemane."

Yochanan nodded approvingly and said, "This is what he taught us on our way."

> "I am the vine of truth and my Father is the vinedresser. He removes every branch in me not bearing fruit and he prunes every one that is bearing fruit that they might bear more fruit. You are already pure because of the word that I have spoken to you. You grow in me as I do in you. As the branch is not able to bear fruit of itself unless it grows in the vine so neither can you, unless you grow in me. I am the vine; you are the branches. The one growing in me as I do in him, bears much fruit. For apart from me you can do nothing. If anyone does not grow in me he is placed aside like the withered branch that they gather and cast into the fire to be burned. If you grow in me, and my words grow in you whatever you wish...ask, and for you, it will happen. By this my Father is glorified, that you should bear much fruit and so you shall be

---

2. Peace be upon you Eve (Living One)

my disciples. As the Father has loved me I also have I loved you. Grow in my love. If you keep my commandments, you will grow in my love, just as I have kept my Father's commandments and grow in his love. These things I have spoken to you, that my joy might be in you, and that your joy may be full."[3]

Polycarp completed his last scratch of the quill on the parchment and looked toward Yochanan. "I find it interesting that Yeshua used a vine analogy while on the way to a garden."

"Yes Saphar. He maximized all of what we were experiencing to communicate the truths of Adonai. The metaphor also spoke to what had happened during the Seder. He removed the unfruitful Yehuda branch and moved forward with the branches, which eventually, would become fruitful. Additionally, he was revealing that the way creation grows physically, is the way new creations grow spiritually. Do you see this Saphar?"

"I believe so Rabbi. When we truly believe or have the seed of faith, we will keep what he has commanded. Keeping his commands provides refreshment to our thirsty souls as if we were drinking living water. This obedience causes maturity in Adonai, which allows us to increase in our love for others. This love attracts those around us and will cause a fruitful harvest of souls. This harvest reproduces that same seed of faith, continuing a cycle of spiritual life. Also, there is no greater joy than plucking a soul away from the Slanderer."

"Indeed young Rabbi," said Yochanan, as he motioned toward the quill and parchment.

> *"This is my commandment, that you love one another as I have loved you. No one has greater love than this, that someone should lay down his life for his friends. You are my friends if you do what I command you. I call you servants no longer, for the servant knows not what his master is doing. However, I have called you friends, for all that I heard from my Father I have made known to you. You did not choose me, but I chose you and commissioned you that you should go and should bear fruit and that your fruit should grow. So now, whatever you might possibly request of the Father in my name, he might give you. I command these things so that you will love one another."*[4]

3. John 15:1–11
4. John 15:12–17

Yochanan stopped at this point and stared out back at the garden for a moment. Polycarp waited patiently and then Yochanan spoke as he slowly moved toward his chair.

"I just now realized that this was the third time he told the eleven of us that if we remain focused on him and obey his commands that whatever we would ask in his name, the Father would provide." Yochanan looked upward and prayed, "Adonai, in the name of Yeshua, please provide success for this project. Amen." Yochanan sat down in his chair and looked at Polycarp and said, "We hung on his every word as soon as he spoke. . .for the most part. I am not sure why I did not understand this before."

"Rabbi, you and the other Apostles have done amazing things over the years that no one else could do, and no one else will do until Messiah returns."

"Of course, Saphar but so many times we were. . .distracted by the world."

"But he called you his friend."

Yochanan smiled, thankful for his scribe. He turned his endearing emerald eyes toward Polycarp and said, "Thank you, my friend. . .let's continue."

Polycarp smiled and made himself and his tools ready.

> *"If this world detests you, know that it has detested me before it detested you. If you were of this world, the world would somehow love you as its own. However, now you are not of this cosmos, because I singled you out from the cosmos, this is why the world detests you. Remember the word I spoke to you that a servant is not greater than his master. If some persecuted me, they will also persecute you and if some kept my word, they will also keep yours. However, all who will act against you do so on account of my name because they have not known the one who sent me. If I had not come and proclaimed to them, they would not have been gripped by sin. But now they have no excuse for their sin. The one who detests me also detests my Father. If I had not done deeds among them that none other could do they would not be gripped by sin. However, now they have both perceived and detested both me and my father. But in order that this saying might be fulfilled which is in the same scripture that was written; 'They detested me without cause.' But when the Advocate comes, whom I will send to you from the Father, the Spirit of truth, who goes forth from the Father, he will testify*

concerning me. However, you will also testify, because you have been with me from the beginning."[5]

"Rabbi, by 'cosmos' or 'world' Yeshua meant the people in the world correct?"

"In part Saphar, remember also that the Slanderer is trying to control this fallen cosmos and there is an unseen spiritual realm amidst this physical realm. When Yeshua revealed himself, the entire cosmos took notice. It was very clear that he was different from those in this present world. His words and actions illuminated how short we fall from the righteousness of Adonai. He proved that the entire cosmos needs redemption. Until that final redemption, he empowered us to offset the Slanderer's evil and spread the good news of Messiah to the known world. Then, shortly after he rose, he gave the Spirit during Shavuot to both restrain the Slanderer and fill believers until Messiah's return. We have the privilege of proclaiming these truths until he comes again. However, what is also true is that many refuse to believe, and those who do believe will face persecution. We must stay the course despite this persecution and continue to proclaim the truth." Yochanan continued dictation.

---

5. John 15:18–27

52

Overcomer of the Cosmos

"I have spoken these things to you that you might not stumble. They will expel you from the synagogues. Indeed, an hour is coming when whoever has killed you will think it is a blessing to Adonai. Now, they will do these things because they do not know the Father, nor me. However, I have said these things to you that when the time comes you might remember that I said these things to you. Also, I have not spoken these things to you from the beginning, because I was with you. Now, however, I am going away to the one who sent me, and no one asks me 'Where are you going?' But because I have said these things to you, sorrow has filled your heart. However, I tell you the truth, it is beneficial for you that I should depart. Indeed, if I do not depart the Advocate will never come to you. However, if I go, I will send him to you. Now after arriving, he will convict the cosmos concerning sin and righteousness and judgment. Concerning sin, because they truly do not believe in me. Concerning righteousness also, because I go away to the Father, and you will see me no more. Concerning judgment also, because the ruler of this cosmos has been judged.[1]

Yochanan paused at this point and waited for his scribe to finish. "It is my turn to ask you a question Saphar."
"Yes Rabbi?"

---

1. John 16:1–16:11

"Why did Yeshua have to leave for the Spirit to come?" Polycarp sat up and leaned back slightly on his chair, which made the wood back supports creak quietly. He looked at Yochanan and answered immediately.

"Without his sacrifice, there would be no atonement. Even if the Spirit was fully given before the cross, it could not come and abide with those who were not covered by his sacrifice. Once atonement was made, the Spirit could abide in the world, restrain evil, and simultaneously encourage spiritual maturity in believers. In addition, Messiah accomplished what he had come to do in this present world. He was ready to perform his intercessory task at the right hand of Adonai. With the sacrifice complete, the Spirit could convict and empower while the Son intercedes until he returns." Yochanan again smiled, nodded and rose from his chair and continued dictation.

> "Now, I have many things to say to you, but you cannot bear them now. However, when the Spirit of truth has come, he will guide you in every aspect of the truth. Indeed, he will not speak on his own but whatever he might hear he will speak. He will also make known to you the things that are to come. He will glorify me, for he will receive that which is mine and make it known to you. All of what the Father possesses is mine which is why I said he will receive that which is mine and make it known to you.[2]

Polycarp's eyes widened as he finished these verses and quickly looked at Yochanan and said, "Rabbi. . .are you able to see the future?" Yochanan chuckled slightly and turned toward Polycarp.

"How the Ruach[3] revealed truths to the prophets of old is similar to how truth is revealed to the eleven. I see what I am meant to see, and yet, I am still limited in what there is to see. Understand Saphar, the special portion of the Spirit given to the eleven was because of our weakness compared to the task before us. Here is what the Master said next."

> "Shortly you will behold me no longer, because I am going to the Father. However, shortly you will again perceive me." Then the disciples said to one another, "What is this that he says to us, 'Shortly you will behold me no longer, because I am going to the Father. However, shortly you will again perceive me?'" Then they said, "What does he mean by 'shortly'? We do not know what he is saying." Yeshua knew that they desired to question him, so he said to them, "Do you inquire among yourselves concerning that I said 'Shortly you will

---

2. John 16:12–15
3. Spirit in Hebrew

> behold me no longer, because I am going to the Father. However, shortly you will again perceive me?'" Truly, truly, I say to you, that you will mourn and wail, however, the cosmos will rejoice. You will be grieved, but your grief will become joy. When a wife is giving birth, she has pain because her hour has come. However, when she has delivered the child, she no longer mentions the anguish, because of the joy that one has been born into the world. Indeed, you also have grief now, however, I will see you again, and your heart will rejoice, and nothing will be able to remove your joy. Now in that day you will ask nothing of me. Truly, truly, I say to you, whenever, whatever you ask of the Father in my name, he will give it to you. Until now you have not asked for anything in my name. Ask, and you will receive, that your joy may be complete."[4]

Yochanan stopped his pacing and lowered himself back into his dusty chair. "Saphar, you understand that when he said, 'You will behold me no longer,' he was referring to his crucifixion, and when he said, 'Shortly you will again perceive me' was his resurrection, correct?"

"Yes Rabbi."

"It was not so clear to us at the time. Yeshua himself told us earlier that, we could not bear many things. We needed to see the redemption of Messiah to awaken our minds to look beyond our physical limitations. Only then could we take advantage of what he had given us in this conjoined physical and spiritual world. Let's continue with his words my friend."

> "These things I have spoken to you in allegories. An hour is coming when I will no longer speak to you in allegories but will speak to you openly concerning the Father. I will announce this to you. In that day, you will request things in my name, however, I say to you that I need not ask the Father on your behalf. Indeed, the Father himself loves you because you have loved me and have believed that I came from Adonai. I came from the Father and have come into the cosmos, and now I am leaving the cosmos and going to the Father." His disciples say to him, "Behold, now you speak openly and not in allegory! Now we know that you know all things and do not need anyone to question you. Because of this we believe that you came from Adonai." Yeshua answered them, "Now you believe. Behold, an hour is coming, and has come, when you will be scattered to your own families and will leave me

---

4. John 16:16–24

alone. However, I am not alone, for the Father is with me. These things I have said to you, that you might find peace in me. In the world, you have tribulation but take courage, I have overcome the world."[5]

Polycarp looked up, as he switched papyrus sheets, with a puzzled look. Yochanan was looking beyond the adobe walls still ruminating on Yeshua's words of overcoming the world when he noticed his scribe's interrogative expression.

"Are you wondering why Yeshua said that he would not need to pass on requests to the Father 'in that day'?"

"Exactly Rabbi, why would he pass on requests and then stop?"

"First, let me mention that Yeshua spoke allegorically before he accomplished redemption because he wanted to provide souls every chance to let the Spirit reveal the truths of Adonai. Second, 'In that day' was after his atonement, which means that believers in Messiah are now acceptable before Adonai because of his sacrifice. Those who have been covered by the life of Messiah are able to approach Adonai."

Polycarp slowly nodded and then the same puzzled look slowly came upon his face.

"Rabbi, some have taught that Yeshua is at the Father's right-hand interceding for us as I suggested earlier. If we can go directly to Adonai in prayer how is Yeshua interceding for us?" Yochanan's gleam returned to his eye revealing the tickling of his intellect.

"While we are able to approach Adonai's throne because of Messiah[6] the Accuser is still traveling here and there. If he were to bring a charge against any believer, Yeshua is there as our advocate. He is before the Father interceding for us to offset the many accusations of the serpent. Only he can do this because of what he did at the cross.[7] The sacrifice of the Melchizedekian Priest provides believers spiritual access, through prayer, into the Holy of Holies while in Olam Haze. In addition, since our Priest is at the Father's right hand he will vouch for his sheep at the final judgment and provide us the pasture of Olam Habah. However, before Yeshua made this sacrifice to sit with the Father he prayed one last time for us and all who would believe."

Polycarp dipped his quill.

---

5. John 16:25–33
6. Hebrews 4:16
7. See Romans 8:33–34

53

Timeless Prayer of the Redeemer

Yeshua spoke these things and then lifted his eyes to the sky and said, "Father, the hour has come. Glorify your Son that the Son might glorify you. Indeed, you have given him authority over everything physical to give eternal life to all whom you have given him. Now, this is eternal life, that they should know you, the only true Adonai, and whom you have sent, Yeshua Messiah. I glorified you on the earth, having completed the task that you gave me to do. So now Father, glorify me along with yourself with the glory that I had with you before the cosmos existed. "I manifested your name to the people whom you gave to me from the world. They were yours, but you gave them to me and they have kept your word. Now they know that all that you have given me is from you. For the words that you gave me, I have given to them and they received them. Now they have truly known that I came from you and they believed that you sent me. I am praying concerning them. I am not praying concerning the world but for those whom you have given me, for they are yours. All that are mine are yours and all that are yours are mine and I have been glorified by them. Now, I am no longer in the world and yet they are in the world. But I am coming to you Holy Father so keep watch over them in the name that you gave me that they may be one like us. When I was with them I was keeping them in the name that you gave me. I have guarded them and not one of them perished except the son of destruction, that the scripture might be fulfilled. However, now I am

> *coming to you and these things I speak in the world, that they might have my joy flowing in them. I have given them your word. Now the world has hated them because they are not of the world, just as I am not of the world. I do not ask that you take them out of the world, but that you should keep them from the evil one. They are not of this cosmos, just as I am not of this cosmos. Set them apart by the truth of your word which is The Truth. As you sent me into the world, so also, I have sent them into the world. And for them I set myself apart that they also might be set apart by truth.*"[1]

Yochanan again sat silent and stared through the front door of the adobe looking back in time. He was standing on the hill of the Mount of Olives with a gentle breeze blowing from the west through the trees. The branches were slightly bowing up and down around Yeshua. His priestly arms stretched over the eleven and his eyes were wide open looking upward as he prayed.

Polycarp, focused on his Rabbi wondered what was flowing through his mind. Then Yochanan's eyes darted quickly toward Polycarp. This slightly startled the scribe and caused a drop of ink to fall from the quill toward the page. He quickly moved his hand to intercept and the drop struck his middle knuckle instead of the parchment.

"Yes Rabbi?" he said quickly.

"Yeshua completed his mission and so must we, no matter what the costs."

"Of course...Rabbi...may I ask a question?"

Yochanan sat back a little deeper in his chair while nodding and listening.

"How could the Master and the eleven be in the world but not of the world? Was it that they were physically in Olam Hazeh but because of their belief were somehow spiritually in Olam Habah?" Yochanan smiled and responded.

"What you have stated in your question is basically correct. Why it is correct, is because the Father now sees us as redeemed and not condemned. We remain physically in this present world while we are simultaneously, spiritually connected and destined for the world to come due to the faithfulness of Messiah. Those redeemed, are no longer...congruent with this present fallen world. The Spirit provides a spiritual mindset for the believer and cultivates desires more compatible of what is to come rather than what lies behind. Do you understand young rabbi?"

---

1. John 17:1–19

"Indeed, I do!"

"Excellent. Now, after he completed his prayer for us, he then graciously prayed for those who would believe through our message. He prayed for those in the future that had not yet heard the word that we, or our future disciples would speak."

> "However, I do not ask for these alone, but also for those believing in me through their message. That they might all be one, just as you, Father, are in me, and I am in you, that they might also be in us. That the world might believe that you have sent me. The glory which you have given me I have given to them that they might be one as we are one. I am in them and you are in me, that they might become perfected in unity that the world might know that you sent me and loved them as you loved me. Father, whoever you have given me I wish that they also might be where I am. That they might be with me in order that they might behold my glory that you gave me before the foundation of the cosmos because of your love for me. Righteous Father, although the world has not known you, I have known you and these you sent me also know you. I have made known to them your name and I will continue to make it known in order that the love which you have loved me with may be in them, just as I am in them."[2]

Polycarp finished his strokes and looked up at Yochanan. After recognizing that Yochanan was waiting for any comments or questions, he spoke.

"Was there some other significance that he chose to pray for the eleven in an olive grove?"

"It seems you have a spark of an idea Saphar, continue."

"Well, olives are the fruit of the branch which make the oil for anointing and healing. However, crushing the olives first is necessary to produce the oil, which provides the ability to heal. The Master, crushed for our healing, was the spiritually anointed one of Adonai. Was this foreshadowing the future of the eleven?"

Yochanan responded, "We did not realize it at the time but yes, and much of that has already come true." He paused as his mind pulled up the images of the other apostles. Tears welled up in his wrinkled eyelids. He thought of those who had already fallen for choosing Messiah. He knew their martyrdom was their privilege but he still missed his friends. Several tears rolled through his wrinkled cheeks and fell on his tallit. After a moment, he dabbed his tears, broke the silence, and looked toward Polycarp.

---

2. John 17:20–26

"There is another reason the Master chose the grove. It provided an illustration of the unity that he had with the Father, the unity we had with the Son, and the unity that was possible for all who believe. As he just instructed, he is the vine and we are the branches. Every part of the olive tree shares the spark of life from Adonai that makes it a living tree. A grove is not a grove unless there are many trees. Each tree shares and depends on that spark of physical life, which is the life-giving spark from the Father. Having the same source of life unifies. It is similar with the Father and believers. The spiritual spark of life for us is the faith we have in Messiah and what he accomplished. Every believer of the past, present and future depends on this spiritual spark of faith for life eternal. The power of Messiah, and what he has done, unifies all who believe throughout time. However, the ultimate realization of our redemption will be in Olam Habah."

"I see that now Rabbi, thank you." The two paused in thought until Polycarp broke the silence.

"Would you like to break for mid-day Rabbi?"

"Yes, of course Saphar. Are you going across town to check on our scribes?"

"I would like to, their new hours are early with a presence in the market during lunch and then late in the afternoon." Yochanan nodded and then added,

"Please invite them to the evening meal."

Polycarp nodded, put away his tools, relocated his station and set out preparations for the mid-day meal. He then loaded some grapes, figs and challah in a cloth bag and filled a wineskin with water before leaving the adobe.

54

Arrested

Earlier, as a slight sliver of the shining sun shone, three stealthy silhouettes entered the clematis cave. They lit their lamps and set up for another day of training. They had covered much ground in a short amount of time. Junia, as a Greek, committed herself to Messiah long ago and with this commitment, Hebraic learning at every opportunity. She also raised Irenaeus speaking and writing both Hebrew and Greek. They mastered the abecedaries, with proper strokes, of both Hebrew and Greek, as well as the formation of both languages with vocabulary.

Ya'aqobe also covered general and specific orthography and reviewed several works of Greek prose and poetry. Their most recent lesson attended to scribal signs and the strict guidelines for ruled lines, guide dots and spacing. Today they would be reviewing several Hebrew works in different genres and the scribal responsibility of the accuracy of the recording of events. Their morning of learning was productive and enjoyable. They were now able to translate accurately Hebrew to Greek and Greek to Hebrew in the strict scribal tradition. As they finished their morning lesson, they again made reconnaissance outside the cave, stowed their tools and made their way to the marketplace.

Polycarp took the most direct route to the marketplace in hopes of seeing the three scribes. As he entered the fringe of the market where the leather goods were, he smelled the pungent odor of the skins and oils used for softening the hides. He made his way past the fabric dealers and with his hand brushed away the small colorful threads and lint in the air as he walked. He made it to the center of the market where the produce vendors had set up booths and tables. The bright vibrant colors of all the different fruits and vegetables made the whole scene quite appealing. However, he did not have need to purchase anything today. He ate his lunch along the way and had sufficient supplies back at the adobe. He knew, though, that the three scribes would be hungry and this would be his best chance to meet up with them if they had not already come and gone.

Amidst the shouts of the vendors trying to entice him to spend his money on their goods, he heard Ya'aqobe's unmistakably deep voice.

"We'll take three figs each, a loaf of challah and. . .that big bunch of Misket[1] grapes." Polycarp walked up to the booth of the vendor where Ya'aqobe, Junia and Irenaeus were standing.

"A good choice of grape Master Scribe," said Polycarp. The three turned toward Polycarp and smiled simultaneously. Ya'aqobe finished his transaction and the four scribes walked to the fringe of the market to discuss the morning events.

The morning had gone well for both parties and neither had seen any signs of the Pharisees or representatives from Domitian. Ya'aqobe shared Chavah' s news and said a prayer for them all, the Elder, and the project. Polycarp extended the evening meal invitation and then bid them farewell until evening. The three scribes continued to eat their lunch in the sunshine of the market.

Polycarp decided to go to the corner near Ya'aqobe's adobe where he previously overheard the Pharisees. Arriving at the corner and slowly peering around, Polycarp saw Yehuda, Ya'aqobe's neighbor, talking with someone. The plumed helmet, leather armor and side sword made it clear that this someone was a Roman messenger. The two men then exchanged small papyri scrolls and the messenger gave Yehuda a small maroon cloth pouch that had gold twisted string for ties to cinch it close. It was about the size of an apple and looked like a typical moneybag. They were discussing something, but Polycarp was too far away to hear. He could see Yehuda pointing toward the outskirts of the enclave toward the general direction of the cave.

"Does Yehuda know about the cave?" thought Polycarp.

Polycarp slipped back around the corner and made his way behind the row of adobes across the street. He came to the same alleyway where the Pharisees were perched to spy on Ya'aqobe. Instead of Pharisees, Polycarp saw Chavah in the alley and she seemed to be listening in on the conversation between Yehuda and the messenger. He said a prayer for Chavah and then serpentined his way through the enclave to find Ya'aqobe. He relayed what he saw to Ya'aqobe and asked him to extend the invitation for the evening meal to Chavah. Upon finishing their meal, Ya'aqobe made his way to

---

1. Most aromatic of the white grape varieties in Turkey

Chavah's as Junia and Irenaeus hiked the back loop toward the clematis cave.

Polycarp arrived back at the adobe just after Yochanan sat down in his chair. He was waiting for his scribe. Polycarp reported the news to Yochanan and let him know that he extended the invitation for the evening meal to Chavah. He then reset his station for dictation. Yochanan, sitting on the edge of his chair, pondered Polycarp's report.

"It seems as if our own Yehuda (Judas) is living up to one of his predecessor's actions. This provides even more reason to be diligent in our undertaking. It was good for you to invite Chavah, thank you Polycarp" Yochanan sat back in his chair and again started dictation.

Having said these things Yeshua went out with his disciples beyond the winter stream of Kidron.² In that place, there was a garden which he and his disciples entered. But Yehuda, who was betraying him, was also aware of the place because Yeshua often gathered together there with his disciples. Now Yehuda, having procured a cohort of soldiers, specifically from the chief priests and the Pharisees, arrives there with lanterns and torches and weapons. Now Yeshua, knowing all that would happen to him, came forward and said to them, "Whom do you seek?" They answered him, "Yeshua of Nazareth." He said to them, "I am." Now Yehuda, who was betraying him, was also standing with them. Immediately, as soon as he said to them, "I am," they stumbled away from him and fell to the ground. Then he questioned them again, "Whom do you seek?" And they said, "Yeshua of Nazareth." Yeshua answered, "I have told you that I am. Therefore, if it is me you seek, allow these men to depart." This was in order that the word he had spoken might be fulfilled. He said, "I have not lost one of those you have given me." Then Shimon Kaypha, having a slaughter knife, ᴬᴬ drew it and struck the high priest's servant and severed his right ear. Now the servant's name was Malchus. Then Yeshua said to Kaypha, "Put the slaughter knife into the sheath. Shall I not drink the cup that the Father has given me?" Then the cohort commander and the soldiers of the Judeans apprehended Yeshua and bound him. They led him away to Annas first, for he was the father-in-law of Caiaphas, who was high priest this year. Now It was Caiaphas who gave counsel to the Judeans that it would better that one man should die on behalf of the nation.²

2. John 18:1–14

"Rabbi, what made Yehuda and the soldiers stumble and fall to the ground?"

Yochanan thought for a moment and said, "Understand Saphar that everything that happened during that time and afterwards was surreal. I can only report my thoughts on the matter. They did fall back when he uttered that word. I believe Yeshua let loose a bit of power he had been restraining all these years when he spoke. No one truly understood what had happened, so they simply got up and did what they came to do.

"What about Caiaphas Rabbi? He did not understand that Yeshua was the Messiah so what did he mean when he said that it would be better that one man die for the nation?'"

"If you remember Saphar, Caiaphas also said this just after Yeshua raised El'azar. Since he was High Priest that year the Father used his vessel to prophesy in two different ways that Caiaphas did not understand. First, from a physical perspective, that the death of Yeshua would appease the Romans from fully taking over Israel. Second, from a spiritual perspective, that Yeshua' s sacrifice would redeem the nation through his death." Yochanan started again.

55

Inspected

Then Shimon Kaypha and another disciple were accompanying Yeshua. Now this other disciple was known to Annas, a chief priest, so he also entered with Yeshua into the court of the High Priest. However, Kaypha stood outside at the door. Then the other disciple, who was known to the chief priest, went out and spoke to the doorkeeper and brought in Kaypha. Then the doorkeeper, a maidservant, says to Kaypha, "Are you not also of this man's disciples?" He says, "I am not." Then standing by, were some servants and officers. Having made a charcoal fire, because it was cold, they were warming themselves. Now Kaypha was also with them, standing and warming himself. Then Annas questioned Yeshua regarding his disciples and concerning his teaching. Yeshua answered him, "I have spoken openly to the world having always taught in a synagogue or in the temple, where the Judeans always come together. Also, I have uttered nothing in secret, why do you question me? Question those having heard what I spoke to them; they know what I said." After having said these things, one of the officers standing by slapped Yeshua saying, "Is this how you answer a chief priest?" Yeshua answered him, "If I spoke evil, give evidence of the evil, however, if I spoke rightly, why strike me?" Annas then sent him bound to Caiaphas the High Priest. Then Shimon Kaypha was standing and warming himself. Those around said to him, "Are you not also of his disciples?" He denied it and said, "I am not." After this, one of the servants of the chief priest, being a *kinsman of the one who had is ear severed by Kaypha says, "I saw you earlier with him in the garden." Then Kaypha again denied it and immediately the Crier shouted.*[1]

Yochanan paused and slowly rose from his wooden cotton padded chair and again turned toward the garden in the back yard as Polycarp voiced another question.

"Could Annas could not answer Yeshua? Is this why he abruptly sent him to Caiaphas?" "In part, Saphar, remember that Annas wanted Yeshua dead because many Jews believed he was the Messiah. While Annas could not immediately bring an accusation to mind, the Sanhedrin had gathered with Caiaphas, and Annas wanted to hurry the process along."

"Rabbi, were you the other disciple with Peter?" Yochanan stared through the rear window looking back to that evening when he was in the courtyard of Annas. He slowly turned his head toward Polycarp and nodded his head.

"Annas and I share a distant lineage which was one reason why I was let into his courtyard with Yeshua. The other reason they allowed me access was to be a witness for the accused. Jewish law allows witnesses for the accused because, eventually, there will be witnesses summoned against the accused."

"I cannot imagine how Peter felt," said Polycarp thoughtfully.

"That was a sad morning for him indeed, but he soon realized who Yeshua wanted him to be and he did greater things after the resurrection."

"Please hand me that last bottle of ink Rabbi." Yochanan took the last bottle off the rough, worn bookshelf and handed it to Polycarp, who nodded toward Yochanan that he was ready.

Then, after Caiaphas, they led Yeshua to the praetorium. However, it was dawn, so they did not enter into the praetorium in order that they would not become defiled, so they might eat the Passover. Then Pilate came out to them and said, "What accusation do you bring against this man?" They answered him, "If this man were not causing evil, we would not have delivered him to you." Then Pilate said to them, "Take him yourselves and judge him according to your own law." The Judeans said to him, "We are not permitted to put anyone to death." This was to fulfill the word that Yeshua had spoken to show by what kind of death he was going to die. Then Pilate entered again into the praetorium and summoned Yeshua and said to him, "Are you the King of the Jews?"

---

1. John 18:15–27

> Yeshua answered, "Do you ask this of yourself or did others say this concerning me?" Pilate answered, "I am not a Jew, am I? Your nation and the chief priests have delivered you to me. What have you done?" Yeshua answered, "My kingdom is not of this world. If it were of this world, my servants would contend by any means that I might not be betrayed to the Judeans. However, my kingdom is not of this world." Then Pilate said to him, "So you are a king!" Yeshua answered, "You say that I am a king. I have been born unto this world. Also, I have come into this world for this; that I might give evidence of the truth. Everyone who is of the truth listens to my voice." Pilate says to him, "What is truth?" Now, having said this he went back to the Judeans and says to them, "I find no guilt in him. However, you have a custom that I should free one man for you at the Passover. So, do you wish me to free for you the King of the Jews?" Then they cried out again saying, "Not this one, but Barabbas!" Now Barabbas[2] was a marauder.[3]

Yochanan was sitting deeply in his chair as a yawn came to his jaw. Polycarp paused, switched inkwells and cleaned his quill before responding to the dictation.

"Rabbi, at Passover, the lamb was to be inspected to be found flawless before sacrificing. It seems obvious now that the leadership was fulfilling the necessary Passover requirements of examining Yeshua as the spiritual paschal lamb. Did anyone realize this was happening at the time?" Yochanan paused briefly before he responded.

"No one fully understood what was truly happening. While we recognized Yeshua as Messiah, the spiritual foreshadowing of the lambs escaped us. During this time, there were thousands of lambs being lead to the temple for sacrifice. We did not fully understand this physical picture of the spiritual mission of Messiah until his resurrection. Overwhelmed with what was going on around us, we even missed the irony of Barabbas.[4] However, you are correct about the inspection of the lamb. After this inspection Pilate formally announced that he could find no fault with Yeshua." Polycarp readied his quill.

---

2. Hebrew for Son of the Father

3. John 18:28–40

4. The crowd chose to let loose an imposturous son (Bar) of the father (Abba) instead of the real Son of the Father.

Then, at that time, Pilate took Yeshua and flogged him. Then, having twisted together a garland of thorns, the soldiers put it on his head and wrapped him in a purple robe. Then they came up to him and said, "Hail, King of the Jews!" while they slapped him. Then Pilate went out again and says to them, "Behold, I bring him out to you that you might know that I find him without guilt." Then Yeshua stumbled out, wearing the thorny garland and the purple robe while he said to them, "Behold the man!" Then when the chief priests and officers saw him, they cried out shouting, "Crucify, crucify!" Pilate says to them, "You take him and crucify him. Indeed, I find no guilt in him." The Judeans answered him, "We have a law, and according to the law he ought to die because he appointed himself as the Son of Adonai." Then when Pilate heard this answer, he dreaded even more. So again, he entered the praetorium and says to Yeshua, "Where are you from?" But Yeshua did not give him an answer. So, Pilate says to him, "You won't speak to me? Don't you understand that I have power to pardon you and power to crucify you?" Yeshua answered him, "You would not have any power over me if it were not given to you from above. Therefore, the one having delivered me to you has the greater sin." Pilate sought to pardon him from this circumstance but the Judeans cried out saying, "If you release this man, you are not a friend of Caesar. Everyone who appoints himself a king opposes Caesar." Then Pilate, having heard these words, brought out Yeshua and sat down upon the judgment seat. This was in the area they were referring to as The Mosaic Pavement or Gabbatha in Aramaic. Now it was Preparation Day for the Passover, about the sixth hour and he says to the Judeans, "Behold your King!" Then they shouted out, "Raise him, raise and crucify him!" Pilate says to them, "Shall I crucify your King?" The chief priests answered, "We have no king but Caesar." Then, at that time he delivered him to them that he might be crucified.[5]

The two rabbis had tears welling in their eyes at this point and they both simply sat in silence, consumed in their own thoughts of regret, gratitude and wonder for their Messiah. After some time, Polycarp questioned Yochanan with a bit of anger in his voice.

"Was the flogging and mockery simply part of the crucifixion process? And why did Pilate fall into deeper dread when he found out that Yeshua claimed to be the Son of Adonai?"

5. John 19:1–16

"No one truly knows the heart of anyone except Adonai, Saphar. However, I suspect that Pilate genuinely thought there was nothing that Yeshua did that was worthy of death, especially crucifixion. His was a feeble attempt to pacify the leadership with the mockery of Yeshua. As far as his heightened dread, his wife had warned him not to have anything to do with Yeshua. Pilate believed in many deities, so, sentencing a god to death made him quite fearful of any divine retribution." Polycarp was still a bit upset as he summarized.

"Just so I understand completely Rabbi. The Jewish leadership, in order to maintain their power and control claimed Caesar as their king instead of Adonai. Also, even though Pilate knew this was a Judean ruse to abuse power, he still cowered to their cruel desires."

"Yes Saphar."

"So, the perfect Lamb of Adonai passed inspection and was led to the altar of the cross. I know it had to happen this way, but that knowledge does not remove the indignation." Polycarp gathered himself and filled his quill.

56

Tormented

Then they took Yeshua and, carrying his own cross, he descended to the place called The Skull or the area referred to as Golgotha in Aramaic. There they crucified him with two others. One on one side, one on the other side with Yeshua between them. Also, Pilate then wrote a title and put it on the cross which read, "Yeshua of Nazareth, the King of the Jews." Then many of the Jews read this title because the place where Yeshua was crucified was close to the city and it was written in Aramaic, Latin and Greek. Then the chief priests of the Judeans said to Pilate, "Do not write, 'The King of the Jews,' but that, 'This man said, I am King of the Jews.'" Pilate answered, "What I have written I have written." Then when the soldiers crucified Yeshua, they took his garments and made four portions, one for each soldier. Now his tunic was seamless, woven from top to bottom continuously. Therefore, they said to one another, "Let us not divide it but cast lots for it for whose it will be." This was in order that the Scripture might be fulfilled that said, "They divided my garments among them, and for my clothing they cast a lot."[1] Now the soldiers, indeed, did these things. Also, Yeshua's mother and aunt had been standing by the cross; Miryam the wife of Clopas, and Miryam Magdalene. Yeshua, upon seeing his mother and the disciple whom he loved standing by her, says to his mother, "Woman, behold, your son." Then he says to the disciple, "Behold, your mother." And from that hour the disciple received

---

1. Read all of Psalm 22

> her as his own. After this, knowing now that all things had been accomplished, Yeshua says, "I thirst." This was in order that scripture might be fulfilled. A jar full of vinegar had been set by so they filled a sponge with vinegar, having put it on a hyssop stalk, and brought it to his mouth. Then, when Yeshua received the vinegar, he said, "It has been finished," and having bowed his head he yielded up his spirit.[2]

Again, water welled in their eyes, but this time during the dictation joy was also present in their tears.

"What a dichotomy," Yochanan said softly with a very weak chuckle. He had leaned forward in his chair and rested his forearms on his thighs with his head down gazing far beyond the dirt floor beneath his calloused feet.

"While Pilate tried to get even, as best he could, with the Judean leadership, the slain lamb of Adonai was not only atoning for the cosmos but also caring for his mother."

"I remember seeing her when I was a child," said Polycarp. "You took good care of her Rabbi."

Looking up Yochanan said, "Thank you Saphar, she also took good care of me. She spent the last nine years of her time in Olam Hazeh in this small enclave in the adobe where Chavah now lives. Miryam helped every day in the synagogue and discipled many of the Way." Yochanan sat upright and nodded once while looking at Polycarp.

> Now because it was preparation day the Judeans, in order that the bodies would not remain on the crosses for the Sabbath, the Great Sabbath day, asked Pilate that their legs might be broken and the bodies removed. Then the soldiers came and indeed broke the legs of the first one and also the other one that was crucified with him. However, upon coming to Yeshua, when they saw he was already dead, they did not break his legs. Nevertheless, one of the soldiers pierced his side with a spear. Then blood and water came out immediately. Indeed, the one who experienced this has borne witness and his testimony is genuine. Indeed, he remembers this truth and testifies so that you also might believe. Now, these things took place that the Scripture might be fulfilled: "Not one of his bones will be broken."[3] Now, additionally, another Scripture says,

---

2. John 19:17–30
3. Read all if Psalm 34

> "They will look on the one they have pierced."[4] *Now after these things, Joseph from Arimathea, who concealed being a disciple of Yeshua for fear of the Judeans, asked Pilate that he might remove Yeshua's body. Then Pilate gave him permission and he came and took away his body. Now Nicodemus also came, the one who came to him by night at the beginning. He was bearing a mixture of myrrh and aloes of about one hundred litras.[5] Then they took Yeshua's body and bound it in linen wrappings with the spices, as is the custom of the Jews for burial preparation. Now there was a garden in the place where he was crucified and in the garden a new tomb, in which no one had yet been laid. Therefore, because of the Judean preparation day they laid Yeshua in that place because the tomb was near.[6]*

After scratching these last words with his quill, Polycarp responded during the shuffling of papyrus sheets as he renewed his writing surface.

"So many prophecies were fulfilled with his death and resurrection. While the sadness of his crucifixion cannot be escaped, the joy of the redemption of the world must be mentioned to all who will listen."

"Indeed Saphar, the prophecies he fulfilled proclaim the truth of Messiah like the heavens declare the glory of Adonai. These truths and his redemption happening during a triple Sabbath further confirmed him as Messiah." Yochanan's head was turned toward the fire pit but at this statement, his eyes darted toward Polycarp. He had a sly smile and his eyes had that mesmerizing emerald gleam that Polycarp enjoyed.

Polycarp's head perked up as he questioned, "Triple Sabbath Rabbi?"

"Yes, my young Rabbi. You know that we recon days from sundown to sundown and that not all Sabbaths are on the seventh day, Yom Shabbat,[7] correct?"

"Respectfully, of course Rabbi, days occur sundown to sundown, and any given Sabbath feast day could be on any other day of the week. This, of course, depends on what day of the week we first sight the moon after the spring solstice."[8]

---

4. Read all of Isaiah 53
5. A litra equals about 12 ounces
6. John 19:31–42
7. Saturday
8. The spring solstice is the beginning of the year and the first sighting of the moon afterwards is the first month.

"Correct," responded Yochanan, who then continued. "Were you aware that there is only one feast where three consecutive Sabbaths are possible?" Yochanan paused as Polycarp pondered for a bit and then responded.

"No, however, I understand that truth now Rabbi. It is ironic that you bring this up on this very day. Do you mind if I think this through out loud?"

"Not at all Rabbi," said Yochanan smiling and relaxing back in his chair as Polycarp spoke.

"Yeshua was crucified during the preparation day before Passover which was Yom Rivee-ee.[9] The first Sabbath of the triple Sabbath was, of course, Passover on Yom Chamishi.[10] The second Sabbath was the first day of Unleavened Bread on the following day, Yom Shishi.[11] Then the last of the triple Sabbath was Shabbat.[12] This is why Miryam found the empty tomb on the first day of the week Yom Rishon."[13]

"Excellent Saphar, we all knew he spent three days in the tomb according to the prophecies. But, how amazing it is that Adonai caused every aspect of his atonement to be the year where a triple Sabbath was possible? He caused the alignment of the celestials for the proper month, and orchestrated the day of crucifixion in order to provide Messiah a triple Sabbath after his hard-fought mission of redemption."[AB]

Polycarp, filled with wonder at this thought, had another thought come to his mind.

"Rabbi, do you find it interesting that Nicodemus, the one who prepared his body for burial, and therefore resurrection, was the one that Yeshua said needed to be born again?"

"Obviously we all need to be born again but I believe I see your point young Rabbi. The one told the need to be born again, helped prepare the Master to be 'born again' or resurrected. Thank you for that good observation. Let's continue that thought with recording his resurrection."

---

9. Wednesday
10. Thursday
11. Friday
12. Saturday
13. Sunday

57

Resurrected

Now on the first of the week, while it was still dark, Miryam Magdalene comes early to the tomb, and sees that the stone had been removed from the tomb. Then she runs and comes to Shimon Kypha and to the other disciple who Yeshua loved, and says to them, "They have taken away the Master from the tomb, and we do not know where they have laid him." Then Kypha and the other disciple went out and came to the tomb. Now the two ran together but the other disciple ran faster than Kypha and came to the tomb first. Then having peered in, he sees the linen wraps lying there, however, he did not enter. Then Shimon Kypha comes, following him, and entered into the tomb and sees the linen wraps lying there. Now the face cloth, which was upon his head, was not lying with the linen wraps but was by itself having been rolled up separate. Then, at that time, the other disciple, who came to the tomb first entered and he saw and believed. Indeed, they did not yet understand the Scripture, that it was necessary for him to rise from the dead. Then the disciples went back to their homes.[1]

Polycarp, surprised, looked up at Yochanan after he finished and said, "Rabbi, since I know that you were the other disciple, could you explain what you meant when you said you believed? Did you not believe Yeshua was the Messiah before this?" Yochanan was sitting during his question. After slowly raising upright, he again answered Polycarp.

1. John 20:1–10

"What is belief? Is it a singular point in time or is it iterative and progressive? I know you see my point Saphar. You believe things now about Adonai that you did not when you first had faith in the truth of Messiah. I am no different. Before his death, I believed that Yeshua was the Messiah. I believed he could raise others from the dead after I saw El'azar rose. However, for someone to resurrect themselves, in my mind, was an entirely different type of power. But that was the day I finally believed he could raise himself from the dead." Yochanan started his usual pacing about the adobe as he continued.

"The three of us made it to the cave as soon as possible. Seeing the wrappings lying in the tomb reminded me of the swaddling cloth of his birth in a feeding trough. After remembering some of his statements over the past three years and seeing the face cloth rolled up neatly, I was convinced that he rose from the dead. I did not believe that his body was stolen as some proposed."

"Rabbi, do you know exactly when he rose?"

"Not definitively, but my suspicion is that he rose after the end of the triple Sabbath in the evening of the first day of the week. He rose like a thief in the night, stealing death away from the cosmos. After seeing the empty tomb I immediately went back to inform his mother. However, it was Magdalene who was the first to see him raised"

> *Miryam, however, stood outside the tomb weeping. Then as she wept she peered into the tomb and she sees two messengers in white, sitting. One at the head and one at the feet where the body of Yeshua had lain. Then they say to her, "Woman, why do you weep?" She says to them, "Because they have taken away my Master, and I do not know where they have laid him." Having said these things she glanced back and sees Yeshua standing there but did not know that it was Yeshua. Yeshua says to her, "Woman, why do you weep? Whom do you seek?" Thinking that it was the gardener, she says to him, "Sir, if you have carried him away, tell me where you have laid him, and I will take him." Yeshua says to her, "Miryam." Having turned completely around she says to him in Aramaic, "Rabboni!" (That is to say, teacher). Yeshua says to her, "Do not touch me, for I have not yet ascended to the Father. However, go to my brothers and say to them, 'I am ascending to my Father and your Father, to my Adonai and your Adonai.'" So Miryam Magdalene comes bringing word to the disciples, that she has seen the Master and that he spoke these things to her. Then it was the evening of the same day,*

the first of the week. Because of the fear of the Judeans the disciples already shut the doors. Then Yeshua entered and stood in their midst and said to them, "Peace be with you." When having said this, he showed them both his hands and his side. Then the disciples rejoiced, having seen the Master. Then Yeshua said to them again, "Peace be with you. As the Father has sent me, I also send you." After having said this, he blew into them and said to them, "Receive the Holy Spirit. If you release anyone of their sins, they are released. If you retain any they are retained."[2]

Yochanan stopped his pacing and again sat down as Polycarp waited in readiness for dictation. "Relax a moment, Saphar." Polycarp tapped his quill on the round opening of the rectangular glass bottle to drain the tip of the quill. He then set the quill in its rest and sat back a bit at his station causing the backrest to creek in its usual fashion.

"For this project, we are only providing a concise, limited record of the Masters mission. To record all that he did would be impossible, and to comment on all that we could is a larger task. However, in order that you may know the meanings of the key things of this particular event let me mention two teaching items."

"Of course, Rabbi, I have my note codex."

"First, do you know why Yeshua did not want Miryam to touch him?"

"That was one of my questions Rabbi."

"The answer to this question requires a proper understanding of what Adonai means by clean and unclean. The Torah's laws regarding cleanliness, given by Adonai, provides guidance in physical cleanliness and defilement while in Olam Haze. The laws for cleanliness do not pertain to sin and righteousness. Many have confused these two sets of laws, if you will, assuming if someone is unclean, they are sinful and if they are clean, they are righteous. Please correct those who believe this, as it is a misunderstanding of Torah. Regarding Yeshua' s death and resurrection, the Torah clearly states that,

> *Whoever touches the dead body of any person shall be unclean seven days. He shall cleanse himself with the water on the third day and on the seventh day, and so be clean.*"[3]

---

2. John 20:11–23

3. Numbers 19:11–12 ESV

Yochanan leaned forward in his chair abruptly, looked at Polycarp and said with vigor. "Now, even though Yeshua did not touch a corpse. . .he was a corpse! He had truly died and just then resurrected. When Miryam saw him, he may have just cleansed himself with water since it was three days after his death. However, he still had four more days to honor the command. If Miryam touched him she would have become unclean, which Yeshua wanted to avoid during Unleavened Bread. He appeared to the disciples immediately, without physical contact to impart the Holy Spirit. He then appeared a second time, five days later, after honoring the command. After fulfilling the command, anyone could touch him without becoming unclean. His satisfaction of the command relates specifically for Tauma which we will cover in a moment. The second matter is about Yeshua imparting the Holy Spirit to those of us in the room."

"That was the other question I had Rabbi."

"I suspected Saphar. Now since Tauma was not there and we lost Yehuda to the evil one, there were only ten disciples present. However, as you know, a group of ten constitutes a minion and therefore a legal body. Yeshua had a mission for us. He knew that the only way we would be able to accomplish this mission was with a special portion of the Spirit. We were to be his Sanhedrin. We were to organize the Way, spread the good news of Messiah, disciple both Jews and Gentiles, and make legal rulings for the people from Jerusalem. This is why he said 'If you release anyone of their sins, they are released. If you retain any they are retained.' We would need his legal authority to make legal judgements for the cases brought before us."

"I understand Rabbi." Polycarp paused as the understanding in his face slowly turned to a puzzled look. Hesitating to ask his next question, he looked at Yochanan, who was slowly stroking his bristly beard as he sat back in his chair. Polycarp perceived his patience and asked the question rolling around in his mind.

"How did Yeshua. . .I mean. . .what did it look like when he breathed the Spirit into you and the others?" Before Yochanan could respond Polycarp quickly added, "And why did he breathe the Spirit? I apologize for the additional question Rabbi."

"No need to apologize. I am sure when the various congregations read this account they will have many of the same questions."

"In that small room he said he was sending us as the Father sent him. Then, without touching us, he exhaled and said, 'Receive the Holy Spirit.' With this, I felt a spiritual refreshing in my soul. This refreshing was a quickening of joy, anticipation, confidence and power that I had never experienced. It was a physical and spiritual breeze invigorating my entire being, like some spring mornings. I suppose it was similar to what Adonai did to

Adam when he breathed physical life into his form. That spark of life eventually perpetuated and filled all the souls of this world. The Son breathed spiritual life into us to spread the good news about Messiah. That good news will fill the world to come with transformed souls." The two sat in silence pondering this thought. "We are close to being done Saphar, are you ready to continue?" Polycarp wet his quill and made himself ready.

>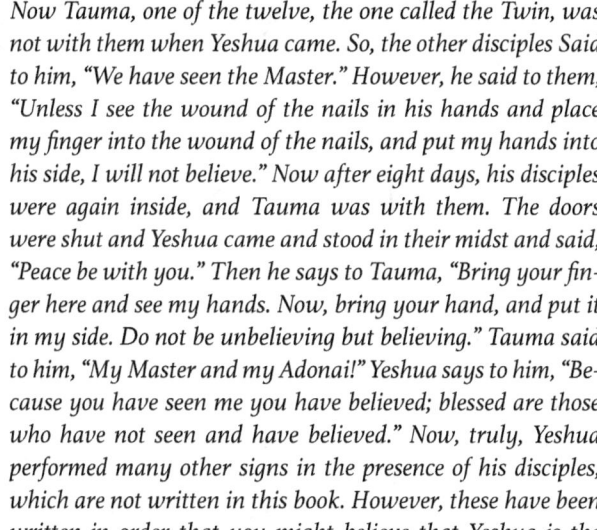
> Now Tauma, one of the twelve, the one called the Twin, was not with them when Yeshua came. So, the other disciples Said to him, "We have seen the Master." However, he said to them, "Unless I see the wound of the nails in his hands and place my finger into the wound of the nails, and put my hands into his side, I will not believe." Now after eight days, his disciples were again inside, and Tauma was with them. The doors were shut and Yeshua came and stood in their midst and said, "Peace be with you." Then he says to Tauma, "Bring your finger here and see my hands. Now, bring your hand, and put it in my side. Do not be unbelieving but believing." Tauma said to him, "My Master and my Adonai!" Yeshua says to him, "Because you have seen me you have believed; blessed are those who have not seen and have believed." Now, truly, Yeshua performed many other signs in the presence of his disciples, which are not written in this book. However, these have been written in order that you might believe that Yeshua is the Messiah, the Son of Adonai, and that by believing you might have life in his name.[4]

"It is amazing that Yeshua appeared in their midst again, so Thomas could touch him, after the time of purification. His care and concern for our souls is unfathomable. I have learned so much from this project, thank you for letting me a part of creating this record Rabbi."

"You are welcome Saphar, but we are not quite done. Let us prepare for the evening and finish up in the morning."

---

4. John 20:24–34

58

Chavah's News

"But I have news for the Elder now Ya'aqobe!" said Chavah slightly shaking.

"I know Chavah, and he knows some of that news already, but he must finish this afternoon's dictation, do you understand?"

"I suppose, but when can I see him Ya'aqobe?"

"Chavah, before you told me this news I was coming to invite you to the evening meal with the Elder and ourselves. He will want to hear everything you have to report. Thank you for looking out for the Elder's best interests. We will come by in a few short hours and we will all join the Elder together." Chavah looked into Ya'aqobe's deep hazel eyes and found comfort in his gentle gaze.

"Alright Ya'aqobe, I will be waiting here and praying."

"I thank you for your prayers Chavah. We will see you soon."

When Ya'aqobe was done visiting Chavah he went directly to the cave and found his sapharim ready for the final lesson. Their previous lessons had made them proficient in identifying mistakes such as minuses, pluses, scribal notations and differences in sequence. Melan and Hylinana had taught them the essentials of their crafts and they could manage making their own writing surfaces, quills and reeds. They would spend the final lesson on the importance of the m'koriy and the strategy for its mass production and delivery.

There would be two routes for delivery to the eighteen churches of Asia Minor, which had substantial congregations of the Way. Someone would need to travel the southern route with nine copies and deliver one copy each to Laodicea, Colosse, Lystra, Derby, Tarsus, Antioch, Damascus, Samaria, and finally Jerusalem. Another messenger would travel the northern route

Chavah's News

with the same number delivering a copy to Philadelphia, Sardis, Thyatira, Pergamos, Troas, Philippi, Thessalonica, Corinth, and then finally Rome. It would be necessary for the northern messenger to solicit a courier in Thessalonica to deliver a copy to Corinth since it was such a deviation from the Roman road.

At the end of the day, Junia and Irenaeus completely packed all their tools and supplies and made a final exit from the clematis cave. They made their way around the back loop and stowed their precious cargo in their adobe. Ya'aqobe gathered what he could and settled in his mind that he would return for his small library of scrolls tomorrow. As he exited the cave, he realized that after the mid-day meal he neglected to take the back loop to the cave and shuddered at his forgetfulness. He determined to use the loop on the way back to his adobe and hoped that, earlier, he went unnoticed. After the three scribes washed and took care of necessities, they met at Chavah' s adobe. She had been ready for some time, anxiously waiting. The company then made their way through the marketplace toward the Elder's adobe.

The two Rabbis returned from a quick visit to the bathhouse and were busy preparing for their visitors. Polycarp was on the breezy rooftop setting challah, raisins, almonds, figs, smoked sardines, and grilled mackerel on the golden table. Yochanan restored the room to its living condition and was about to bring some lemon, wine, and water to the rooftop when he heard, a "Knock, knock, knock" on the newly hinged door. He set his items down, crossed the living area and grasped the rusty metal latch of the door opening it for his guests.

"Shalom Elder," said Ya'aqobe. Ya'aqobe, Junia, Irenaeus, and Chavah were all standing at the doorstep with various items for the evening meal.

"Shalom my friends please come in and make your way to the rooftop."

"Elder?" said Chavah immediately, "there is something we must discuss."

"You are right Chavah, all of us must discuss many things tonight. However, let us welcome each other on the rooftop, thank Adonai for his blessings, and talk about these matters after being well fed."

With this statement, Chavah realized that her Roman report was only one of the important things under consideration.

"I understand, Elder and thank you for your invitation."

"We are glad to have you Chavah. Polycarp!" bellowed Yochanan. Polycarp had finished dressing the table and poked his head down through the hatch of the roof. His oval head, dark hair and long neck looked as if it was hanging from the ceiling. His eyes darted, and he noticed Chavah and said, "Shalom Chavah, I will be right there Elder."

After helping Chavah to the rooftop, Polycarp joined the rest of the tribe at the golden table. As everyone was standing around the rectangular table Yochanan chanted the blessing for the meal. "Baruch atah Adonai Eloheinu, Melech haOlam, HaMotzi lechem min haAretz Ve'noten lanu echem min haShamayim." As before Polycarp translated, "Blessed are you, Adonai, our Adonai, King of the universe, who brings forth bread from the earth, and gives us Bread from Heaven." They all sat down, filled their plates and cups and started the meal. A short time into the meal Yochanan looked at Polycarp and nodded.

"Chavah," Polycarp said, "I have already reported to the Elder that I saw the Roman messenger talking with Yehuda earlier today. I know that they exchanged messages and payment but we are unclear regarding the purpose of the payment. I also saw you eavesdropping on the conversation from the alley across the street." At this Chavah looked worried and the wrinkles on her raw umber forehead turned into deep winding furrows as her concern increased. "Which we are thankful for, if you have some news," continued Polycarp quickly, which eased her furrows and frown to a relieved smile.

"As you know I do have some news," said Chavah. "First of all, thank you Elder for my home and its location. . .and this meal tonight." Yochanan smiled. "Polycarp, I am thankful that you were spying on me as I eavesdropped on my neighbor's private conversation." Everyone at the table smiled at this comment except Polycarp who chuckled aloud. Chavah's smile and tone morphed slowly into a matter of fact presentation as she continued.

"Yehuda does know about the cave and told the Roman soldier that Ya'aqobe was taking trips there with a boy and woman. While this was little concern to the soldier, what Yehuda said next piqued the soldier's interest. Yehuda told him that Ya'aqobe used to be a Master Scribe and about the scrolls he saw Ya'aqobe carrying toward the direction of the cave. He said that he knew Ya'aqobe to be a member of the Way and that the scrolls undoubtedly were seditious writings of the Way that Ya'aqobe was using to lure Jews away from the faith." As Chavah paused Yochanan asked a question.

"Chavah, did the soldier say where he was from?"

"Yes, at the beginning of their conversation he and another had been dispatched by the Chief Priests from Jerusalem." Ya'aqobe looked at Yochanan and spoke.

"Yehuda must have informed one of the guards at the garrison, who sent word to the Jerusalem cohort, who informed the Sanhedrin." Yochanan nodded in agreement and then slowly turned again to Chavah with another question.

"Is that all you have to report Chavah?"

"Unfortunately, no Elder, Yehuda asked about what the soldier was going to do about. . ." Chavah stopped suddenly and looked desperately at Yochanan as tears welled up in, and over her puffy eyelids. She put her face in her calloused hands and started to cry.

Chavah was sitting at Yochanan' s left side and Yochanan gently put his hand on her shoulder and softly said, "Chavah, there is nothing out of Adonai's control; do you believe this?" Chavah slowly lifted her head and nodded as the tears slowed. "Please continue, what did Yehuda ask?" After a moment Chavah wiped her tears, regained her composure and continued.

"He asked what they were going to do about you." The entire table looked toward Yochanan in surprise. Yochanan acted as if this news was as important as the day's market report from Polycarp and calmly responded.

"What did the soldier say, Chavah?"

"He said that others from Rome would be handling 'that matter.'" Yochanan sat back, turned his gaze from Chavah, looked deep into one of the lit candles on the golden table, and slowly stroked his lower beard.

"Chavah," said Ya'aqobe, "Did the soldier say anything about what they were going to do or when?" Chavah moved her head slowly from side to side and then responded.

"That is all I know. . .what are you going to do?"

Polycarp interjected, "We are going to finish this lovely meal and then finish the project just as planned," he said boldly.

Chavah turned her gaze from Polycarp to Yochanan and said questioningly, "Project, what project?" Chavah had missed the Sabbath services where Yochanan gave a quick overview of the project. Polycarp provided a detailed explanation and recapped the past week for Chavah. A bright twinkle started to form in her eyes. She now understood the burden of those sitting beside her. She turned toward Yochanan and exclaimed,

"Elder, what can I do to help!"

"Chavah, you have already helped. In the light of your recent news the less you know the better, should the worst happen. What you can do is to continue to keep your eyes and ears open for any other news." Chavah looked around the table and suddenly realized the groups business was not complete.

"I will Elder and thank you for the meal. If Polycarp could help me down I will be on my way and help how I can."

"I will not only help you down but walk you home Chavah," said Polycarp.

"The help down will do, I can still make it home by myself. Right now, you belong here, shalom my friends."

59

Project Planning

Polycarp returned to his seat and most of the group sat calmly praying and pondering the situation in silence. After a moment, Irenaeus was looking around the table from person to person unknowingly tapping his fingers on the table softly. It was obvious that he had something on his mind so Yochanan gave him the opportunity. He broke his gaze from the flame of the candle and looked into Irenaeus' eyes.

"Do you have something on your mind, young scribe?"

"I understand that it is imperative that we complete the project but how are we going to do that now in light of this news?" Yochanan looked directly at Ya'aqobe.

"Are your scribe's ready, old friend?"

"They are Yochanan,"

"The m'koriy[1] will be about twenty codex pages, how much time for one copy?" Ya'aqobe thought for few seconds while looking at his new scribes with a thoughtful visage and then responded.

"Individual direct copy would take at least four hours."

"What about dictation?" replied Yochanan.

"Dictation would be quicker, perhaps three hours per copy." Yochanan turned his gaze back to Irenaeus finally answering his question.

"I will review the m'koriy this evening. You, your mother, and Ya'aqobe will rise at the first hour to start your day. Go to the synagogue as soon as possible and set up three complete scribal stations. Polycarp will meet you at the synagogue sometime between the second and third hour."

---

1. Mi-kor-ee—The volarge or original

Junia sat forward on her chair, putting her left hand on the table. Her olive skin and slender fingers provided a pleasing contrast on the golden table. As she did this, she enthusiastically inquired.

"Does this mean you are done with the record Elder?" Yochanan looked at Polycarp and responded making eye contact with everyone at the table.

"I still have a postscript, so to speak, to complete the pattern of the overall record but this will not take long. Polycarp and I will complete that this evening. By the time you set up, he will deliver the complete record with my review and blessing. Once you all are there, Ya'aqobe will dictate and you three will provide as many copies as possible. Your goal is four copies each for tomorrow for a total of twelve copies. I will be preparing for someone to travel both routes and will relieve Ya'aqobe after nine copies are complete. I know you have more questions. However, for now, if we could step forward one day at time I believe this strategy will help keep our focus narrow to the task at hand."

"I agree," said Ya'aqobe, while Polycarp and Junia nodded in agreement.

Ya'aqobe continued, "It is a good plan to accomplish what Adonai desires. I suggest we spend some time in prayer and then look for sleep sooner rather than later to ensure we are fresh for tomorrow." Irenaeus looked toward Yochanan and spoke once more.

"Thank you Elder for your guidance." He then turned toward Ya'aqobe and said, "And thank you Rabbi for teaching us and helping us be a part of this great work."

The two rabbis nodded and then Ya'aqobe prayed for some time pleading for the Fathers blessing, protection, and guidance. After prayer, Yochanan encouraged them to take the rest of the food upon the table for their breakfast and said a blessing upon each one as they crossed the entry door threshold departing for their own adobe.

After Polycarp closed the door, he turned toward Yochanan to ask a question. He was leaning on one of the adobe columns looking through the window into the far away night.

"Do you think the Ephesian Garrison will help the soldiers from Jerusalem?"

"They do not have a choice Polycarp. However, how they help is another matter. You were young then but I am sure you remember the tension that existed between the garrison and the enclaves when we arrived."

"Yes. I also remember that you met often with Stephanos."

Yochanan turned toward his friend and responded.

"When Stephanos and I first met there was an instant mutual respect that I was not anticipating. It was as if the Father had prepared him to be receptive to work with a Jewish leader in order to calm the chaos. We met once a month and discussed how to bring peace to our corner of the city. Together we helped bring shalom to the enclaves and the gospel has thrived because of that atmosphere. He remains a reasonable man, so I am hopeful that, while acquiescing to outside requests, he remains reasonable and understands the power of peace."

"Such will be my prayers Rabbi."

Polycarp finished readying his station as Yochanan moved and leaned against the back wall of the adobe near the window to the garden. He then quickly summarized their outline in preparation for their last session.

"As you know Saphar we have used the outline of B'resheet[2] as a framework for our record. Our introduction recorded six events in the Masters life that paralleled the six days of creation. The 'Toledot' divides the body of B'resheet and we have divided our record by the major feasts in Jerusalem for the three years of the Masters amazing ministry. This account deserves a proper closing analogous with our pattern of B'resheet. There is an event where the Master revealed himself to some of his disciples. This event is very similar to the closing account in B'resheet." Polycarp's curiosity was peaked at this point and made himself ready for the last session of dictation as Yochanan began.

2. Genesis

60

Yeshua and Yehoshua

^{AC}*After these things Yeshua revealed himself again to the disciples at the Sea of Tiberius. Now he revealed himself in this manner. Those present were Shimon Kypha, Tauma called Thomas, Netan'el[1] of Cana in Galilee, and the sons of Zvad'yah,[2] and two others of his disciples. Shimon Kypha says to them, "I am going to fish." They all said to him, "We will also come with you." So, they left, stepped into the boat and caught nothing the entire night. Now, at this time, morning had already come and Yeshua stood on the shore. However, the disciples did not know that it was Yeshua. Then Yeshua says to them, "Children, do you not have any food?" They answered him, "No." Then he said to them, "Cast the net to the right side of the boat, and you will gather." So, they cast and they were not able to haul in the catch because of the number of the fish. Then the disciple whom Yeshua loved says to Kypha, "It is the Master!" When Shimon Kypha heard that it was the Master, he put on his outer garment, for he was mostly bare, and cast himself into the sea. Then the other disciples arrived in the boat for they were not far from the shore. Indeed, they were about two hundred cubits away dragging the net with the fish. Then when they stepped out onto the shore they see a ready charcoal fire with fish upon it and bread. Yeshua says to them, "Bring some of the fish that you have just caught." So, Shimon Kypha went aboard and hauled the*

1. Nathaniel
2. Zebedee

> *net full of large fish to the shore. Although there were so many fish, one hundred and fifty-three, the net was not torn. Yeshua says to them, "Come, have breakfast." However, knowing it was the Master, none of the disciples dared to ask him, "Who are you?" So Yeshua comes and takes the bread and gives it to them, and the fish in the same manner. This was now the third time Yeshua revealed himself to the disciples, after being raised from the dead. Then, after they had dined, Yeshua says to Shimon Kypha, "Shimon, son of Yochanan, do you love me more than these?" He says to him, "Yes, Master; you know that I cherish you." He says to him, "Tend my lambs." He says to him again, a second time, "Shimon, son of Yochanan, do you love me?" He says to him, "Yes, Master; you know that I cherish you." He said to him, "Shepherd my sheep." He says to him the third time, "Shimon, son of Yochanan, do you cherish me?" Kypha was grieved because the third time he said to him, "Do you cherish me?" Then he said to him, "Master, you know all things, you know that I cherish you." Yeshua says to him, "Tend my sheep. Truly I say to you this will be, that when you were younger you dressed yourself and walked wherever you desired. However, when you get old, you will stretch out your hands and another will dress you and bring you where you do not desire." Now he said this indicating how he would glorify Adonai by his death. Then, having said this, he says to him, "Follow me." Then Kypha, having turned, sees the disciple whom Yeshua loved following. This is who had reclined on his chest at the Seder and said, "Master, who is it that is betraying you?" Then, Kypha, having seen him, says to Yeshua, "Master, what about this one?" Yeshua says to him, "If I desire him to remain until I come, what is that to you? You follow me!" Then the word went out among the brothers that he was the disciple that could not die. However, Yeshua did not say he could not die, only, "If I desire him to remain until I come, what is that to you?"*[3]

After these words, Yochanan breathed in deeply and let out a long sigh. "Now Saphar, we have finally finished." Polycarp sat back at his station, reached his arms overhead in a prolonged stretch and said,

"There is something satisfying about completing the m'koriy."

Some time went by while both Rabbis were lost in various thoughts about the past week. Polycarp was staring into the flame of a candle when Yochanan questioned Polycarp.

3. John 21:1–23

"What are your thoughts Saphar?"

"I was thinking that the outline of the account makes the record easy to memorize. I can see the wisdom in the organization." Polycarp looked directly at Yochanan and continued. "The analogous closing is the narrative of Yehoshua[4] in Egypt, when he finally revealed himself to his brothers, correct?"

"That is the narrative I had in mind. What are the parallels you see between the two?" Polycarp looked up toward the ceiling thinking and simultaneously stretching his long neck. After a short time, he responded.

"As Adonai allowed Yehoshua to be imprisoned for the physical salvation of Israel so Adonai allowed Yeshua to be imprisoned for the spiritual salvation of the cosmos."

"Yes, continue Saphar."

"During Yehoshua's time, there was a physical famine in the entire world and the brothers were seeking food. During Yeshua's time there was a spiritual famine in the entire world and the disciples were also seeking food." Yochanan nodded in agreement, as another comparison came to Polycarp's mind.

"Just as Ya'aqobe's sons did not recognize their brother Yehoshua so the apostles did not recognize Yeshua. Also, as Yehoshua provided food for his brothers so Yeshua provided food for his disciples."

Yochanan smiled and said, "Anything else Rabbi?"

Polycarp thought a bit more and then continued.

"Although we did not record it here, as Ya'aqobe was reunited with his son Yehoshua, so Adonai was reunited with his son Yeshua."

Yochanan laughed out loud and said, "Well done Saphar. Now, hand me the m'koriy and I will provide my own toledot, or postscript, as in B'resheet. Ready yourself for bed and I will lay the complete record on the bookshelf. Take it to the synagogue tomorrow at the appointed time and be diligent in helping Ya'aqobe."

"Yes Rabbi."

Yochanan sat down in his chair and carefully turned to the last page and reviewed the last account. He then grabbed a flat board as a lap desk and the quill and ink from the small shelf to the left of his chair. Dipping the quill in the inkwell, he set ink to parchment and finished the record with his own hand.

---

4. Hebrew for Joseph

> *This is that disciple who is bearing witness concerning these things and who has written to you. Indeed, all have seen that his testimony is true. Now there are also many other things that Yeshua accomplished. If every one of these should be recorded, not even the world itself would have space for the books to be written.*[5]

Yochanan waited for the ink to dry. He then set aside the lap desk, quill and ink and stood slowly. He laid the final manuscript on the larger bookshelf, laid himself down on his mat and immediately fell into a deep, sound sleep. Polycarp returned from washing and saw his master and the m'koriy in their proper place. He covered Yochanan with a blanket, blew out all but one candle and put himself to bed.

---

5. John 21:24-25

61

Propagation Preparations

Yom Chamishi[1]

Yochanan awoke from his deep sleep later than usual. While his slumber was sweet, once awake, the thoughts of Chavah's news immediately raced to the forefront of his mind. Stirring with a sense of purpose, he looked immediately toward Polycarp's mat while rising to his knees. He felt shadowed with aloneness even before he saw the empty mat. A premonitory feeling of their imminent separation shivered through his soul. He rose slowly from his knees and sat in his chair as he pondered the racing reflections. His thoughts, in the form of questions, started with his concern for Ya'aqobe.

"Why are the Chief Priests working with the Roman Praetorian in order to find Ya'aqobe? Do they still see him as such a threat? Are they coming to take him to Jerusalem for another trial before the Sanhedrin? What else did the Roman soldier know about me and would someone be coming from Rome to...'deal with the matter?' What *was* the 'matter' in their minds? Was Domitian increasing his persecution of the Way? If he does increase persecution does this change anything?"

He paused at this last thought and then spoke aloud, "Even if both of us are arrested, it changes nothing. We must continue." Yochanan's face filled with fortitude as he rose and made himself ready for the day.

Polycarp had risen early, eaten quickly, carefully packed the m'koriy, and made his way to the synagogue. He arrived somewhere between the first

---

1. Hebrew for Fifth Day—Thursday

and second hour. He grasped the iron latches on the double wooden entry doors and pushed them both wide open. The gathering hall was the size of two regular homes, had a high ceiling, and constructed completely out of dolomitic limestone. This gave the interior space and exterior façade beautiful hints of orange hues in the sunlight. Stone seating terraced the sidewalls and ornately carved wooden benches lined the main grey cobblestone floor. Across the room and opposite the entry door was the Bema[2] where an elaborate cabinet housed the local Torah scroll. Just in front of the bema was the Teba[3] and behind the Bema was the preparation room. This room was as wide as the synagogue but quite a bit narrower and used for prayer, storage, and service supplies.

Ya'aqobe, Junia, and Irenaeus had come early and set up scribal stations in the preparation room. There were three stations on the wall opposite the Bema wall. The sapharim would have their backs to the Bema while facing the rear exterior wall of the synagogue. Ya'aqobe would be between the stations and the rear wall on an elevated stool to read the m'koriy aloud for the scribal dictation. From this position, he would also be able to view the production of the copies to ensure accuracy. Polycarp gave the m'koriy to Ya'aqobe and the four scribes finished preparing their stations. After everything was in place, Ya'aqobe took his seat and said, "Let's begin."

While the scribes were diligently making accurate copies, Yochanan was preparing supplies for two messengers. He sourced provisions from the market and the garden out back. He cleaned all the food and then packed everything in pouches. The pouches, and other supplies, he placed in two saddle packs. He spent the morning ensuring that there was enough food and water for two people per saddle pack for two weeks. After several hours, he was confident that the preparations for the trips were complete. All he needed now were the eighteen copies of the m'koriy, willing souls, and transportation. It was now past mid-day so he decided to pack a lunch and go to the synagogue to check on the progress of the scribes. Once there, the Shamash[4] greeted him at the front door. He informed him that the scribes were almost complete with the second set of copies and asked Yochanan if he could wait a short while. Yochanan nodded, thanked him for his help with the project, and sat in one of the benches in the back of the synagogue.

Not long afterwards all four scribes filed out of the preparation room, each one stretching in a different fashion. Ya'aqobe was arching his back, Polycarp was reaching high in a prolonged arm stretch, Junia was bending

---

2. The elevated platform in a synagogue from where scripture is read.
3. A lectern, typically on the floor from where the synagogue service is lead.
4. Synagogue Caretaker

down and touching her toes and Irenaeus was slowly twisting his torso left and right. Irenaeus was the first to see Yochanan.

"Good afternoon Elder, you came for the mid-day meal I hope."

"Indeed, I did young scribe." The company went outside and sat on the front steps of the synagogue for a mid-day meal. After Yochanan gave thanks, he asked how the dictation was going. The three younger scribes all turned their attention toward Ya'aqobe, who had just inserted a large piece of challah in his mouth. He struggled to chew quickly as the others smiled at the entertainment. After swallowing and drinking some water, he responded.

"These three are doing fine. The first copy took a bit longer than the second but that was to be expected. I believe we have a realistic schedule and should be able to complete twelve copies as planned. Are you still coming around the eleventh hour to participate?"

"Yes," replied Yochanan, smiling at the other three who had mouths full of food.

"Thank you Elder that will give me opportunity to retrieve my scrolls from the cave."

During the meal, Yochanan informed them of his preparations, his need for horses, and his hopes for volunteers during this coming Sabbath service. Junia's eyes widened when he had mentioned the need for transportation and spoke after he finished.

"I have two horses that are fine animals and would be good for such a trip. They are yours as you need them."

"That is most gracious of you Junia, thank you for your continued sacrifice."

"Not at all Elder, Irenaeus will have them ferried and waiting at your adobe after we finish the day's work." She nodded toward Irenaeus when she said this and Irenaeus nodded and smiled in agreement. After the meal, Yochanan prayed a blessing for each scribe and then left them to their work. The four scribes again locked themselves in the preparation room while Yochanan made his way back to his rooftop for an extended time in prayer.

Chavah finished her mid-day meal and was perched on the rooftop peering for any movement in her part of the enclave. After some observation of the usual people coming and going she suddenly saw two fully armed Roman foot soldiers turn the corner where Polycarp had been before. They were walking toward Ya'aqobe's adobe. One was Stephanos, the captain of the cohort from the local garrison and the other she did not recognize. They did not seem to be in a hurry and in fact, they seemed a bit nonchalant as they stepped on to Ya'aqobe's stoop and knocked on the door. They waited an unusually long amount of time on the stoop before looking inside and around the other adobes. The captain noticed Chavah on the rooftop and yelled in Aramaic, "Have you seen Ya'aqobe?" Chavah shook her head from side to side and then moved further toward the center of the rooftop out of view from the street. The soldiers had a brief exchange in Greek, which Chavah could not distinguish, and then continued down the road and moved to the rear of the row of homes. Chavah repositioned herself again at her observation post near the front parapet, wondering if she should go and tell Yochanan. Knowing they would be in dictation, she decided to wait.

Having prayed for hours, Yochanan slowly raised himself from his knees and lowered himself through the roof hatch and down the ladder. He sat in his chair as he ate some of the grilled mackerel, dates and challah. He then left the adobe for the bathhouse to wash and take care of necessities. Afterwards he made his way to the synagogue to relieve Ya'aqobe. When he arrived this time, the scribes were already on the front steps finishing a late afternoon meal.

"Shalom Elder," said Polycarp. "We have nine copies completed and will be ready shortly for another session."

"Excellent," said Yochanan. Ya'aqobe stood up and greeted Yochanan.

"Thank you for coming. They are getting faster while maintaining accuracy, you should be very proud."

Yochanan smiled and said, "I am not only proud but thankful for each of you. Now, Ya'aqobe, I know you are anxious to return the scrolls in the cave to your adobe. You are relieved. I will see you tomorrow morning, Adonai willing."

"Thank you Elder, I think I shall spend some time here in the synagogue praying before retrieving the scrolls."

"Very well my friend," responded Yochanan.

"Good night to you all," said Ya'aqobe. The three scribes thanked Ya'aqobe, regrouped and filed back into the preparation room for dictation with Yochanan.

62

The Southern Messengers

Ya'aqobe spent a bit more time on the front steps thinking about the past week. He smiled, got up slowly and went to the bema to pray. After about an hour, he left the synagogue and started toward the market. He purchased selected nuts and dried fruit from the vendors and took his time as he made his way around the backside of the enclave toward the cave. Finally, reaching the cave, he went inside and lit the lamps. Going through his scrolls, he grasped the first book of Psalms, sat down at a scribal station and reread The Shepherd Psalm. While he memorized this Psalm long ago, he felt compelled to read the text.

> *Yahweh is my shepherd; I shall not want. He makes me lie down in green pastures. He leads me beside still waters. He restores my soul. He leads me in paths of righteousness for his name's sake. Even though I walk through the valley of the shadow of death, I will fear no evil, for you are with me; your rod and your staff, they comfort me. You prepare a table before me in the presence of my enemies; you anoint my head with oil; my cup overflows. Surely goodness and mercy shall follow me all the days of my life, and I shall dwell in the house of Yahweh forever.*[1]

Ya'aqobe spent some time pondering the Psalm and why he was suddenly so drawn to the words. He then got up from the station and carefully, with some nostalgia, packed his library in the bag he had brought when they relocated to the cave.

1. Psalm 23 ESV

Back at the synagogue, the scribes were diligent and efficient in their task and close to completion with the fourth set of copies. Chavah was still poised on her rooftop even though sundown was approaching. She only lapsed in her observation twice. Once to go the aphedron and once seduced by the sun to slumber. She continued to be frustrated at herself for her short nap.

As Ya'aqobe held the library bag in his right hand, he held aside the clematis with his left arm while exiting the cave. Once outside he turned to ascend to the plateau but stopped and shuddered at what he saw.

Leaning against the limestone wall, outside the cave, were the two Roman soldiers. They had been watching the cave from the other side of the plateau. After seeing Ya'aqobe enter the cave, they walked the rim and calmly waited for him to exit.

"What did I tell you Titus? Here he is, and he has everything packed for us," said Stephanos, the Captain of the guard.

"You were right," said Titus, one of the Roman envoys from Jerusalem. Ya'aqobe's shudder slipped away as he suddenly felt a depth of peace that he had never felt before. While it was a peace that he could not understand or explain, it was not completely foreign to him. He knew the peace had come from Adonai.

"Well Ya'aqobe," said Stephanos, "Your secret is now known. I did not know you were a wanted man. The Sanhedrin does not forget easily and they want you returned to Jerusalem."

"I understand," replied Ya'aqobe confidently.

"Give the bag to Titus and come with us to the holding pen." Ya'aqobe gave the bag of scrolls to Titus and then held out his hands as an offering for shackles. Stephanos looked at Titus and asked,

"What say you Titus, do want this old man's hands bound? He might assail you!" Titus just laughed and softly barked an order.

"Follow me old man." Titus started climbing toward the plateau with Ya'aqobe close behind. Stephanos verified that the cave was empty and then joined the other two, staying behind Ya'aqobe. Once they reached the plateau, they took the most direct route to the barracks and the holding pen.

Chavah was about to leave the rooftop when she saw the soldiers and Ya'aqobe emerge from the rear of the line of adobes, walking toward the barracks. This time she did not hesitate in deciding what she needed to do and said aloud to herself, "I must inform Yochanan." She quickly broke down her observation post, shuffled down the stairs and left her adobe immediately. She went up the alley where she had eavesdropped on the soldiers, made her way through the market, and headed straight for the synagogue. When she arrived, the Shamash, Gaius, greeted her and was about to suggest she wait when the preparation room door opened. Yochanan and the scribes emerged having completed three more copies. Chavah bolted toward Yochanan, brushing the shoulder of Gaius as she passed. Gaius started toward Chavah but stopped when he saw Yochanan holding up his hand signaling him to be patient. Once Chavah reached Yochanan she said with desperation,

"The soldiers have arrested Ya'aqobe and taken him to the barracks!" As Yochanan received this news, he paused, breathed in deeply and then exhaled slowly. Everyone in the room was looking at Yochanan for direction for some time as he pondered this news. Finally, Yochanan spoke.

"Was Stephanos one of the soldiers Chavah?"

"Yes Elder."

"Thank you for bringing this news Chavah. Please go and tell all those in the enclave who know Yeshua as Messiah what has happened. They deserve to know that Roman eyes are watching the Way."

"Yes Elder." As Chavah went to inform the community about Ya'aqobe, Yochanan turned to the three scribes and Gaius.

"I suggest you all pray for this situation. I am going to talk with Stephanos." The company was surprised at this action but yielded to their Elder's wisdom and remained quiet. Yochanan left the synagogue and headed for the barracks as the others gathered in the preparation room to pray.

It was a short walk from the synagogue to the barracks. As Yochanan rounded the corner of the building that housed one hundred Praetorian soldiers, he felt the peace of Adonai infuse his spirit. A calm confidence came over him as he noticed Stephanos and Titus at the other end of the building shutting the gate of the holding pen. Stephanos turned, saw Yochanan and waited for him to make his way to where they stood. As Yochanan approached, Stephanos spoke.

"Titus, this is Yochanan, the Jewish Elder of the enclave. Yochanan, this is Titus, the Praetorian Envoy from Jerusalem." Titus only turned his head to look at Yochanan as Stephanos continued. "News in your little enclave travels quickly. I knew you would come, but I did not expect to see you so soon."

"Our people have great love for one another Stephanos."

Titus responded in a strong accusatory tone toward Yochanan.

"Is that why your leaders in Jerusalem desire one of their own to stand before the Sanhedrin for sedition?" Yochanan responded with the same calm confidence that filled his soul.

"I am not here to try and change your minds about Ya'aqobe Master Envoy, simply to present a request." Titus felt a calm come over him as Yochanan spoke. With this, he slowly relaxed while being suddenly intrigued with Yochanan.

Stephanos noticed the slight change in Titus and said, "Go on, Elder."

"Ya'aqobe does not see himself as impaired in any way but he is older and will require a bit more attention than your typical captive. While I do not question your ability to care for him during the journey, I would like to offer an akolouthos[2] to assist during the trip to Jerusalem." Yochanan paused slightly, noticed their interest, and then continued.

"This person will have his own transportation and carry provisions enough for himself and Ya'aqobe for the entire journey." Titus looked at Stephanos with a questioning sideways glance. Stephanos perceived that Titus was curious for his opinion but he first questioned Yochanan.

"Who do you have in mind for this akolouthos?"

"Polycarp," said Yochanan.

Stephanos then turned to Titus, looked him in the eye and said, "Polycarp is harmless and would relieve you of the burden of the old man. However, this decision is yours ... 'Master Envoy,'" said Stephanos in a joking manner. Titus smiled at Stephanos' mocking of Yochanan' s earlier address.

Titus thought for a moment and then responded to Yochanan, "We leave at first light, make sure your akolouthos is on time or we leave without him."

Yochanan looked Titus in the eye and said, "He will be on time Master Envoy." Yochanan then turned again to Stephanos and calmly looked him in the eye and waited. At this, Stephanos barked at the guard attending the gate of the holding pen while nodding toward Yochanan.

"Allow the Elder one turn of the small sand glass with the prisoner." The guard raised his right forearm, pounded his fist against his chest, and then opened the gate to let Yochanan inside to see Ya'aqobe.

Yochanan stepped inside and saw Ya'aqobe sitting on the dirt floor in a small cell with a bowl of water by his side and a clump of bread in his left hand. Ya'aqobe smiled when he saw Yochanan and said in Hebrew, "Shalom old friend."

Yochanan smiled and responded, "Shalom old friend."

Ya'aqobe looked into Yochanan' s eyes and said, "An appropriate word choice as I have felt a depth of Adonai's peace since they found me at the cave. I know you understand that they are taking me to Jerusalem. They will need to stop for supplies in every major town on the way." A gleam came to his eyes. He smiled, tilted his head a bit to the right and said, "How are you going to get me nine copies of your record of Messiah?"

---

2. A religious attendant

Yochanan smiled at his friends understanding, tenacity and willingness and then responded.

"Polycarp will be joining you in the morning as your akolouthos and will have supplies and the copies for you to deliver to the congregations of the Way."

Ya'aqobe looked toward the guard at the door, smiled and said, "If we do not see each other again I want you to know I am thankful for you and your ministry over the years."

"I echo the same for you my friend. However, whether in this life or the next, we will be reunited."

"Amen," said Ya'aqobe.

Yochanan grasped his hand through the bars for a moment and then rose and left the holding pen as the guard was opening the door. He left immediately for the synagogue.

At the synagogue, he found the others still in prayer when he knocked on the preparation door. As they came out into the great room Yochanan informed them about Ya'aqobe.

"They are taking Ya'aqobe to Jerusalem and stopping at every town where we wish to provide a copy of the m'koriy." Irenaeus immediately stepped forward and spoke up.

"How can I help Elder? Should I go with Ya'aqobe and the soldiers?" Yochanan looked at Junia who seemed to respect Irenaeus' request.

"Thank you for your offer Irenaeus but I need you to bring your horses to my adobe and remain here to create the remaining copies."

Polycarp smiled and then asked, "When do I leave Elder?" Junia and Yochanan looked at Polycarp and each let a slight smile come to their face.

"You leave in the morning, at first light. You are now Ya'aqobe's akolouthos, the soldiers are expecting you. I have enough supplies packed for you both in one of the saddle packs. Stow nine copies of the m'koriy in a shoulder bag. In the morning load one of the horses with a saddle pack, and get to the holding pen before sunrise. Do you remember all of the homes and leaders of the Way in each of the cities from our trip to Jerusalem last Passover?"

"Yes Elder."

"Good." Yochanan turned toward Irenaeus and Junia.

"Please bring your horses to our adobe one hour before sunrise tomorrow. Make sure you sleep well for the three of us will need to start early in order to provide six more copies."

"Yes Elder," they said in unison. Yochanan and Polycarp went to double check supplies while Junia and Irenaeus returned to their adobe.

63

Copies Complete

Yom Shishi[1]

Junia could hardly sleep. She was in and out of slumber throughout the night. Two hours before sunrise she was up, ready for the day, and already had the horses waiting in the front of their adobe. Irenaeus had ferried them when they arrived home last night. He was still sleeping while Junia was on the rooftop staring into the cosmos and occasionally praying. Irenaeus woke up early and did not take long to prepare for the day. After his breakfast, he joined her on the rooftop.

"Should we go early mother?"

"I suppose, we'll take our time and walk the horses. They have quite a trip before them." The two stepped down the exterior stone staircase and picked up their bags with supplies and meals. Each one grasped the reigns of a waiting horse and started toward Yochanan' s adobe.

Polycarp woke about an hour and a half before sunrise and turned to see Yochanan sitting in his chair, staring at the embers of the fire. He turned toward his scribe and greeted him.

"Good morning young Rabbi, I want you to know how thankful I am for you and I truly believe you are living up to your name. You have produced and will produce much fruit for the kingdom."

"Thank you Elder." He said standing and stretching. "However, I would be lost without your teaching and guidance over the years. So, thank you."

---

1. Hebrew for Sixth Day—Friday

The two smiled softly and made themselves ready. Checking the supplies and the copies of the m'koriy a third and final time, they were confident in the preparations. They brought everything outside as Junia and Irenaeus were walking up to the adobe.

"Shalom," said Polycarp.

"Shalom my brother," said Junia.

Irenaeus handed Polycarp the leather reigns to one of the horses and said, "This is Elpida, she has a winsome spirit and will give you hope along the journey."

Polycarp smiled and responded, "Thank you, my friends."

Irenaeus helped Polycarp load the saddle packs on Elpida and Junia greeted Yochanan. The mood was somber yet hopeful and the band of four made their way to the synagogue, leaving one horse behind.

Unable to express their love adequately, the farewells at the synagogue had few words, however, there were many tears. Yochanan prayed over Polycarp one last time before he made his way to the barracks. Once there, he saw Titus and his aid who was readying the horses.

"I take it you are Polycarp?" said Titus.

"Yes, Master Envoy." Titus chuckled and went to retrieve Ya'aqobe. Titus removed an iron skeleton key from his waist pocket and unlocked the cell. He grasped Ya'aqobe's arm and brought him outside. Leading him over to Polycarp, he barked another order.

"The old man is your responsibility, make sure neither of you are a burden." Polycarp nodded and then helped Ya'aqobe onto a waiting Roman horse while slipping some honeyed challah in Ya'aqobe hands. The two looked at each other briefly and a slight, sly smile came to their faces.

"All is ready," announced the Envoy's aid. Polycarp, Titus, and the aid mounted their horses. The trip began and the messengers of the southern route slowly departed.

Back at the synagogue, Junia, and Irenaeus went into the preparation room and stopped suddenly as they saw Polycarp's empty station.

They paused for a moment and then Junia looked at Irenaeus and said, "He would want us to be diligent today and finish strong."

Irenaeus nodded in agreement and the two replenished their supplies and made themselves ready with a new determination. Yochanan entered, took Ya'aqobe's position on the elevated stool and opened the m'koriy.

"I know much has transpired my dear scribes, but we must continue to spread the good news of Messiah."

Irenaeus replied with a strong voice, "We are ready Elder."

Yochanan was a bit surprised at his spirit and decided the rest of his encouraging speech was unnecessary. He smiled and began dictation.

The news about the arrest of Ya'aqobe gave the enclave a concerned but prayerful ambiance. Lit candles were in almost every window letting those outside know of prayers inside. After spreading the news, the night before, Chavah started her day by preparing a meal for the scribes and Elder. She woke later than usual, and it took her some time to gather the provision for what she hoped would be a welcomed mid-day meal. While she was at the market people stopped her frequently to ask if there were any updates on Ya'aqobe or Yochanan. It was around mid-day when she arrived at the synagogue with her offering for the Scribes and Elder.

Inside the preparation room, the three stayed focused all morning and had produced two more copies each. Nine copies were on their way to the southern towns with Polycarp. These four copies, with the other three produced the previous day made seven. There were only two more copies needed to provide the nine for the northern towns. Yochanan stretched his arms overhead while on the stool and then said,

"After a mid-day meal we will finish our task. Thank you for your hard work and determination." The three exited the preparation room to see Chavah sitting in the last row of the synagogue with a large basket.

"Good afternoon, I hope you are hungry," said Chavah. Smiles came to their faces as they walked toward Chavah. They all thanked her and the three decided that her intentions must have been inspired. Junia and Irenaeus ate most of the food they brought during dictation while Yochanan had forgotten to bring food entirely. Smiling, they moved outside to the synagogue steps, prayed, ate, and wondered about Ya'aqobe. Chavah informed them of her evening visits to the many households of their friends and neighbors. Yochanan thanked her and told her that he would extend his appreciation tomorrow during the Sabbath service. After the meal, they all relaxed for a short while in silence. Then Yochanan looked at Junia and Irenaeus and they knew that he was getting anxious for the completion of the copies. They all rose, thanked Chavah and went back to their stations. Chavah packed the lunch leftovers in the basket and went back to her adobe.

The next hours went quickly, and the required copies were finally complete. The nine precious scrolls were stowed in a shoulder bag and Yochanan put the M'koriy in a special leather pouch just the right size for the codex. They were relaxing in the preparation room feeling glad about what their hard work had produced when suddenly there was a "Knock, knock, knock" on the solid wood preparation door. Junia opened the door to reveal the Shamash. He stepped inside, looked directly at Yochanan, and gave him a message.

"Elder, the captain of the guard, Stephanos, is outside requesting your presence." As the others looked at Yochanan, he rose from the elevated stool and said,

"Let's all go see what the captain desires."

64

The Northern Messengers

They all left the preparation room, crossed the large stone room of the synagogue and walked toward the outside steps with Yochanan leading the way. Stephanos was on his horse, in the road at the edge of the bottom step waiting. Yochanan continued to the edge of the top step as the others paused about halfway between the steps and the front door of the synagogue.

"Good afternoon captain." Stephanos looked at Yochanan, shifted his gaze to the group behind him and then again looked at Yochanan.

"Yochanan, we have coexisted here because you and I have kept our heads amidst the turmoil around us. Our past success is due to being honest and direct with each other."

"I agree Captain. However, with this greeting you obviously have some news for me." Stephanos shifted in his saddle and seemed somewhat disappointed as he said, "There are two emissaries from Domitian at the barracks that have been sent to bring you to Rome."

"No!" shouted the three observers in Hebrew. Yochanan, still looking at the captain, held up his hand for them to calm themselves.

"Thank you for informing me Stephanos but why did they not come here themselves?"

"They understand that you are the leader of this community and removing the leader of any community could be potentially. . .volatile. So, they sent me in hopes that you would come willingly to the barracks for them to deliver Domitian's. . .request."

"Request?" laughed Yochanan. "You should be a politician Stephanos I think you have missed your calling." Stephanos smiled slightly and leaned back in his saddle.

Yochanan looked back at those behind him, turned back toward Stephanos and said, "I will be at the barracks shortly Captain." Stephanos nodded, turned his horse and rode away to the barracks. As Yochanan walked back to his friends, Junia spoke first.

"I understand that there was no other choice Elder but is there something we can do?"

"Even if there was something you could do to change the events I would not want you to change anything." Gaius, Junia, and Irenaeus looked confused for a moment and then Junia snickered briefly and commented.

"Of course, I understand now. I would not have chosen this, but I trust the choice of Adonai." Gaius and Irenaeus were still pondering these words as Yochanan slimly smiled and then addressed Junia.

"Explain it to Gaius and Irenaeus while I go to the barracks. I suspect I will be returning shortly but departing tomorrow for Rome." Yochanan left to meet the emissaries. Junia turned toward the others and explained.

"Adonai provided Roman protection yesterday for Ya'aqobe to deliver the copies to the southern cities. He is now providing similar protection for Yochanan to deliver copies to the northern cities." Gaius and Irenaeus nodded and understood completely. Irenaeus had a thoughtful look on his face as he addressed Junia.

"Yochanan will be in custody like Ya'aqobe correct?"

"I suppose, yes my son."

"Then Yochanan will need an akolouthos to help deliver the copies just as Ya'aqobe needed Polycarp."

"Again, I suppose," she responded distantly. Irenaeus looked into his mother's eyes and responded.

"I know you understand what I am asking."

"I do Irenaeus and if Adonai truly wants you to go I will not stand in the way. However, for now let us all pray for the Elder and if. . .when. . .he returns we will discuss this further."

While the three entered into the synagogue to pray, Yochanan was praying on his way to the barracks for guidance and protection for those he would leave behind. He had decided to charge Junia with the synagogue services while away and would need to cover some details before tomorrow. He came to the far corner of the barracks where Ya'aqobe had been just yesterday. As he turned the corner, he saw two soldiers he could not identify. They were dressed in a darker leather armor than the rest of the garrison. They also wore boots instead of sandals, a long sword, and pugio instead of a gladius. He could only assume these were the emissaries.

As he approached, the emissaries turned toward him and questioned him.

"Are you Yochanan, the Elder?"

"I am" said Yochanan. At this point Stephanos came out of the barracks and joined the other soldiers.

"You do not disappoint Stephanos," said one of the emissaries turning toward Stephanos. Stephanos turned to Yochanan.

"Elder this is Aelius and Festus from Domitian's court. They will be taking you to Rome." Festus stepped a bit closer to Yochanan and spoke.

"It was wise of you to come of your own volition. I hope you will not be troublesome during the journey." Stephanos interjected at this point.

"Yochanan will most likely have an akolouthos with him, someone with his own transportation and supplies, enough for himself and the Elder for the entire trip."

"Is this standard practice Stephanos?" said Aelius. Stephanos shot a quick glance at Yochanan and responded.

"I do not know about other places but this enclave prides itself in being self-sufficient. If you would rather provide for the Elder on your own, that can be arranged."

Festus responded.

"The akolouthos is acceptable. He will be to our advantage, as we must stop in each town between here and Rome for our own supplies. When can you be ready?" Yochanan answered Festus.

"The preparation will require the rest of the evening Master Emissary."

Festus paused and looked Yochanan in the eyes for a few seconds and then said, "You came willingly today. If I have your word you will come tomorrow morning, we can avoid the holding pen and you can help your akolouthos prepare."

"You have my word," said Yochanan, while keeping eye contact. "Very well, we leave one hour after dawn." Yochanan nodded, turned, and made his way back to the synagogue.

"Knock, knock, knock." Junia and the others heard the rap on the preparation door. They opened it and saw Yochanan standing in the doorway with a short smile. Relieved, everyone came out of the preparation room and started moving toward the front door. Yochanan explained the brief interchange with the emissaries and Stephanos' help with suggesting an akolouthos. As they departed the synagogue, Irenaeus looked at Junia and gently grasped her arm stopping her just before the steps. Junia looked at Irenaeus and then slowly posed a question for Yochanan.

"Elder, will you take Irenaeus as your akolouthos?" Yochanan was leading the way and about to move down the steps but stopped when he heard this request. They could not see his reaction but his eyes closed for a brief prayer of thanks and a joyful smile came to his face. As he turned, he opened his eyes and the smile faded as he soberly addressed both Junia and Irenaeus.

"Is this the will of Adonai for you both? Are you prepared, Irenaeus, to leave your mother for a week or two. . .or more? And you Junia, to be without your son?" Junia, a bit surprised, responded first.

"He is of age and able take care of himself and yes, the Spirit has given me peace about this trip." Yochanan switched his gaze from Junia to Irenaeus as Irenaeus spoke.

"Adonai put this desire in me just before Polycarp left with Ya'aqobe. It is as if he was preparing me for what I should do." Yochanan looked them both in the eyes and his neutral expression turned into a smile as he spoke.

"I have sensed the same and it gives me great joy to see Adonai's leading in your lives." He then looked directly at Irenaeus and said, "Let us have one last meal together and then we shall prepare for tomorrow. Gaius, please join us for the evening meal and we can talk about the services while I am gone.

"Thank you for the invitation Elder."

"Gaius, do you mind paying Chavah a visit to let her know what has transpired and to ask her to inform the enclave?"

"Not at all Elder, I will do that now."

Gaius was quick in his errand and soon they were all on the rooftop sitting at the golden table missing Ya'aqobe and Polycarp. The meal was bittersweet but the group was confident that Adonai was involved in the project. Their confidence was strong even though their Elder and leader would soon be before one of the most ruthless dictators of their time. After the meal, Irenaeus double-checked the supplies and Dunemā, the other horse that Junia offered.

Yochanan informed Junia and Gaius of his decision for Juina to facilitate the Sabbath services. Although Gaius was puzzled initially, he understood Junia's past dedication and had seen Adonai work through her in discipling those in the enclave. Persecuted early on with the Way, she remained steadfast in her faith, learning, and leadership. She was discipled by Yochanan and had discipled many Greek men, women and children throughout the years. After discussing some details on the liturgy, Gaius would open the service by conducting the formal prayers and Junia would read the Torah and provide observations. Gaius would then close the service by leading the assembly in reciting selected Psalms. After discussing these details, Yochanan went to the shelves behind the door, lifted the m'koriy, which was contained in the leather pouch, and set it in Junia's capable hands.

"Thank you Elder, we will not waver from the truth."

Yochanan smiled. It was now late in the evening so everyone went to their own adobes with Junia and Irenaeus to return at first light. Yochanan lay down in his mat, alone for the first time in many years. He shed some tears, prayed away his fears and slipped into slumber.

65

The Enclave Apostle

Yom Shabbat[1]

As a sliver of sun started to shine, the shimmering sky allowed the clarity of the star's salience to be particularly articulate. Reality robed itself in the surreal and existence became especially acute. It was another memorable morning where sentience was superlative. This was felt...experienced...simultaneously across the enclave by the followers of the Way.

Yochanan, Junia and Irenaeus woke within the same moment before dawn and each prepared themselves for the day. Clean and with their hunger satisfied, the mother and son crossed the dirt roads toward the Elder's adobe. Yochanan was ready and praying on the rooftop when the two arrived. He noticed their arrival and closed the hatch behind him as he descended the ladder. As he stepped over the threshold, he knew that Gaius would honor his request to look after the adobe in his absence. Walking in silence, the three arrived at the synagogue where Chavah and most of the enclave gathered to say goodbye to Yochanan and Irenaeus. After tearful farewells, Yochanan laid hands on Junia and Gaius and prayed a charge over them in front of all the people. Irenaeus gave his mother one last hug before they were ready to leave. Yochanan gave a comforting look to Irenaeus and asked a question.

"Shall we go Saphar?" Irenaeus smiled and said,

---

1. Hebrew for Seventh Day—Saturday

"Where you go, I follow Rabbi." The two left the synagogue and started on their northern journey.

Junia nodded toward Gaius and Gaius called everyone to gather in the synagogue for the Sabbath service. After everyone settled inside, Junia stood behind the Teba and spoke to the congregation. "You have known in part about the project some of us have been working on over the past week. The project is the Elder's record of the good news of the arrival and mission of Messiah. We do not know what awaits Ya'aqobe and Polycarp in Jerusalem. However, they and their Roman protection will be stopping in Laodicea, Colosse, Lystra, Derby, Tarsus, Antioch, Damascus, and Samaria. Polycarp will deliver a copy of Yochanan' s gospel to the congregations of the Way in those towns. Simultaneously, as you have seen, Yochanan and Irenaeus, along with their Domitian protection, are starting for Rome. They will be stopping in Philadelphia, Sardis, Thyatira, Pergamos, Troas, Philippi, and Thessalonica. Irenaeus will deliver a copy of the gospel to those congregations and a messenger from Thessalonica will deliver a copy to Corinth. While it is unfortunate that they are traveling on Shabbat, we are confident that Adonai is with them. These four messengers, these angels, need our prayer. We will continue with our normal liturgy next Sabbath but today let us take this day to pray for any and everything that comes to mind for our beloved Elder, our Master Scribe, our Rabbi and our younger scribe as they spread the good news of Yeshua HaMeshiac."

The congregation prayed throughout the day and into the beginning of the evening before they dispersed slowly, family by family, and returned to their homes. By this time, Ya'aqobe and Polycarp were more than half way to Laodicea and Yochanan and Irenaeus were close to Philadelphia.

Discover the details of the adventures of the Northern and Southern messengers in the second book of the Johannine trilogy, *A Novel Commentary—First, Second, and Third John—The Lady Junia*.

Endnotes

A. See Ross, Allen, *Creation and Blessing*, Baker, Grand Rapids, 1988, Pages 103–104 where, whatever is waste and void is clearly more than just the earth alone.

B. Certain Greek words such as Θεὸς, Ἰησοῦ and Χριστοῦ will consider the current cultural Hebraic intention for interpretation and will use the proper Hebrew or Aramaic terms (אֲדֹנָי, יֵשׁוּעַ, and המשיח respectively) throughout the translation.

C. Strong's 1096 *gínomai* – properly, to *emerge, become, transitioning* from one point (realm, condition) to another. 1096 (*gínomai*) fundamentally means "*become*" (becoming, became) so it is *not* an exact equivalent to the ordinary equative verb «to be» (*is, was, will be*) as with 1510/*eimí* (1511 / *eínai*, 2258 /*ēn*).

D. ἀνθρώπων is also used to convey "mankind." Strong's 444 ánthrōpos – man, also the generic term for "mankind"; the human race; people, including women and men (Mt 4:19, 12:12, etc.).

E. Strong's 1849 eksousía (from 1537 /ek, "out from," which intensifies 1510 /eimí, "to be, being as a right or privilege") – authority, conferred power; delegated empowerment ("authorization"), operating in a designated jurisdiction.

F. See Hendrickson, *BDB*, Peabody, 2010, Page 956 where רָקִיעַ is defined as an extended surface. This is touched on by the philosophical (metaphysical) notion of extension popularized by Descartes (physically) and Kant (conceptually). Essentially, the space of the physical universe (שָׁמַיִם) is extension. This area that is seen as a stranded surface to Elohim is perceived as the macrocosm of outer space to creation.

G. Strong's 3439 monogenés (from 3411 /misthōtós, "one-and-only" and 1085 /génos, "offspring, stock") – properly, one-and-only; "one of a kind" – literally, "one (monos) of a class, genos" (the only of its kind).

H. Strong's 2859 kólpos – properly, the upper part of the chest where a garment naturally folded to form a "pocket" – called the "bosom," the position synonymous with intimacy (union). Choosing "cleft" provides the probable intended comparison of Moses and Messiah. Moses was hidden in a cleft as the glory of Yahweh passed but Messiah is in the very cleft of Yahweh where his glory is revealed.

I. "Ἰουδαῖος (Heb. יְהוּדִי) pr. *one sprung from the tribe of Judah, or a subject of the kingdom of Judah.*" See Moulton, *The Analytical Greek Lexicon*, Zondervan, Grand Rapids, 1978, Page 202. Judah was the largest surviving tribe at the time. The specific name for this ruling tribe was popularized to reference all the sons of Jacob; the Jews. John, mostly, uses the word throughout his gospel, specifically referencing the current ruling tribe rather than the nation as a whole.

J. See *BDB* for קָוָה.

K. Τῇ ἐπαύριον – Literally "the next," is an adverb of time used for "Tomorrow." However, this phrase is used four times in this section and it is clearly atypical. It appears in verses 29, 35, 43 and 2:1. Τῇ ἐπαύριον is typically translated "the next day" even though the word for "day" only appears in 2:1. If this is accurate then this is the second day of John's record; the day before and "the next day" introduced by verse 29. Τῇ ἐπαύριον of verse 35 would indicate the third day and the Τῇ ἐπαύριον of verse 43 would indicate the fourth. The problem presents itself in verse 2:1 where Καὶ τῇ ἡμέρᾳ τῇ τρίτῃ is translated "On the third day." How can this refer to the third day when sequentially, according to typical interpretation, it should be the fifth day? Verse 35 helps by adding πάλιν, "the next again," which could bring the days in this section to four instead of five. However, this count still contradicts the "third day" of 2:1. It should also be noted, again, that ἡμέρᾳ is only used in Verse 2:1 so the "next" in verses 29, 35 and 43 is still unspecified.

One possible answer to this confusion is John's outline relating to the three couplets of the six days of creation. The two events of the first couplet and the two events of the third couplet come one after the other without interruption. However, the two events of the second couplet are separated by parenthetical statements. The first parenthetical statement is between the first and second couplet (1:24–28) and the second parenthetical statement is between the two events of the second couplet (1:35–42). Within this construct "the next" of verse 29 introduces the first event, "the next again" of verse 35 introduces the parenthetical narrative and "the next" of verse 43 introduces the second event. This observation allows "the third day" of 2:1 to stand without contradiction while staying consistent with the six-day couplet parallel.

Comparison					
Τῇ ἐπαύριον assuming ἡμέρᾳ			Τῇ ἐπαύριον meaning "next"		
Day Count	"Day" Interpretation	Reference	Next Interpretation	Day Count	Events
1	Baptist Testimony	John 1:1-28	The first set	1	Light and Glory
2	The next day	John 1:29-34	The next	2	Water
2	The next day again	John 1:35-42	The next again	2	Water
3	The next day	John 1:43-51	The next	2	Illumination
4	The third day	John 2:1-12	The third set	3	Life
A few days more	Passover	John 2:13-25	Passover	A few days more	Renewal

L. נֶפֶשׁ חַיָּה – See Strong's 5315 and 2416, literally "old soul."

M. Τί ἐμοὶ καὶ σοί (Dative) γύναι οὔπω ἥκει ἡ ὥρα μου.
What? Not for me or you mother, for my hour has come

N. κρίνῃ - Strong's 2919 krínō – properly, to separate (distinguish), i.e. judge; come to a choice (decision, judgment) by making a judgment – either positive (a verdict in favor of) or negative (which rejects or condemns). Translating κρίνω as "separate," and its forms, allows consistency in the translation of this word for 3:17-19.

O. Ἰουδαίων – In this narrative, contextually, the word refers to the Sons of Jacob.

p. εἰς τὸν αἰῶνα, literally "for this age." In this present world, water provides physical life and Jesus provides spiritual life. In the world to come the א and the ה will provide the spring of the water of life (Rev. 21:6).

q. What day did the apostles consider the Sabbath?
1) Acts 20:7a - Ἐν δὲ τῇ μιᾷ τῶν σαββάτων συνηγμένων ἡμῶν κλάσαι ἄρτον. μιᾷ is a dative adjective for σαββάτων and hence means the first Sabbath. ἡμέρα is not present in the text so the reading "the first day of the week" contradicts the straightforward meaning of the Greek text.
2) 1 Corinthians 16:2 - κατὰ μίαν σαββάτου. Again, ἡμέρα is not present and literally reads "according to the first (main) Sabbath," which was during the week, as opposed to the festal Sabbaths. The Modern Greek Bible interprets κατὰ μίαν in this normal sense.
3) Revelation 1:10 - ἐγενόμην ἐν Πνεύματι ἐν τῇ κυριακῇ ἡμέρᾳ, "I was in the Spirit in the day of the Lord." See Matthew 12:8 - "For the Son of man is Lord even of the Sabbath day." And Isaiah 58:13 - "If thou turn away thy foot from the Sabbath, from doing thy will on my holy day; and call the Sabbath the delightful, holy, glorious day of the LORD; and shalt honor him by not doing thine own ways, nor seeking thine own will, nor speaking thine own words." (JB2000)

r. Μετὰ ταῦτα ἦν ἡ ἑορτὴ τῶν Ἰουδαίων - RP Byzantine Majority Text 2005. "The" feast of the Judeans, i.e. Yom Kippur.

s. ὅτι οὐ μόνον ἔλυεν τὸ σάββατον – "ἔλυεν"- IAI3 – Loosened. Strong's 3089 - to loose any person (or thing) tied or fastened. The ordinance of not carrying a mat on the Sabbath was not from the Torah. Jesus did not "break" the Sabbath, but loosened the pharisaical ordinance put in place as a fence for the command of not working on the Sabbath.

t. ἀπῆλθον εἰς τὰ ὀπίσω – Literally "departed to the back" meaning that there were essentially two groups following Jesus. The smaller group of apostles was traveling by Jesus' side and the larger group of disciples was behind this smaller group.

u. Ἀπεσταλμένος is from ἀπό and στέλλω – Literally meaning, set apart (i.e. sanctified), which seems more applicable when referring to inanimate objects such as a pool of water. ἁγιάζω is used for human sanctification and ἀπόστολος is used for human commissioning. The Pool of Siloam was both provided and set apart by Adonai which was probably supposed to bring

Endnotes

the light and water of the creation event and Yeshua's recent declarations to the readers mind.

V. There were three types of excommunication from the synagogue; 30 days, another 30 days and indefinitely. Anyone would have a severe disadvantage without the support of the synagogue. It provided education, instruction, and a communal center which cared for the physical needs of the people. It was also the city citadel of civil influence and protection in a tumultuous Roman environment. See Schurer, *A History of the Jewish People in the Time of Jesus Christ*, Hendrickson, Peabody, 2009, 2nd Div., V2, 52–83.

W.

Divisions of Genesis		
Verses	Colophon	Name(s) of God
1:1–2:4	Heaven & Earth	אֱלֹהִים
2:5–5:2	Adam	יְהֹוָה & אֱלֹהִים
5:3–6:10	Noah	יְהֹוָה & אֱלֹהִים
6:11–10:1	Noah's Sons	יְהֹוָה & אֱלֹהִים
10:2–11:10	Shem	יְהֹוָה
11:10–27	Terah	No Name
11:27–25:19	Ishmael & Isaac	יְהֹוָה & אֱלֹהִים & אֲדֹנָי
25:20–37:2	Jacob	יְהֹוָה & אֱלֹהִים
37:2–50:26	Joseph	יְהֹוָה & אֱלֹהִים & אֲדֹנָי

X. μοι ἐντολὴν δέδωκεν - Strong's 1785 entolé (a feminine noun derived from 1722 /en, "in," which intensifies 5056 /télos, "reach the end, consummation") – properly, "in the end," focusing on the end-result (objective) of a command, hence injunction.

Y. See Leviticus 8 and how this relates to Moses preparing the priests for service. As a side note, "clean" and "unclean" in the Tanakh is typically restricted to the physical rather than the spiritual.

Z. χειμάρρου τῶν Κέδρων

AA. Μάχαιραν - Strong's 3162 máxaira – properly, a slaughter-knife; a short sword or dagger mainly used for butchering.

AB. The year 30 AD is the only year where Nissan 14 falls on a Thursday between 24 and 41 AD.
The solstice falls on March 23:
https://www.timeanddate.com/calendar/seasons.html?year=1&n=110
The Full moon occurs on April 6th which would be Passover (Nissan 14-See Lev. 23):
https://www.moonpage.com/index.html?go=T&auto_dst=T&tzone=ut&m=4&d=6&y=0030&hour=17&min=29&sec=50
The day of the week for April 6th, 30 AD was a Thursday:
https://www.timeanddate.com/calendar/index.html?year=30&country=34
Keep in mind these tools are using Gregorian numbered dates for calculation which will not provide accurate numbered dates for those days in any given month. However, the series of seven days in a week remains the constant and is what is important for this observation. Messiah was crucified on a Wednesday and raised after three consecutive Sabbaths on Saturday after sundown in the year 30. This is the only year where this was possible in a span of 17 years.

AC. "In the estimate of the majority of NT scholars, chap. 21 is an addendum to the gospel, whether it be described as an appendix, a postscript, or an epilogue, and whether it be put to the account to the Evangelist or to a later editor of the Johannine school." Beasley-Murray, *Word Biblical Commentary, John*, Word, Waco, 1987, 395.

Bibliography

Beasley-Murray, George R., *Word Biblical Commentary, John*, Word, Waco, 1987.
Blumenthal, George S,. *The Aleppo Codex*, Ben-Zvi Institute, Jerusalem, 1958.
Brown, Francis. et al, *The Brown, Driver, Briggs Hebrew and English Lexicon*, Hendrickson, Peabody, 2010.
Dodd, C. H., *The Interpretation Of The Fourth Gospel*, Cambridge, New York, 1965.
Durant, Will & Ariel, *The Story Of Civilization*, Simon and Schuster, New York, 1944.
Good News, *The ESV Global Study Bible*, Crossway, Wheaton, 2012.
Jewish Publication Society, *The Holy Scriptures According To The Masoretic Text*, JPS, Philadelphia, 1917.
Keil, C. F. & Delitzsch, F., *Biblical Commentary on the Old Testament*, Eerdmans, Grand Rapids, 1949.
Martini, Carlo M. et al, *Nestle-Aland 27th Edition Greek New Testament*, Deutsche Bibelgesellschaft, 1993.
Moulton, Harold K., *The Analytical Greek Lexicon*, Zondervan, Grand Rapids, 1978.
Robertson, Archibald, *Word Pictures in the New Testament*, Baker, Grand Rapids, 1932.
Robinson, Maurice A., and Pierpont, William G., *The New Testament in the Original Greek*, Chilton, Southborough, 2005.
Rodkinson, Michael L., *The Babylonian Talmud*, 1918.
Ross, Allen, *Creation and Blessing*, Baker, Grand Rapids, 1988.
Schurer, Emil, *A History of the Jewish People in the Time of Jesus Christ*, Hendrickson, Peabody, 2009.
Stendal, Russell M., *The Jubilee Bible*, Life Sentence, Abbotsford, 2000.
Strong, James, *The Exhaustive Concordance Of The Bible*, Hunt & Eaton, New York, 1894.
Taylor, Charles, Who Wrote Genesis? Are the Toledoth Colophons?, *Journal of Creation* 8 (1994) 204–11.
Westcott, Brooke Foss, *The Epistle to the Hebrews*, Eerdmans, Grand Rapids, 1892.

www.ingramcontent.com/pod-product-compliance
Lightning Source LLC
Chambersburg PA
CBHW051635230426
43669CB00013B/2307